Supervision of Dance Movement Psychotherapy

Supervision of Dance Movement Psychotherapy is the first book of its kind to explore the supervisory process in the psychotherapeutic practice of movement and dance. Helen Payne brings together international contributors to discuss how the language of the body plays an important part in the supervisory experience for psychotherapists and counsellors.

Contributors consider a variety of models and examine the role of supervision in a range of professional and cultural settings, forming a theoretical base to current practice in dance movement psychotherapy. Chapters include:

- an overview of supervision in dance movement therapy
- working psychotherapeutically with the embodied self
- transcultural issues
- the use of authentic movement in supervision
- a novice practitioner's experiences.

Outlining key concepts from both theory and practice, this book contributes towards a deeper understanding of the mentor–trainee relationship and the curative power of movement and dance. Supervisors and supervisees in dance movement psychotherapy as well as the arts therapies, counselling and psychotherapy will find it invaluable.

Helen Payne is an accredited psychotherapist and senior registered dance movement therapist. She holds a Chair in Psychotherapy at the University of Hertfordshire, facilitates authentic movement groups and runs a small private practice.

Supervision in the Arts Therapies
Series Editor: Joy Schaverien

'This splendid series breaks new ground in its depth, breadth and scope, guided by Joy Schaverien's recognition that the time is right for a comprehensive, multi-faceted study of supervision in the arts psychotherapies. With each volume, the reader is invited to imagine, explore, and reflect on the expressive qualities of a particular art form in clinical supervision, turning special attention to art, music, dance, drama, and sandplay through contributions by leading experts from different parts of the world. These five volumes will make a lasting contribution as essential reading for supervisors and supervisees across the psychotherapies. The series also contributes towards a deeper understanding of the mentor–student relationship and the healing power of the arts.'

Joan Chodorow, Jungian Analyst and former President of the American Dance Therapy Association

'This new series of *Supervision in the Arts Therapies* is both timely and necessary. Now that all the arts therapies are established as state registered professions in their own right, there is a lack of resources that can support both the more advanced practitioner and the student. The writers of these individual titles are leaders in their respective fields both as researchers and practitioners. These publications make very important and innovative steps, and should be read by everyone in related fields of work.'

Dr Sue Jennings, Consultant Dramatherapist and Supervisor

This innovative series comprises five edited volumes, each focusing on one of the arts therapies – art, music, drama, dance or sandplay – and reflects on the dynamic nature of the presentation of that art form in supervision. The series reveals similarities and differences encountered in the theory and practice of supervision in each modality and within a range of contexts, and with diverse client groups.

Supervision in the Arts Therapies makes a timely contribution to the literature and will be essential reading for experienced practitioners and students of the arts therapies, as well as psychotherapists and other professionals engaged in supervision.

Titles in the series

Supervision of Art Psychotherapy
Joy Schaverien and Caroline Case

Supervision of Music Therapy
Helen Odell Miller and Eleanor Richards

Supervision of Dramatherapy
Phil Jones and Ditty Dokter

Supervision of Dance Movement Psychotherapy
Helen Payne

Supervision of Sandplay Therapy
Harriet Friedman and Rie Rogers Mitchell

Supervision of Dance Movement Psychotherapy

A practitioner's guide

Edited by Helen Payne

Routledge
Taylor & Francis Group

LONDON AND NEW YORK

First published 2008
by Routledge
27 Church Road, Hove, East Sussex BN3 2FA

Simultaneously published in the USA and Canada
by Routledge
270 Madison Ave, New York, NY 10016

*Routledge is an imprint of the Taylor & Francis Group,
an Informa business*

© 2008 Selection and editorial matter, Helen Payne; individual
chapters, the contributors

Typeset in Times by
RefineCatch Limited, Bungay, Suffolk
Printed and bound in Great Britain by
TJ International Ltd, Padstow, Cornwall
Paperback cover design by Sandra Heath

British Library Cataloguing in Publication Data
A catalogue record for this book is available from the British Library

Library of Congress Cataloging-in-Publication Data
Supervision of dance movement psychotherapy : a practitioner's
guide / edited by Helen Payne.
    p. ; cm.
  Includes bibliographical references and indexes
    ISBN 978–0–415–41343–5 (hardback) – ISBN 978–0–415–
41344–2 (pbk.) 1. Dance therapy–Study of teaching–Supervision.
2. Dance therapists–Training of. I. Payne, Helen, 1951–
  [DNLM: 1. Dance Therapy–organization & administration.
2. Dance Therapy–education. 3. Psychotherapeutic Processes.
WM 450.5.D2 S959 2008]
  RC489.D3S87 2008
  616.89′1655–dc22   2007051267

ISBN: 978–0–415–41343–5 (hbk)
ISBN: 978–0–415–41344–2 (pbk)

To all clients, supervisees and supervisors everywhere.

Contents

List of figures   ix
Notes on contributors   x
Preface to the series and this book   xiv
Preface   xvi
Acknowledgements   xviii

1 Supervision in dance movement psychotherapy: an overview   1
HELEN PAYNE

2 Spontaneous symbolism in clinical supervision:
moving beyond logic   18
BONNIE MEEKUMS

3 The supervision process in training   33
ROSA MARIA GOVONI AND PATRIZIA PALLARO

4 Supervision in dance movement therapy:
a proposed model for trainees   49
DITA JUDITH FEDERMAN AND LEE BENNETT GABER

5 Forgotten moments in supervision: the challenge
for their recuperation   61
HEIDRUN PANHOFER

6 From here and elsewhere: transcultural issues in supervision   76
ISABEL FIGUEIRA

7 The contribution of authentic movement in
supervising dance movement therapists   89
WENDY WYMAN-McGINTY

8 We could dance at the opera house: a novice
   practitioner's experience of in-session supervision in training   103
   MAGGIE YOUNG

9 The Balint group model applied to dance/
   movement therapy supervision   118
   IMKE A. FIEDLER

10 Interactive reflections: moving between modes of
   expression as a model for supervision   137
   PENELOPE A. BEST

11 Three makes one: a journey of growth through supervision   154
   KEDZIE PENFIELD

   Appendix   168
   Author index   177
   Subject index   181

Figures

9.1   Steps and levels of countertransference analysis   127
9.2   The concept of the mirror phenomenon   130
9.3   The concept of the reciprocal mirror phenomenon   131
10.1 Inter-creative conversation within RCPM supervision   142
11.1 Triangular space of supervision   156
11.2 The outcome of the triadic relationship   158

Notes on contributors

Penelope A. Best, PGCE, MCAT, HEAM, SnrDMT, is a senior dance therapy clinician, trainer, supervisor and DMT programme consultant. She is Director of first Polish Dance and Movement Psychotherapy training, Warsaw; core tutor on Dance Therapy programme, Rotterdam, the Netherlands; trainer for Italian DMT supervisors; and runs a private individual/group supervisory practice (RCPM). She is currently Honorary Research Fellow, School of Human and Life Sciences, former coordinator of PGDip/MA Dance Movement Therapy, Roehampton University, and consultant evaluator, researcher and mentor for national projects on creativity. She was formerly a Visiting Research Fellow, Open Creativity Centre, Open University, UK.

Dita Judith Federman is an accredited dance movement therapist, psychotherapist and senior supervisor in DMT. She graduated in psychology, and holds a Masters degree in Expressive Arts Therapies. She has worked within psychiatric settings and with children in Kibutzim. She is a Ph.D. candidate at the University of Roehampton, UK. For the past 13 years, she has been Director of the DMT training programme at the University of Haifa. She has published several articles on movement therapy. She is associate editor of the scholarly journal *Body, Movement and Dance in Psychotherapy*.

Imke A. Fiedler, M.Sc., MA, ADTR, is a certified psychotherapist. She has worked as a clinical dance/movement therapist in psychiatric and psychosomatic clinics. In 1990 she co-founded a private training institute for dance/movement therapy. She is currently Director of 'Tanztherapie Zentrum Berlin', an approved training institute by the German Dance Therapy Association. She is the author of various articles and chapters on dance therapy in Germany. She has a private practice for individuals and supervision, and is currently studying for an MA in supervision specialising in the integration of movement into supervision processes.

Isabel Figueira, MA (DMT) from the Laban Centre, London, is coordinator and supervisor for the postgraduate course in DMT and Non-Verbal

Communication, Universidade Autónoma de Lisboa and teaches on the DMT postgraduate course in Barcelona. She has worked in a psychiatric team with anorectic in-patients and currently with out-patients suffering from depression, fibromialgia and psychosomatic complaints, and in a day hospital for acute and chronic psychotics. She is a member of the Nucleo of Transcultural Psychiatry specially created to treat immigrant and refugee patients. She is involved in DMT research with trainees and supervisees, has published articles and contributed to the recent book *El cuerpo en Psicoterapia*, edited in Barcelona. She is a founding member and President of the Portuguese DMT Association and a member of the international board for the journal for *Body, Movement and Dance in Psychotherapy*.

Lee Bennett Gaber, Ph.D., is a Senior Clinical Psychologist and Supervisor in psychotherapy. He has been a Senior Teaching Fellow within the Department of Psychology, University of Haifa since 1975. From 1975 to 1999 he was also Chief of Clinical Psychology, Rambam Medical Center and the Faculty of Medicine, Technion Institute of Technology, Haifa, and held the post of Supervising Psychologist for Northern Israel in the Ministry of Health. He was a Senior Research Associate in Sir Martin Roth's Department of Psychological Medicine, Newcastle-upon-Tyne, where he received his postgraduate degree. He is also engaged in private practice.

Rosa Maria Govoni, MA, M.Sc., Dip. DMT, ADTR, is a Registered Psychologist and Psychotherapist in Italy. She studies authentic movement with Janet Adler, Joan Chodorow, Tina Stromsted and Zoe Avstheih, and teaches the discipline. She has published articles in *DMT* and is teacher and clinical supervisor at Art Therapy Italiana, where she is Director of the DMT Department as well as teaching DMT-related matters in many different national and European schools and settings. She is coordinator of DMT Professionals at Centro di Psicoterapie Espressive ATI in Bologna, Italy, where she works in private practice. She has collaborated with many National Health clinical projects for different populations such as autistic and psychotic, handicapped children, disturbed adolescents, eating disordered, and breast cancer survivors. In 1997 she founded the Italian Professional Association of Dance Movement Therapists (APID), being vice-president for three years.

Bonnie Meekums, Ph.D., SRDMT, UKCP, is a registered psychotherapist. She has been developing her approach to DMT for around 30 years, and to DMT supervision for around 15 years. She began her academic life as a physiologist/biochemist, then trained in dance and theatre at the groundbreaking Dartington College of Arts. Her research career has similarly spanned a wide spectrum from experimental science to narrative research. Her published books include *Creative Group Therapy for Women Survivors* *of Child Sexual Abuse* and *Dance Movement Therapy* as well as many articles, and she sits on the international boards for *The Arts in Psychotherapy* and *Body, Movement and Dance in Psychotherapy*. Bonnie currently teaches both in Poland and at the University of Leeds (UK). Her personal interests include being a mother and a Quaker, dancing, and walking in the hills.

Patrizia Pallaro, Ph.D., LCMFT, ADTR, is a licensed psychotherapist and registered dance/movement therapist in the USA, a registered clinical psychologist in Italy, and maintains a private practice in Maryland at the Moving The Self Psychotherapy Center (www.movingtheself.org), where she integrates authentic movement principles into her clinical work, training and supervision. She is a writer and editor; sits on the editorial boards of several academic journals; a faculty member of the Dance/Movement Therapy programme at Art Therapy Italiana, a postgraduate training psychotherapy school in Bologna, Italy (www.arttherapy.it); and a Fellow of the International Psychotherapy Institute (www.theipi.org).

Heidrun Panhofer, MA, MSR, ADMTE, trained as a Dance Movement Therapist at the Laban Centre in London and has worked with a wide variety of clients in the UK, Germany and Spain. She is coordinator and lecturer of the Master and Postgraduate Programme of DMT at the Autonomous University in Barcelona. She co-founded the Spanish DMT Association and served during four years as its president. In 2005 she edited the first book in the Spanish language on DMT, *The Body in Psychotherapy: Theory and Practice of DMT*. As a lecturer in DMT she works at different universities and institutes in Europe, and has been a member of the organising committee for the first Luso-Hispanic Symposium for DMT in Barcelona in 2005 and of the First National Congress for Creative Arts Therapies in Spain in 2006. She is currently studying for a Ph.D. at the University of Hertfordshire, UK.

Helen Payne, Ph.D., M.Phil., Adv.Dip., Laban Cert., SRDMT, UKCP, is a accredited psychotherapist and a Fellow of ADMT UK who pioneered the development of DMT in the UK. She began the professional association, training, research and publications, and is Professor of Psychotherapy at the University of Hertfordshire where she supervises Ph.D. candidates. She trained in Laban movement, person-centred counselling and group analysis, and practises her own form of authentic movement. She offers clinical supervision as well as movement psychotherapy in private practice in which she integrates authentic movement with her clinical experiences with autistic children, young people, and those with learning difficulties, eating disorders and psychotics. She is editor-in-chief of the new international journal *Body, Movement and Dance in Psychotherapy* (www.tandf.co.uk). Her latest edited volume is entitled

Dance Movement Therapy: Theory, research and practice published by Routledge.

Kedzie Penfield, ADTR, ADMT UK, CMA, MPA, UKCP and BCP registered, has worked freelance and as a staff member in various statutory and voluntary organisations fulfilling different roles of therapist, supervisor and trainer. She has a private practice in dance movement therapy, psychoanalytic psychotherapy and arts therapy supervision. She has contributed chapters to both editions of *Dance Therapy Theory and Practice* edited by Helen Payne, and to *Where Analysis Meets the Arts* edited by Yvonne Searle and Isabelle Streng. From her base in Edinburgh she continues consulting in German throughout Europe.

Wendy Wyman-McGinty, Ph.D., licensed clinical psychologist, certified Jungian analyst, ADTR, MA, maintains a private analytic practice in West Los Angeles, CA, USA, and is a member of the faculty at the C.G. Jung Institute of Los Angeles. She has also served on the Faculty of the Dance Departments at UCLA and Santa Monica Community College, where she taught dance therapy and modern dance. For the past 30 years she has worked with numerous clinical populations, including children, substance abusers and adult psychiatric in-patients. Currently she lectures primarily on authentic movement in analysis, and has published articles and presented her work in the USA, Australia and Europe.

Maggie Young, MA, BA, Cert. Dance Therapy, NSW Cert., Alexander Technique Teachers Cert., member, Dance Movement Therapy Association of Australia, member, Australian Society of Alexander Teachers, works as a freelance drama and dance consultant and as a dance movement therapist in youth and community centres with the elderly and disabled in Australia while writing and staging community plays and teaching the Alexander Technique. She has presented papers at International Drama Congresses and published articles on drama as a methodology for teaching English as a second language to Aboriginal students. Her special interest is in developing programmes for 'youth at risk' based on her knowledge of circus skills, her internship with Bread and Puppet Theatre, and currently dance/movement therapy. She is a member of DTAA and AUSTAT and work as a dance movement therapist.

Preface to the series and this book

Supervision of Dance Movement Psychotherapy is a title in the five-volume series *Supervision in the Arts Therapies*. The series was conceived as a result of collaboration with colleagues from the fields of art and music therapy, drama and dance movement therapy, as well as the related discipline of sandplay therapy. This led to creative discourse regarding the similarities and differences among the roles of the various arts media in therapy and supervision. The common element in the practices explored in this series is that, in each of the arts therapies an object, sound or action (or series of objects, sounds or actions) mediates psychological processes within the context of a therapeutic relationship. The evidence is that there is a developing body of theory specific to the fields of supervision in the arts therapies but there is relatively little literature on the subject. Thus the idea of a series of books on *Supervision in the Arts Therapies* was envisaged and, with the encouragement of Joanne Forshaw at Routledge, the series came into being.

It is a great pleasure to introduce this, the first book on the professional practice of *Supervision of Dance Movement Psychotherapy*. Dance movement psychotherapy offers the opportunity for a very particular experience which is qualitatively different from other forms of psychotherapy, and this is reflected in supervision of the practice. Professor Helen Payne, the editor of this book, is a leading practitioner, researcher and theorist in the field of dance movement psychotherapy and she has assembled a group of contributors who are all highly experienced dance movement therapists, from widely diverse international backgrounds. This has resulted in a book that is an exciting and lively contribution to the literature in this expanding field. It is anticipated that, along with its companion volumes in the series, *Supervision of Dance Movement Psychotherapy* will be of interest to a wide readership: supervisors and supervisees, whether experienced practitioners or students of dance movement psychotherapy. However, the anticipated readership is not limited to this group; it includes practitioners of the other arts therapies, as well as analytical psychology, child and adult psychotherapy, counselling and integrative arts therapy. All who supervise dance movement therapists, and all who are interested in understanding its role in profes-sional practice, will find this book inspiring and an essential companion to supervision.

Joy Schaverien
September 2007

Preface

I was invited by Professor Joy Schaverian, art psychotherapist and series editor for the supervision books in the arts therapies, to edit this volume at an auspicious time. It was when we were both delegates and presenters at the United Kingdom Council for Psychotherapy's (UKCP) annual conference entitled 'About a Body: working with the embodied mind in psychotherapy'. This was a gathering of many verbal psychotherapists interested to learn about the place and nature of the body in psychotherapy, and coincided with the launch of the new international journal *Body, Movement and Dance in Psychotherapy*. I had also been busy compiling the entirely new book on UK dance movement therapy practice, *Dance Movement Therapy: Theory, research and practice*, published by Routledge. I accepted Joy's invitation willingly, excited by the challenge of editing another illuminating and hopefully useful book at this time of increasing interest in the embodied self. The prospect of being involved in a series with our sister arts therapies (art, music and drama) stirred me still further. The timing was synchronous, since the rest of the psychotherapy community appeared to be delving into the way we can use the body and movement in therapy, and more DMT training programmes were being developed worldwide.

In addition, it is a time of change for the UK dance movement therapy (DMT) profession. For example, the membership recently elected to change the term 'therapy' in DMT to 'psychotherapy'. Consequently the new UK term for DMT is now dance movement psychotherapy (DMP); hence the title of this book as a reflection of the change. The way the term is written varies around the globe: for example, dance therapy; movement therapy; dance movement therapy; dance-movement therapy; or dance/movement therapy. The name given to the work however needs to fit into the overall philosophy, subculture and policies of the setting in which it is practised. It might not be appropriate to include the term *dance* in many settings since it can demotivate possible participants from even coming into the space. Others though are positively delighted that the word *dance* is included in the title of the sessions; it is whatever this term conjures up for them which excites them to attend at all. The skill is in when the practitioner uses the terms *dance*, *movement* or both in the light of her/his perception of the context for the work. The term *therapy* may be equally difficult for participants to make sense of, since this term is also used in 'drug therapy', 'occupational therapy' and 'speech therapy', for example. The creative arts therapies are more closely aligned to psychotherapy than any of these disciplines. Historically the arts therapies have been built on much of the theorising found in the specialist forms of psychotherapy and counselling, hence the change of title for the professional association in the UK.

Supervision has been little researched and studied despite so many emphasising its importance in both training and subsequent clinical practice. I was struck by the limited number of texts in the psychological therapies (including the arts therapies) on the subject.

I would like to encourage practitioners and trainers to research the area of supervision much more systematically. A number of questions come to mind: for example, why is it that supervision is seen as so crucial to effective practice; what can we gain, as psychotherapists, from it; how does it help our patients/clients; what are the methods and models most helpful for trainees' developing and/or experienced clinicians and how might they be different; what are the outcomes we expect and do these match the actual outcomes; and are there differences in the efficacy between group or individual supervision? Some of these questions are raised and solutions or responses posed as answers in this book. Other chapters raise more questions.

I hope you will find the book helpful and informative. It has been designed with the trainer, clinician and student in mind. Those from other disciplines of psychotherapy might find the ways to work with the embodied mind helpful to incorporate into their own practice of supervision.

I would anticipate, in the future, postgraduate training programmes for those experienced practitioners wishing to learn how to supervise in dance or movement psychotherapy might be offered, in which case this volume would be extremely useful as a text.

Hopefully, whatever your stage of training and experience, this book will take you further in your considerations of what it is to be supervised and be a clinical supervisor.

Helen Payne

Acknowledgements

First, I would like to thank the authors for their insightful, creative stories about supervision. It was very enriching to work with the various people in dance movement psychotherapy from diverse countries, a new experience for me. Second, to show my appreciation to the publishers for all their hard work in getting the book into print. Third, without the sustaining efforts offered by the University of Hertfordshire together with my research assistant Sabine Fichter the book would not have been produced, so much gratitude is due. Finally, thanks to my family and friends for their recent support which has enabled me to complete this task.

Note

Please be aware that authors have assured me that all names and other identifying details in client/supervisee material documented in this book have been changed or omitted to preserve their anonymity and confidentiality.

Chapter 1

Supervision in dance movement psychotherapy

An overview

Helen Payne

Introduction

Welcome to this book, the first to document the art and science of professional (rather than management) supervision in the field of dance and movement psychotherapy (DMP). As one of the five volumes on arts psychotherapies supervision it will make a permanent impact as fundamental reading for supervisors and supervisees across the psychotherapies. This book contributes toward a deeper understanding of the mentor–trainee relationship and the curative power of movement and dance.

The terms DMT and DMP are used interchangeably. The discipline is known worldwide by various other terms, specifically: dance-movement therapy; movement therapy; movement psychotherapy; dance therapy; dance movement therapy and dance/movement therapy. However, to reflect the new title of DMP recently adopted by the UK professional association (ADMT.UK), it has been decided that this will be the term used in the title to this book, the introductory chapter and in the other authors' chapters who responded that this was acceptable to them. As the book includes international contributions, the other terms in common use have been left as written by those authors.

The contributors have been selected from an international community of senior clinical practitioners. We welcome them to this volume from different parts of the globe: Australia; Germany; Israel; Italy; Portugal; Spain; the UK; the USA; and they have been diligent in bringing to readers their own models of supervision in DMP. Some approaches have been systematically researched; others are based on many years of supervisory experience, from private practice to training. Uniquely, we have one chapter from a novice practitioner describing her fears, hopes and experiences during her training as an apprentice with a DMP trainer in a clinical setting. I have been impressed by the thoroughness of the descriptive analysis of the ways in which these authors speak about supervision.

This chapter presents: (1) definition and goals of supervision; (2) an analysis of the nature of supervision from the chapters and beyond to guide the reader through the book, highlighting specifically relevant themes; (3) a summary of the benefits for the readership from this ground-breaking book; (4) a delineation of the aims of the book; and (5) a synopsis of each of the chapters as they appear sequentially.

An outline of definitions, goals and the nature of supervision in DMP is now presented. This serves as an introduction to this volume for dance movement psychotherapists, body psychotherapists and arts therapists as well as verbal psychotherapists/counsellors who may also be interested in the nature of the embodied self.

Definition and goals of supervision

What is supervision?

Research (Gelso and Carter, 1985; Robinson *et al.*, 1990; Horvath and Symonds, 1991; Clarkson, 1996, 2003; Martin and Garski, 2000; Paley and Lawton, 2001) has demonstrated that it is not the approach but the therapeutic relationship variables (working alliance) and client motivation in psychotherapy/counselling which determine outcome. Therefore the nature of supervision in any form of psychotherapy needs to reflect this finding and is equally complex. Supervision, whatever form it takes, is intended to be in the service of the client by providing the supervisee with a safe container for the honest communication of clinical practice.

Clinical professional supervision ('super vision') contributes to both supervisee and supervisor seeing the bigger picture. It is a process of facilitation of the supervisee's capacity to work responsibly, empathically and beneficially with the client who is the focus of a shared concern. It is normally undertaken both during and following training (career-long) whereby an experienced dance movement psychotherapist collaborates with a less equally experienced dance movement psychotherapist to assist her/him in: (1) refining their practice, (2) understanding more of their personal and unique elements which form part of that practice, (3) dealing with anxieties inherent in the practice, and (4) facilitating them to use the supervisory process to achieve a greater clinical understanding.

It has relationship, didactic, supportive, challenging and explorative functions. From a psychodynamic perspective supervision may be seen as a relationship between the supervisor and a therapeutic alliance (the 'client') in a triadic design. Whatever the theoretical orientation it is a confidential working relationship between two or more people in which resources of both (or all if a group) are shared and directed towards giving fresh and diverse perspectives on the practice and work concerns brought to regular sessions by one of them.

Supervision may also be defined broadly as the education and training of the dance movement psychotherapist through the sharing of client material with the supervisor (and other supervisees). The DMP supervision process may teach fundamental (at initial training stage) and advanced levels of professional ethical practice in the understanding and techniques of embodied psychotherapy. It may involve the supervisee in ethical decision-making concerning practice and engage her/him in numerous professional issues. In undertaking supervision it is hoped the supervisee will develop a healthy investment in practising insightful, ethical psychotherapy and evolve a benign, well-functioning internal supervisor (Casement, 1985, 1990). This model has been explored in relation to authentic movement and supervision (Payne, 2001b).

This development of a capacity for self-supervision while in practice is crucial if the practitioner is to become a more competent and confident psychotherapist. The novice practitioner on placement, during training, usually learns by example, such as during their own dance movement therapy process for personal therapy, in an experiential DMP group on the programme or during clinical in-session supervision. The latter is a type of apprenticeship role, where the supervisee is neither client nor taking full responsibility for the group process. Debriefings following the sessions take place with the group facilitator, who is normally an experienced and registered dance movement psychotherapist. This process has been described in depth in earlier writings (Payne and Wright, 1994).

In essence I see supervision as key to continuing professional development (CPD) for qualified practitioners leading towards improving quality and promoting effective ethical practice. In my view, it is incumbent upon a clinician, once graduated from training, to arrange regular supervision.

In psychodynamic theory unconscious processes are crucial to therapeutic outcome. Supervision in this model is an enabling space to reflect on these processes and any interpretations of them offered in the service of the client. The idea of 'parallel process' (Mothersole, 1999) as an integral-relational organising principle for psychotherapy can assist clinicians in thinking about session content and the therapeutic alliance. Supervision gives the opportunity for the process and relationship to be explored by becoming aware of the mirroring of these processes which can take place between supervisor and supervisee.

The concepts of the body-self, the interpersonal self and the intrapsychic self are articulated by Wendy Wyman-McGinty (Chapter 7, this volume) as a way of assessing the individual in relationship to his/her body, to others, and to inner states of mind. Within these underlying concepts definitions emerging in this volume include supervision as:

- a multi-phased process between words and movement;
- a form of movement expression as the primary organisation of experience in the pre-verbal stage of human development;

- related to neurological and psychological growth, acknowledging the cultural context in which these processes take place;
- acknowledging the setting as a facilitating and holding environment modulated by the client's needs, characteristics and potential;
- making conscious movement as a modality of analysis in order to grasp the complexity of interaction (body, movement, psyche, word) between patient/client and therapist in the setting;
- making conscious use of the body as a receptive instrument for kinaesthetic empathy and imagination, for somatic countertransference;
- an opening for supervisees to perceive themselves, the other, and the unknown and to enter into a 'potential space' of transitional phenomena;
- providing supervisees with a place to sustain the ability to relate to dissociated split-off parts and repressed or inhibited ones, the 'shadow'.

To sum up, the contributors to this book appear to engage with the setting, professional growth, relationship, the 'shadow' and movement in providing professional DMP supervision.

What is the evidence that supervision is effective?

Although it is increasingly being seen as one of the foundations of effective clinical practice in all the psychotherapies (including DMP), very little research has been conducted on capturing the complexities of process and outcomes in supervision. One unpublished study in the UK in DMP supervision (Clarke 1999, 2001) made recommendations to the professional association on supervision as a result of participant observation; interviews with supervisors and analysis of supervisee reflections on supervision sessions. To date there appears to be very limited evidence that clients benefit from therapist supervision, although there is some opinion and research to show that the therapist/counsellor profits.

Of relevance when considering DMP supervision, the evidence of research in supervision from counselling and psychotherapy can be informative. Research in this related field has mainly been to assess the impact of supervision on therapy and counsellor trainees in the USA such as the study reported by Skovholt and Ronnestad (1992) and Ronnestad and Skovholt (1993). This evidence suggests that supervision has a positive impact on the self-awareness, self-efficacy and skill development of the supervisee. Preliminary findings from other evidence suggest that supervision has an influence on theoretical orientation, and that the timing and frequency of supervision can impact on the content and process of supervision. Since the provision of research knowledge from this sister discipline may be useful, a more detailed overview is provided below.

Research is developing in this field as illustrated by the following studies. For example, Grant and Schofeld (2007) conducted a survey to delineate factors associated with the frequency of ongoing supervision among psychotherapists and counsellors; Walker *et al.* (2007) explored gender-related events from female trainee perspectives which were found to be related to trainee self-disclose and the supervisory alliance; and Crocket (2007) presents a discourse analysis on the professional culture of supervision from a supervisory conversation which 'pays attention to the politics of its own production and thus to the culture of supervision that it produces' (ibid.: 19).

Jacobsen (2007) provides a limited qualitative single case study, in which supervision sessions were randomly selected, to explore the parallel process. An independent analyst verifies the author's conclusions of the ways this process manifests, highlighting the potential for supervisors to develop insight into the therapeutic alliance and foster appropriate interventions. In another qualitative study with supervisees working with traumatised clients (Smith *et al.*, 2007) it was found that 'difficult situations' could be categorised into therapist reactions which in turn could be linked to therapist style. It is recommended that supervision enhance constructive coping in accordance with therapist style.

With reference to group supervision, DeStefano *et al.* (2007) in a small pilot study looked at trainees' experience of clinical impasses and the impact of the group on their resolution. Trainees, who experienced the impasse as a failure, sought and received support from group supervision as well as increased self-awareness. Dissatisfaction with the group was also reported, resulting in a recommendation that the developmental needs of the trainee warranting differing supervisory styles be considered. The findings make it clear that a group supervisor for trainees needs to be both a competent clinician and an experienced group facilitator; otherwise the group experience for the trainee may be a destructive one.

Routine outcome monitoring helps actualise the goals of counselling supervision and is reported in Worthen and Lambert (2007). Tracking client treatment response and comparing this with expected outcomes alerts counsellors and supervisors, it is argued, and adds value to supportive supervision consultations. Progress feedback and problem-solving strategies from supervisors was provided immediately for off track cases, resulting in richer and more focused supervision activity. Clients showing negative change had significantly better outcomes.

In a systematic review of the literature on the impact of counselling supervision on the therapist, their practice and their clients (Wheeler, 2003; Wheeler and Richards, 2007) findings from 18 studies included self-awareness enhancement; skills development; self-efficacy; timing and frequency of supervision; theoretical orientation; support and outcome for the client. The authors were critical of the methodology and process of most of the studies with only two reaching their criteria of 'very good'. The analysis of studies reviewed offers insight into what might be most helpful for the supervisee in the short term. Since trainees appear to have been the participants in the main, other influences on the outcomes may have played a part. Supervision may form an integrating medium for the trainee, whereby theory and practice come together.

Despite these encouraging beginnings, due to the dearth of studies across all the psychotherapies (i.e. arts therapies and counselling/psychotherapy), there is an overwhelming and overdue need to research the impact of supervision on qualified and experienced practitioners over a longer term as well as on client outcome.

Others have contributed to the development of an understanding of supervision through their writings, for example, Langs (1994) and Jacobs (1996) in psychoanalytic psychotherapy; Hawkins and Shohet (1989) in humanistic psychotherapy; Kranz (1994) from play therapy; Dryden (1995) from the behavioural school; and Wilkins (1995) from psychodrama.

Counselling authors such as Inskip and Proctor (1993, 1995); Proctor (1994, 2000); Mearns (1995); Juhnke (1996); Orlans and Edwards (1997); Carroll and Holloway (1998, 2001); Webb and Wheeler (1998); Holloway and Carroll (1999); and Wheeler and King (2001) have described their views on the supervisory process. In addition, there is a personal experience of counselling supervision documented by Winter (1994).

Goals of supervision

There may be a number of goals the supervisor intends to fulfil when entering into a supervisory relationship. Goals will, of course, depend on the psychotherapeutic orientation (humanistic, psychodynamic, systemic, behavioural or integrative) of the supervisor. These are some of the goals, in no particular order, which the reader may wish to consider:

1   To enable the supervisee to feel safe, in a confidential environment of exploration and professional/personal development and in the overall service of the client.
2   To facilitate the supervisee to develop an open-minded attitude to dealing with the inevitable anxieties, fear of failure and conflict arising when constantly monitoring material from client work (Ronnestad and Skovholt, 1993), particularly with trainees. This may be by encouraging commentaries on the therapeutic alliance (using the 'me/not me' interface) accommodating associations as relating to the supervisee and the client with unclear mixtures of insightfulness and misrepresentation, and establishing a safe emotional climate.
3   To help the supervisee clarify (and resolve where possible) the conflicts between their intentions, that which the client appears to want/need and the expectations from the clinical work setting.

4 To assist the supervisee to master countertransference as she/he tunes into client material.

5 To examine, retrospectively, interventions made by the supervisee and consider future ethical practice in the light of these interventions.

6 To focus upon the client (who remains anonymous) and the symptom as they unfold symbolically in the interaction within the broader context and setting.

7 To monitor and evaluate the interaction between the client and the supervisee and the supervisee and the supervisor as it may be mirrored in a parallel process (in a psychodynamic theoretical model).

8 To offer support and challenge to the client through providing support and challenge to the supervisee. For example, challenging the supervisee in their belief that there is only one correct response/intervention.

9 To provide a forum for reflexivity on assessment and evaluation, therapeutic intervention, goals and the therapeutic alliance, perhaps augmented through the use of video analysis or examining process notes taken by the supervisee after clinical sessions.

Goals of the supervisee might include:

1 To be attended to and 'overseen' within a supportive, empathic, exploratory and guided approach.

2 To find a tolerance for mistakes and self-doubts and to be able to receive feedback on and/or explore them in the context of the therapeutic alliance.

3 To feel the supervisor as a participant/observer in the therapeutic alliance.

4 To achieve self-understanding and effective clinical techniques/skills.

5 To be able to bring emotional pain and/or anxiety-provoking scenarios to the relationship.

6 To access the personal growth and educational potential possible through supervision.

7 To experience the importance of the interpersonal relationship with the supervisor.

8 To feel understood, respected and constructively criticised, leading towards further learning.

9 To collaborate with the supervisor to assess competencies/learning needs; define goals and procedures for the supervision and to bring further learning needs which are responded to as they arise.

10 To leave the supervision session feeling more confident and that there is something helpful which may be used with a client, either now or later, as a means of understanding what was previously elusive.

An analysis of the nature of supervision

Role of movement

During the process of DMP supervision movement may or may not be utilised. However, Penfield (1994), when speaking about the importance of supervision, encourages movement as a way of nurturing the evolving therapist. The early practitioners in the UK used to meet together regularly to offer support to each other through peer supervision by role playing their clients in movement, the others acting as the therapist or witnesses (Payne, 1984). The professional association (ADMT.UK) has offered supervision groups in which movement has been actively stressed as integral to the supervisory method. Scarth (1995) refers to movement as integral to the process of supervision, and Clarke (1999) documents her experience of 'moving supervision' (ibid.: 110) in one of these ongoing groups facilitated by the author. Other writings have alluded to the significance of therapist creativity in supervision (Lett, 1993) and the need to examine issues as they arise, communication with clients, families and colleagues, and to clarify any power dynamics and those of role/contract/context (Murrow, 1999). If movement is considered during supervision it requires balancing with verbal psychotherapy skills to promote a full engagement with the process.

Group and individual supervision

Supervision will always need to contain some teaching and learning elements, particularly during initial training. In group supervision there is the advantage of learning from others as well as having input on group dynamic theory. The group itself will mirror some relevant dynamics which can be thought about with reference to the supervisee's practice groups. After some time the process and dynamics within an established group of supervisees will become reflective of the actual situation the supervisees and their clients are experiencing. Therefore the way in which the supervisor and the supervisee approach and engage with the process concerned will directly enable supervisees to work more effectively with clients. Supervision is often the vehicle of transformation and integration for the supervisee. It should be a safe environment (Payne, 2001a) where challenging experiences can be put into perspective and built on, reducing stress and increasing competence. The free expression of mistakes, negative feelings, stuckness and other testing matters to the supervisor, without fear of judgement, can enhance the supervisee's journey as a professional.

Individual supervision can be primarily valuable in providing an emphasis on the impact of personal issues in the context of clinical practice. It can also support clinicians in examining staff relationships and organisational dynamics, which may sometimes hinder effective practice and outcome. It may provide more safety (without peer presence) to bring self-doubts, anxieties and uncertainty, and in identifying useful issues to explore in personal therapy.

It is generally proposed that the supervisee's personal therapy is undertaken in conjunction with supervision sessions, as this work may dovetail with matters arising in the supervisory process resulting in increased understanding in, for example, countertransference issues.

Whether group or individual supervision, it is important to agree at the outset the ground rules for working safely together, to clarify the methods that will be used and to outline the boundaries of roles and responsibilities.

The development of the profession

As we move towards the professional state regulation of DMP in the UK (the other arts therapies are already state regulated by the Health Professions Council), a longer-term goal must be the provision of opportunities for the undertaking of systematic research into this pivotal aspect of CPD. Consequently, it is a timely opportunity for clinicians to embark on supervision research, where, together with demands for evidence-based practice and practice-based evidence in recent years, there will be significant implications for training, theory and practice.

There are many methodological challenges, particularly for an approach which uses both movement and words. Studies which embrace the client, supervisee and the supervisor's experiences; the importance of context; the impact on client process and outcome; the nature of the parallel process; somatic countertransference; the communication of our work to others (including the client) – whatever the topic there is certainly plenty of scope in this cutting-edge new area of theory and practice.

Supervision has the potential to help in the calls for greater self-regulation and accountability to patients, organisations and professional bodies which are all a high priority for clinicians.

Professional bodies rely on supervision to underpin safe and ethical practice. Gradually they are making career-long supervision a professional requirement rather than a recommendation. The sister practices of counselling and psychotherapy are moving to supervision as a requirement for all practising clinicians regardless of length of experience, although the psychology profession is still at the stage of recommending it. Supervision is increasingly seen as having a vital role to play in safeguarding the interests of patients/clients and practitioners and valued by groups previously not having thought it necessary. In my own supervisory practice I have noticed an increasing willingness on the part of the National Health Service, and other voluntary health and social care bodies, to finance arts therapies supervision.

ADMT.UK has developed a 'code of professional practice' (ADMT.UK, 1997, www.admt.org.uk) which outlines policies on topics such as professional competence, ongoing professional development, actual procedure, conduct of the therapist, equality of opportunity, confidentiality, insurance, clinical notes and record keeping and implementation. A significant sentence under 'professional competence' reads 'The therapist has a responsibility to arrange adequate supervision. In addition to this specialist advice should be sought where necessary.' The 'adequate supervision' referred to might be considered as one hour of supervision to every eight hours of clinical work. If in group supervision, the number of hours should be multiplied by the number of supervisees in the group. For example, a group of three supervisees needs 4.5 hours per month to ensure each supervisee receives 1.5 hours of individual time per month.

The readers

This book is written and edited with the needs of the client, trainee, supervisee, trainer and supervisor in mind. It is edited with reference to dance and movement psychotherapists, body psychotherapists, other arts therapies professionals, those who use approaches normally associated with counselling/psychotherapy from the psychological therapies and practitioners from the health and social care professions. It is expected that all these readers will benefit from the contents of this volume, which takes the concept of the embodied self further. As client readers, it is hoped you may be able to understand the nature of supervision within the practice of DMP and appreciate that needs are being addressed in a professional manner and within an ethical framework.

As trainees receiving supervision from trainers and experienced practitioners, often for the first time while on placement (in-house or in-session) it is anticipated that you will be able to gain confidence from supervision and develop skills and knowledge of practice in DMP. As you develop through your training, using chapters from this book to guide your reflections on the underlying issues inherent in your supervisory process, you will hopefully gain a deeper understanding of its significance to your professional development. The roots of our clinical practice lie in our capacity to reflect on our practice with curiosity. This can be in a systematic, coherent or even chaotic, creative way. It can be in a group of peers or with one other in a dyadic encounter. Whatever the practice setting, the content, relationship with clients and colleagues or institutional philosophy, personal material will arise. You should feel safe and supported, where mistakes and challenges can be expressed and worked with, all in a collaborative atmosphere. The novice practitioner's perspective is voiced in a number of chapters in this volume, particularly in Chapter 8.

As supervisees, whether recently graduated or well down the path towards an experienced supervisee, this book holds a wealth of ideas and practical suggestions, vividly illustrated through the lived experiences of supervision.

Theoretical notions are clearly outlined together with descriptions and evaluations of processes and models of practice for consideration. For those supervisees engaged in, or considering, research these chapters will provide stimulation for a variety of possible research topics.

As trainers and supervisors it is anticipated that you can identify with, and appreciate, the theory and practice as described, even though your own approach and philosophy may be different. By reading the examples from supervisory practice retold here perhaps your own practice will evolve in a different and imaginative way. It is hoped the suggestions offered and the narrative of the trainee's/supervisee's voice will give plenty of scope for reflection on supervisory processes, whether in a training, clinical health/ social care or private practice context. Those from verbal psychotherapy may find the approach to working with the non-verbal through the bodymind an insightful practice which will inform and contribute to their own interventions as supervisors and supervisees.

Finally, professionals from health and social care will be able to see the impact the supervisory process has on practitioners who use the body and expressive movement and dance as a psychotherapeutic approach to change. In learning to appreciate the work which evolves out of supervision on this process, perhaps a deeper recognition and truer mirroring of the nature and role of DMP might be grasped.

The book highlights some aspects of supervision in DMP to date. In this way it provides the reader with a spur for learning about and enquiring into supervision. It is anticipated that some readers may find questions and topics here to take forward into future research studies.

Aims of the book

A number of aims came to mind while the book was in gestation:

- *To prioritise supervision in the development of the profession.* In developing the professionals the profession is developed. Many qualified practitioners are either required to undertake supervision by their professional associations or to undertake it voluntarily as part of their own continuing professional development. In some countries only students have supervision as part of their training, while in others all levels are required to demonstrate ongoing supervision for their work. Research is required into the effectiveness of supervision and its outcomes before any decision is taken on whether or not it should be made mandatory for all practitioners.
- *To offer an overview of current practice.* By providing an overview of some approaches currently available in DMP training in the wider international community, practitioners and students are able to see where their practice of supervision and receipt of supervision sits. Other approaches may be adopted as well as those psychodynamic ones prevailing in this

book. My own approach is integrative, others may be more person-centred, for example. There are as many approaches to supervision as there are approaches to DMP. Whatever the theoretical orientation though, supervision is essential for ethical practice. As such this overview cannot be comprehensive; it can serve to light the fire in others to begin to articulate this newly developing subject area within DMP professional development. It is highly significant that we are now thinking about supervision in a wider context such as the public domain.

- *To generate an international collective.* This aim is fulfilled by presenting a range of chapters from around the world. Authors come from Europe, the USA, Australia and Israel. In this way we can see what is different and what is similar in our ways of working in supervision despite our cultural differences.

- *To provide for theory and practice.* In offering a breadth of theoretical models and ways of practising supervision in the chapters herewith, it is hoped that readers will expand their knowledge and understanding, find challenges to their current thinking and feel validated by their experiences of DMP supervision.

- *To make links with the theory and practice of verbal psychotherapy.* Authors have referred to several psychotherapeutic theories and research as well as drawing upon their own empirical findings in thinking about supervision. The chapters illustrate an integration between the worlds of symbolic movement and dance and verbal psychotherapy. The hybrid we call DMP contains both the art and science of clinical practice.

- *To give training courses a text to which staff and students can refer.* Currently there are no texts in the supervision of DMP clinical practice. It is hoped that the ideas presented in this book will convey a sense of the kind of supervision practices possible for students and qualified practitioners.

- *To spread the word on the nature and role of supervision.* Related to the aim above, this book can begin to address the dearth of documentation in the public domain on this crucial subject. It is hoped that it will act as a catalyst for research and evaluation on the processes and outcomes of supervision, thereby increasing our understanding of supervision. In addition, clients and others interested in the process of supervision might gain valuable insights into the nature of practice and the way supervision can develop psychotherapists.

- *To offer support and encouragement to those new to the profession.* By including several vignettes relevant to students in training it is anticipated that trainees and trainers will have a greater understanding of the process of learning in DMP and appreciate more ways to support and encourage those new to the profession in their work.

The chapters

The following themes appear to stand out from the contributions in this book: (1) definitions of supervision; (2) movement as part of the supervision process; (3) supervision during clinical training (in-session and in-house); (4) individual supervision in health and social care and private practice; (5) group models of supervision.

The book has been structured into eleven chapters, all from leading, registered, practising trainers and clinical supervisors in dance and movement psychotherapy. There are first- and second-generation writers. Each of the chapters reflects the theoretical and philosophical roots of the author's approach to supervision and offers examples from practice as illustration. The subject is introduced with related literature and examples built in for ease of reference. Analysis and commentary are included. Any notes and references are given at the end of each chapter. Author and subject index are at the back of the book together, with an Appendix of further information on professional associations, journals and training programmes worldwide. The order of the chapters as presented is organised from theoretical issues, to a number of programme-based settings on group supervision in the main section, to, lastly, private practice-based individual supervision.

Below is a description of the chapters in order of their appearance. First, in the dance movement mediated supervisory relationship, embodiment and somatic intelligence are described as fundamental in the subsequent chapter to this one (Chapter 2) by Bonnie Meekums entitled 'Spontaneous symbolism in clinical supervision: moving beyond logic'. DMP supervision, in common with other supervision in the psychological therapies, encourages forms of knowing which emerge from 'not knowingness'. The supervisor becomes witness and co-participant, her own body being part of the process, and this has implications for session content and structure and for supervisor/supervisee self-care. This chapter stresses that creativity and experiential learning (right-hemisphere activities) are key ingredients to conscious understanding of the client–therapist relationship.

Rosa Maria Govoni and Patrizia Pallaro introduce the idea of supervision as part of a training course for dance movement therapists in Chapter 3. They illustrate the importance of good-quality supervision when conducted within a training setting. This can serve graduates as a way of setting up any future clinical practice whereby supervision is at the heart.

Dita Federman and Lee Gaber continue the theme of training by describing the concept of a group intervention model for supervision within a training programme in Chapter 4. Heidrun Panhofer provides us with insight into those forgotten pieces which can be so informative when reflecting on practice in Chapter 5, which focuses again on a training context. Isabel Figueira, in Chapter 6, furnishes the reader with the many nuances present in transcultural supervision within training both from the perspective of a student and trainer.

In Chapter 7, Wendy Wyman-McGinty writes about the contribution of authentic movement in supervising dance movement therapists. This illustrates the importance of an awareness of, and ability to, differentiate between internal feeling states at a somatic level. This, she says, is a finely developed sense of kinaesthetic empathy and attunement, the capacity to tolerate a range of affective material in a non-defensive and containing manner, the ability to track unconscious material on a movement level, and the ability to work symbolically. In learning to track one's somatic countertransference responses, an understanding of when it is helpful to use verbal interpretation or clarification within a session is developed.

In Chapter 8, Maggie Young, who, as an initiate into the profession, follows her process of supervision as a trainee with an experienced dance therapist in a clinical setting within the clinical group itself as well as in a peer group. Her learning reaches forward into her current practice today. In another group model in Chapter 9, Imke Fiedler offers the Balint approach to group therapy as an example of in-house supervision. The hypothesis is that dance/movement therapists need to reflect not only on a psychoanalytic perspective of the client–therapist relationship, but also on their professional role in teams, and to understand institutional structures in order to be more fully supported by the supervision process.

In Chapter 10, Penelope Best informs us about the multiple positions we can take when thinking about our client work as clinical professionals. The different forms of expression adopted to reflect can help us to gain valuable insight into the way forward with the most difficult clients. Chapter 11, by Kedzie Penfield, discusses supervision in the context of private practice. In it she gives us an indication of how we can utilise the supervisory relationship to help us gain a crucial understanding of our work in movement psychotherapy with clients in private practice.

Finally, as our clinical work develops further through practice and research I would like to make a strong plea for experienced practitioners to embark on supervision training. Currently there do not appear to be training courses for dance movement psychotherapists per se. However, there are many short courses and postgraduate certificate programmes in the counselling and psychotherapy world from which much can be learned. I undertook a course at Metanoia in 1987, and, due to my experience in a number of settings and with different client populations, I was able to make the necessary adaptations for supervising other practitioners working in movement psychotherapy.

Offering effective ongoing clinical supervision is a craft in its own right. It is different from personal psychotherapy and from line management. It is often about the relationship between client and therapist and process of therapy, but not always. Setting or organisational issues can have a huge impact on therapeutic outcome and need to be addressed in supervision. Ethical practice requires ethical supervision, and one of the key assessment and monitoring tasks for the supervisor is to ensure that the practice being brought is indeed ethical.

I hope you find this book helpful in your considerations of supervision and that it offers you another insight into the many ways of supporting clients in their journeys.

References

Casement, P. (1985) *Learning from the Patient*. London: Routledge.

—— (1990) *Further Learning from the Patient*. London: Routledge.

Carroll, M. (1996) *Counselling Supervision: Theory, Skills and Practice*. London: Cassell.

Carroll, M. and Holloway, E. (eds) (1998) *Counselling Supervision in Context*. London: Sage.

—— (2001) *Counselling Supervision*. London: Sage.

Clarke, I. (1999) *Supervision in Dance/Movement Therapy*. A dissertation submitted in part fulfilment of the degree of M.Ed., University of Bristol, England.

—— (2001) Supervision in dance/movement therapy. E-motion, ADMT.UK newsletter, 13, 3, 3–5.

Clarkson, P. (1996) Researching the 'therapeutic relationship' in psychoanalysis, counselling psychology and psychotherapy: a qualitative inquiry. *Counselling Psychology Quarterly*, 9, 2, 143–162.

—— (2003) *The Therapeutic Relationship* (2nd edn). London: Whurr Publishers.

Crocket, K. (2007) Counselling supervision and the production of professional selves. *Counselling and Psychotherapy*, 7, 1, 19–25.

DeStefano, J., D'Huso, N., Blake, E., Fitzpatrick, M., Drapeau, M. and Chamodraka, M. (2007) Therapist experiences of impasses in counselling and the impact of group supervision on their resolution: a pilot study. *Counselling and Psychotherapy Research*, 7, 1, 35–41.

Dryden, W. (1995) *Issues in Professional Counsellor Training*. Trainer and supervision Series. London: Cassell.

Gelso, C.J. and Carter, J.A. (1985) The relationship in counseling and psychotherapy. *The Counseling Psychologist*, 13, 2, 155–243.

Grant, J. and Schofeld, M. (2007) Career-long supervision: patterns and perspectives. *Counselling and Psychotherapy Research*, 7, 1, 3–11.

Hawkins, P. and Shohet, R. (1989) *Supervision in the Helping Professions*. Buckingham: Open University Press.

Holloway, E. and Carroll, M. (1999) *Training Counselling Supervisors: Strategies, Methods and Techniques*. London: Sage.

Horvath, A.O. and Symonds, B.D. (1991) Relation between working alliance and outcomes in psychotherapy: a meta analysis. *Journal of Consulting Psychology*, 38, 139–149.

Inskip, F. and Proctor, B. (1993) *The Art, Craft and Tasks of Counselling Supervision: Making the Most of Supervision*. Sussex: Cascade.

—— (1995) *The Art, Craft and Tasks of Counselling Supervision: Becoming a Supervisor*. Sussex: Cascade.

Jacobs, M. (1996) *In Search of Supervision: In Search of a Therapist*. Buckingham: Open University Press.

Jacobsen, C.H. (2007) A qualitative single case study of parallel process. *Counselling and Psychotherapy Research*, 7, 1, 26–33.

Juhnke, G. (1996) Solution focussed supervision: promoting supervisee skills and confidence through successful solutions. *Counselor Education and Supervision*, 36, 48–57.

Kranz, P. (1994) Recommendations for supervising play therapists. *International Journal of Play Therapy*, 3, 2, 45–52.

Langs, R. (1994) Combining supervision with empowered psychotherapy. *Journal of Contemporary Psychoanalysis*, 30, 25–47.

Lett, W. (1993) Therapist creativity: the arts of supervision. *The Arts in Psychotherapy*, 20, 371–386.

Martin, D.J. and Garski, J.P. (2000) Relation of the therapeutic alliance with outcome to other variables: a meta analytic review. *Journal of Consulting and Clinical Psychology*, 18, 3, 238–450.

Mearns, D. (1995) Supervision: the tale of the missing client. *British Journal of Guidance and Counselling*, 23, 1, 421–427.

Mothersole, G. (1999) Parallel process: a review. *The Clinical Supervisor*, 18, 2, 107–121.

Murrow, L. (1999) Dance movement therapy supervision (extract from *Dance Therapy Association of Australia Newsletter*, 1998, 5, 3). *E-Motion, ADMT. UK Newsletter*, 11, 1, 14–16. First published in *Dance Therapy Association, Australia Inc. Newsletter*, July 1998, 5, 3.

Orlans, V. and Edwards, D. (1997) Focus and process in supervision: a personal view. *British Journal of Guidance and Counselling*, 25, 3, 409–414.

Paley, G. and Lawton, D. (2001) Evidenced based practice: accounting for the importance of the therapeutic relationship in UK NHS therapy provision. *Counselling and Psychotherapy Research* 1, 1, 12–17.

Payne, H. (1984) Working in dance movement therapy: the need for support groups, supervision and personal therapy. *ADMT newsletter*, March, p. 6.

—— (2001a) Student experiences in a dance movement therapy group: the question of safety. *European Journal of Psychotherapy, Counselling and Health*, 4, 2, 267–292.

—— (2001b) Authentic movement and supervision. *E-Motion, ADMT. UK Newsletter*, 13, 4, 4–7.

Payne, H. and Wright, S. (1994) The sorcerer's apprentice: learning and teaching in supervised dance movement therapy practice. Unpublished paper, available through the author.

Penfield, K. (1994) Nurturing the working therapist. *ADMT. UK Newsletter*, 6, 4, 4–5.

Proctor, B. (1994) Supervision-competence, confidence, accountability. *British Journal of Guidance and Counselling*, 22, 309–318.

—— (2000) *Group Supervision: A Guide to Creative Practice*. London: Sage.

Robinson, L.A., Berman, J.S. and Niemeyer, R.A. (1990) Psychotherapy for the treatment of depression: a comparative review of controlled outcome research. *Psychological Bulletin*, 108, 1, 30–49.

Ronnestad, M.H. and Skovholt, T.M. (1993) Supervision of beginning and advanced graduate students of counselling and psychotherapy. *Journal of Counselling and Development*, 7, 4, 396–405.

Scarth, S. (1995) Supervision on the move. *ADMT.UK Newsletter*, 7, 2, 12.

Skovholt, T.M. and Ronnestad, M.H. (1992) *The Evolving Professional Self: Stages and Themes in Therapist and Counsellor Development*. New York: John Wiley.

Smith, A.J.M., Klein, W.C. and Hutschemaekers, G.J.M. (2007) Therapist reactions in self experienced difficult situations: an exploration. *Counselling and Psychotherapy Research*, 7, 1, 34–41.

Walker, S., Ladany, N. and Pate-Carolan, L.M. (2007) Gender-related events in psychotherapy supervision: female trainee perspectives. *Counselling and Psychotherapy Research*, 7, 1, 12–18.

Webb, A. and Wheeler, S. (1998) How honest do counsellors dare to be in the supervisory relationship: an exploratory study. *British Journal of Guidance and Counselling*, 26, 4, 509–524.

Wheeler, S. (2003) *A Research on Supervision of Counsellors and Psychotherapists: A Systematic Scoping Search*. Rugby: British Association of Counselling and Psychotherapy (BACP).

Wheeler, S. and King, D. (eds) (2001) *Supervising Counsellors: Issues of Responsibility*. London: Sage.

Wheeler, S. and Richards, K. (2007) The impact of clinical supervision on counsellors and therapists, their practice and their clients: a systematic review of the literature. *Counselling and Psychotherapy Research*, 7, 1, 54–65.

Wilkins, P. (1995) A creative therapies model for group supervision of counsellors. *British Journal of Guidance and Counselling*, 23, 2, 245–257.

Winter, P. (1994) A personal experience of supervision. *British Journal of Guidance and Counselling*, 23, 3, 353–355.

Worthen, V.E. and Lambert, M.J. (2007) Supervision: advantages of adding systematic client tracking to supportive consultations. *Counselling and Psychotherapy Research*, 7, 1, 48–53.

Chapter 2

Spontaneous symbolism in clinical supervision

Moving beyond logic[1]

Bonnie Meekums

Introduction

The purpose of this chapter is to attempt to theorise phenomena associated with spontaneous symbolism within clinical supervision by asking 'what is really going on here?' I will first illustrate the phenomena using a case example taken from my own supervision practice, before critically appraising two potential explanatory clinical theories. I will begin with somatic counter-transference, which has been used to explain embodied knowing within the therapeutic frame (Lewis, 1984). I will then consider empathy, and in particular embodied empathy (Dosamantes-Alperson, 1984; Cooper, 2001) as another key theory of relevance to my question.

After examining these theoretical constructs, I will consider possible mechanisms for the phenomena associated with spontaneous symbolism in supervision, including ideas derived from quantum physics, and Rowan's (2002; Rowan and Jacobs, 2002) concept of 'linking' which Rowan and Jacobs associate with Gestalt field theory. From this I hope to draw some conclusions, and to pose further questions for research.

My approach to movement supervision

I usually work in a room large enough for movement. The supervisee initially discusses issues related to clinical work. Eventually both of us let go of trying to address these issues using left-brain problem-solving techniques, instead instructing the unconscious to reveal a new perspective on them.[2] Together, we engage in a non-led physical warm-up, each listening to our own body while moving. I also begin tuning into my supervisee, balancing this with attention to my own body. The main purpose of the warm-up is to open both of us to the wisdom of the body, and to enter into a right-brain state, sensitive to forms of knowing that extend beyond 'logical' left-brain functions. I quite often notice some symbolic motif in my movement at this point, which I silently observe and then put metaphorically on the back burner for later. The supervisee seamlessly moves into improvisation, while I unobtrusively retreat to a seated position, where I can act as witness[3] and open further to intuitive forms of knowing. What emerges from such immersion in a shared process is a spontaneous symbol or symbols. These symbols may appear as body movement, changes in sensory information, affective change, or visual or (internal) linguistic imagery in what may be described as the 'inner eye' or 'inner ear'. They may be 'received' by either party; my experience is that each of us will often 'receive' a different but complementary part of a jigsaw. The symbols can be conceptualised as a way of seeing things afresh; a new perspective on the supervisee's work situation, as if from a new position in space. The symbolic nature of such insight is often not immediately understood; indeed, I would argue that it is important not to rush to 'understanding' with the left brain. When the supervisee feels that she or he has moved for long enough we begin our verbal evaluation, a kind of sense-making and grounding of the raw material of the world of metaphor.

Case vignette

The following case vignette illustrates my movement supervision practice. It begins after Tanya,[4] a supervisee with whom I had been working for some years, had first checked in and warmed up with me, and then had been moving on her own for a short while.

> I noticed Tanya's arms crossing and uncrossing at the wrists. At the same time, I noticed a tingling in my vagina. I was initially shocked, as I could not detect any obviously seductive symbolism in her movement and I was fairly certain that I was not sexually attracted to her. I decided to accept this as information, the significance of which would reveal itself later.
>
> During our evaluation, Tanya told me that when she had been crossing and uncrossing her wrists she remembered the play *Titus Andronicus*, in which Lavinia is raped and her hands and tongue cut off. She made a link with her practice agency which had been 'raped'; it had been used, but its funding had been brutally cut. I reflected that like Lavinia it might lose its 'hands' (employees).
>
> I shared my embodied experience with Tanya. Was I countertransferentially the rapist? That didn't fit for either of us. We tentatively concluded that my body had symbolised life-affirming energy. Perhaps, like the rape victim who reclaims her sexuality, this was a signal of hope. We both experienced a deep sense of satisfaction at having unravelled these insights, trusting in our own intuitive access to the world of unconscious symbolism, and feeling deeply connected in the process.
>
> It turned out that the centre did not have to close.

The above vignette demonstrates several typical features of spontaneous symbolism in clinical supervision:

- Forms of knowing are in embodied symbolic form.
- The embodied symbols associated with such knowing cannot be forced, but appear as 'received' by the person experiencing them.
- The supervisor must be in a prepared and open state I think of as 'witnessing'.
- Both supervisor and supervisee tolerate 'not knowing' (Bion, 1974, cited in Casement, 1985; Meekums, 2002), accepting the symbol without immediately understanding it.
- Symbols require evaluation of their relevance to the supervisee's work.
- Both supervisee and supervisor experience a deep sense of satisfaction after evaluation.
- The process depends on a trusting relationship between supervisor and supervisee.

I will now examine somatic countertransference as one possible theoretical position from which to understand spontaneous symbolism.

Somatic countertransference: a critical appraisal

Transference refers to the client's reactions towards the therapist associated with the client's (often early) significant relationships (Dosamantes-Alperson, 1987). These reactions are communicated both verbally and non-verbally and are recognisable by both their intensity and tenacity. If a phenomenon is transferential, it will repeat (Winnicott, 1960a). While the term 'countertransference' can have several meanings, for the purposes of this chapter it will be taken to mean the therapist's response to the client's transference.

Jung described transference as an emotional bridge (Mattinson, 1975). These emotions, according to Jung, are deeply rooted in the body. Lewis, a dance movement therapist, provides an early description of what she calls somatic countertransference. Influenced by Jung, she focuses on communication between what she calls the 'somatic unconscious' of the therapist and that of the patient. It is this, she claims, that 'is the most subtle to perceive, but by far, the most potentially transformative' (Lewis, 1984, p. 182). Lewis describes experiences of receiving client material through her head, heart or vagina, and via any of Jung's functions (sensory, cognitive/conceptual, emotional or intuitive as in symbolic images). These phenomena have a quality of 'other than self' (Lewis, 1984, p. 184).

A later discussion by Ross (2000) demonstrates that the term 'somatic countertransference' is also adopted by some psychodynamically orientated verbal therapists. She does not acknowledge the prior thinking within the DMP profession, and defines somatic countertransference rather loosely as 'the physical experience of the therapist in the therapy session' (Ross, 2000, p. 452). Ross sees her own physical experiences as potentially a communication from and about her clients that can and should be thought about and put into words. But does this make it countertransference?

One possible scenario, alluded to by Ross, is that the therapist is playing the role of the mother/container, in relation to the infant/contained. She references the concept of projective identification, in which the therapist has the experience of the client 'getting under [the therapist's] skin' (Ross, 2000, p. 458). Ross does not consider explanations of these embodied phenomena beyond transference theory.

Samuels, a Jungian analyst, discusses syntonic countertransference.[5] The term 'syntonic' is derived from radio communications and denotes 'the accurate tuning of a receiver so that transmission from one particular transmitter may be received' (Samuels, 1985, p. 191). Samuels distinguishes between syntonic countertransference and intuition, as the former necessarily involves emotional processes including projection and introjection and may be experienced by the therapist as intrusive. He uses the term 'intuition' to mean 'a sense of where something is going, of what the possibilities are, without conscious proof or knowledge' (Samuels, 1985, p. 62), and defines empathy as 'putting oneself in the place of, or inside, another person without losing sight of who one is' (Samuels, 1985, p. 147). Intuition, thus according to Samuels, has directionality and purpose, and is future-orientated, while empathy is present-orientated. Despite these helpful definitions, writers from the psychodynamic tradition like Lewis, Samuels and Ross fail to make a clear distinction between empathy and syntonic countertransference.

Sensations in the therapist's body in response to a client could be the result of projective identification. Projective identification may be viewed as a particular form of transference, eliciting corresponding countertransferential reactions in the therapist (Segal, 1993), and is thought to be an unconscious attempt on the part of the client to communicate and contain aspects of experience (Ogden, 1993). The therapeutic aspect of projective identification lies in the possibility of the therapist containing, digesting and slightly modifying the aspect of the client that is being projected. The client eventually internalises this newly modified aspect of self (Lewis, 1984).

In describing her body and in particular her belly as a receptacle of the client's emotional state, it would appear that Ross has developed a finely tuned *empathic* ability to pick up terror ('grips it like a vice'), pain ('silent'), fear ('nausea'), anxiety ('makes me sweat with a particular smell'), and a sexualised environment ('can excite my vagina') (Ross, 2000, p. 462). Ross, however, sees these phenomena in terms of projective identification. She claims that those clients who make use of a therapist that can metabolise the embodied information available through projective identification are those whose mother was not attuned and responsive. This view concurs with Alexandris and Vaslamatzis (1993), who claim that when the main form of communication between therapist and client is non-verbal, 'the patient has suffered from violent, massive, intensive projective identification processes used by the parental figures', and that this occurs 'at the pre-verbal phase, when the child thinks with its body' (Alexandris and Vaslamatzis, 1993, p. 141).

Lewis similarly observes that most often 'it is the wounded split off infant self of the patient that I hold in my uterus' (Lewis, 1984, p. 187). Such containment is not confined to women therapists; one male therapist says he experiences a similar sense of 'holding' or containing certain clients in the centre of his body (upper abdomen/chest area), emanating out into the beyond the body space (Nolan, 2006, personal communication).

Ogden suggests that therapists may find working with projective identification difficult and unsettling, as they experience 'feelings and thoughts that are in an important sense not entirely one's own' (Ogden, 1993, p. 21). The therapist's capacity to think may be impaired in this process.

Explanations of embodied countertransference in terms of regressed clients and impairment of thinking do not immediately fit for spontaneous symbolism in supervision. Supervisees are likely to have engaged in their own therapy making the explanation of regressed states less feasible. Parallel process could be one explanation (in which the supervisee is experiencing the client's regression), but this is not always apparent (as in the vignette above). Spontaneous symbolism does seem to arise from 'other than self', but does not display inner disturbance or impairment of thinking; on the contrary, 'flow states' are typical (Beard and Wilson, 2002, p. 132).

Thus somatic countertransference, while sharing some characteristics with spontaneous symbolism in clinical supervision, is not an appropriate explanatory construct. Samuels' distinction between empathy and intuition is worthy of further consideration, as the latter implies insight that has direction for the future. However, the concept is poorly defined. A far greater literature exists in relation to empathy, and it is to this that we turn next.

Defining empathy

The word 'empathy' was translated in about 1910 from the German *Einfühlung*, meaning 'in-feeling', or feeling into (Shlien, 2001). While person-centred therapists do not accept the concept of transference or countertransference within the therapeutic relationship, empathy is almost universally considered to be an important factor in therapeutic change.

However, this concept is also problematic. Cox and Theilgaard (1987) observe that attempts to define empathy are unsuccessful due to its preconscious and pre-verbal nature. I prefer the term 'non-verbal' or 'paraverbal' (depending on the precise context), to avoid any associations with immature or primitive forms of communication.

Shlien (2001) attempts to normalise empathy. While he acknowledges that 'many definitions are afloat' (p. 38), he does propose his own definition of sorts, framing empathy as a form of intelligence. He subverts the kind of elitism that claims empathy as a preserve of the professional therapist, suggesting that empathy is present in other spheres of experience, including kite flying. A fictional illustration of this point may be found in Khaled Hosseini's (2004) novel *The Kite Runner*, in which Hassan seems to know intuitively where the kite will land. Shlien also cites empathic experiences that are in apparent opposition to the goals of therapy: 'The sadist knows your pain, and takes pleasure in it' (Shlien, 2001, p. 38). The difference Shlien observes is that the sadist lacks sympathy (feeling for), a long derided yet apparently necessary quality in the therapist. Shlien also distinguishes between empathy and understanding, claiming that: 'Understanding is a volitional effort and a service that empathy is not' (Shlien, 2001, p. 41); but is the mere knowledge of another's pain, as Shlien suggests, empathy? Arguably not; in the therapy context the word has acquired a meaning that includes benevolent understanding in addition to Shlien's focus on accurate 'reading'.

Embodied empathy

Cooper, professor of counselling, claims empathy is always embodied, and 'any empathic attunement which does not include a somatic component will only ever be a partial attunement' (Cooper, 2001, p. 225). He recommends that therapists should spend some time relaxing their bodies before sessions, and that bodywork be incorporated into psychotherapy training programmes. Cooper uses the metaphor of a fountain to explain embodied experiencing. The 'waters' of the fountain are only divided into thoughts, emotions and bodily sensations as they fall back to earth; embodiment thus derives from and returns to the source, a more holistic subjectivity.

Pearmain, writing from a psychodynamic perspective, bemoans the 'belated recognition of embodied cognition' (Pearmain, 1999, p. 45). She is aware of the movement aspects of attunement:

> a parent attunes to the infant not only by mirroring the exact gesture but by capturing the dynamic and affective qualities so that a child's shout can be mirrored by a parallel movement of swooping the child up.
>
> (Pearmain, 1999, p. 46)

The embodied nature of empathy was researched by Scheflen (1964). His frame-by-frame analysis of psychotherapy sessions revealed that at moments of deep empathy, therapists shifted their posture to mirror that of the client, literally taking a shared 'position'. Interestingly, his 18 therapists came from a wide range of psychotherapy approaches, but showed remarkable similarity in this respect. More recently, Ramseyer (2006) has used modern digital techniques to demonstrate a similar effect, showing that rapport was associated with synchrony (attuned interactional movements that share certain qualities and occur in response to a partner's movement within a very short time lapse, like an echo) but not mimicry (a deliberate copying, likely to have a longer time lapse). This may be because the roots of embodied empathy lie in early, pre-verbal experience; we have known for some decades that neonates synchronise their movements with adult speech (Condon and Sander, 1974).

Dosamantes-Alperson (1984), a dance movement therapist, makes deliberate use of synchrony. In an early reference to what she calls 'kinaesthetic empathy', she locates it within what Winnicott (1960b) calls the 'holding environment'. She describes how she uses kinaesthetic empathy, re-creating her client's movement in her own body 'in the abbreviated and coded form of incipient body movements' (Dosamantes-Alperson, 1984, p. 156), so that she can sense and respond to the client's emotional state. This process can be partly explained now by neurophysiologic research concerning the existence of 'mirror neurones'. These allow learning by imitation, also firing as 'body memory' when we see someone performing an action that lies within our own repertoire (Rizzolatti *et al.*, 1996).

Cox and Theilgaard (1987) offer another perspective on embodied empathy. Writing from the perspective of largely verbal therapy, they suggest that embodied empathy occurs in relation to words, because as children, when we learn a new word it becomes associated with a complex affective–sensori–motor pattern. If this is true, and it is consistent with established learning theory, then it may be possible for movement to become associated in the reverse direction, i.e. with affective states and even certain words and other symbols. A witness to movement, whose mirror neurones are firing, thus also has associations with certain affective states and possibly words or other symbols through their own lived body experience. However, this indicates the need for awareness and caution; the associations may be uniquely those of the witness, and may not be shared by the person being witnessed.

In an echo of Winnicott's concept of 'being alone while someone else is present' (Winnicott, 1958, p. 30), Cox and Theilgaard suggest that intense empathy may need few or no words. They also suggest that, when successful, it results in tension reduction and a sense of a new fit. This description is interesting, as it resonates with Gendlin's (1981) description of focusing.[6] Gendlin developed an understanding of the 'felt sense', which Pearmain (a psychodynamically orientated therapist) observes offers a way of speaking 'what was unknowable, vague and amorphous in revealing ways' (Pearmain, 1999, p. 47). Gendlin emphasised the importance of allowing time for these amorphous senses to develop and be experienced before labelling them; Pearmain acknowledges that this demands patience and 'a capacity to stay open without knowing' (Pearmain, 1999, p. 47), but that: 'When we suspend semantic labelling then there is more time for a broader gathering of this subliminal process to come forward into awareness' (Pearmain, 1999, p. 45).

It is as if, in focusing, the individual is learning to empathise with, and witness, the self. I would argue that this is a necessary condition for congru-ence, and also for accurate empathy; if the individual is able to distinguish moment-to-moment embodied experiencing by focusing on the 'felt sense', it is easier to distinguish a new event within the interactional sphere, including spontaneous symbolism.

The importance of 'not knowing' is also discussed elsewhere (Bion, 1974, cited in Casement, 1985; Meekums, 2002). My own understanding of the importance of not knowing derives both from spiritual practice,[7] and from my studies with the dancer and choreographer Mary Fulkerson (1982) in the 1970s. Mary used to instruct her students to literally lie in wait for the impulse to move, and to adopt an attitude of 'waiting without expectation'.

The ability to tune into another human being via one's own felt sense and to contain this experience without interpretation (to cope with not knowing) implies acceptance of self and other. It also implies the ability to be alone while someone else is present (Winnicott, 1958, p. 30). This kind of communication is at once both a re-embodying of early and satisfying, deeply connected relating, yet with a highly evolved, some might say transpersonal quality, linking as it does to the spiritual practice of silence and inner attention that can lead beyond the self, to oneness with others and perhaps with the universe. However, before we can conclude this, we need to examine a theoretical debate about the nature of empathy, namely the degree to which empathic experience implies merging. Is empathy 'for real'? Or is it always one step removed, like the actor who steps into a character's clothes, feeling and even moving the body's imprint but never becoming that body?

'As if' or 'for real'?

Rogers maintained the importance of the 'as if' quality in empathy; he had been disturbed by the experience of losing the boundaries of his 'self' with a client. For Buber's 'I–Thou', however, there is no 'as if' (Shlien, 2001). To experience 'I–Thou' 'means touching and being touched existentially' (Schmid, 2001, p. 58). It is also intrinsically tied up, according to Schmid, with the art of not-knowing, and with an expression of love. However, he claims that 'the crucial thing about empathy is that it always tries, but is never able, to reach the other person. There will always remain a difference' (Schmid, 2001, p. 61). For Schmid, then, there is no merging, and possibly not even an overlapping of boundaries. He references Levinas, for whom desire originates in the Other, and is always a movement towards infinity. Coming closer to the Other increases desire, and so true desire is insatiable.

This does not resonate with my experiences of spontaneous symbolism in clinical supervision, which *when shared* are accompanied by a deep sense of satisfaction, a sense of 'rightness' and fulfilment associated with what some label as transpersonal phenomena or flow states. Rowan characterises such experiences of deep connection as 'linking' (Rowan, 2002; Rowan and Jacobs, 2002), 'a way of relating that refuses to take separation seriously' (Rowan and Jacobs, 2002, p. 82).

Casement (1985) advocates the kind of empathy that is 'a capacity to share in the experience of others, not just like our own but as our own' (Casement, 1985, p. 34). The process of moving between thinking and feeling, between empathic identification and separation, is made possible according to Casement by the willingness of both supervisor and supervisee to enter a state of play and reverie. This means not getting caught up in the detail of what is being said (as might happen in verbal supervision at times), but paying attention to form and symbolism.

Thus, for some therapists, empathy must remain an 'as if' experience. Others, both humanistic and psychodynamic, more fearlessly surrender to what Rowan calls 'linking'. Spontaneous symbolism in clinical supervision seems to depend on the latter, which I suggest is only possible when the supervisor has secure boundaries of self that can be reconstructed after each experience of their dissolution.

Possible mechanisms for spontaneous imagery in clinical supervision

The theory of linking proposed by Rowan offers a conceptual framework, but not an explanatory mechanism. *How* can I know what another is thinking or feeling to the extent, for example, that I form pictures in my head, experience embodied symptoms, or 'hear' words that directly address my supervisee before she or he has uttered a word? Mirror neurones, while they explain some aspects of empathic communication, may not fully explain such complex phenomena.

One possibility is the 'quantum self' theory put forward by Zohar, who suggests that consciousness is 'the wave side of the wave/particle duality' (Zohar, 1990, p. 82), and that the *relationship* between two waves/selves becomes a thing in itself, a binding force akin to the love between lovers or Buber's (1937) I–Thou. The whole (relationship) is greater than the sum of its parts, rather as Mozart's *Eine Kleine Nachtmusik* is more than a collection of notes. The aesthetic possibilities are intriguing, and may explain the sense of deep satisfaction and well-being experienced by both my supervisee and myself when we have these moments of deep connection. Zohar suggests that what she calls 'relational holism' is not only the essence of consciousness but of both truth and art, and provides a 'bridge between mind, truth and beauty and the world of matter' (Zohar, 1990, p. 85). It is interesting to note that here she makes a link with creativity. Her theory offers a scientific conception of this bridge between worlds alluded to by several other theorists, and explains the possibility of growth or learning arising from it.

Because wave functions can overlap and become entangled, quantum systems can 'get inside' each other and form a creative, internal relationship of a sort not possible with Newtonian billiard balls. Quantum systems 'meet', and through their meetings, evolve.

(Zohar, 1990, p. 113)

Rowan and Jacobs (2002) offer one idea that resonates with Zohar's (1990) relational holism, and with Samuels' (1985) metaphoric description of syntonic countertransference as a tuned receiver. They reference an idea from field theory (a key theory in Gestalt psychotherapy), that two selves connect on a particular frequency so that neither has to enter the other's space. The relationship may thus be viewed as rhythmic, wave-like and temporal rather than physical, particle-like and spatial. This may partially explain the apparently mystical and transpersonal experience associated with spontaneous symbolism in supervision; wave-like experiencing means consciousness is embodied, but can be simultaneously in all places and connected with all things. Thus, in the relationship with the Other, one reaches a relationship with the cosmos, and infinity.

This idea of linking into something that is rhythmic and wave-like has obvious appeal to dance movement therapists, who feel at home in the world of rhythmic attunement. However, attunement to frequency may not involve any outer movement at all, and inwardly there may be a deep silence and stillness, an emptying yet a sense of complete satiation. It is as if one reaches the place that yang turns into yin (or rather there is no yin or yang).

Discussion

We have seen that somatic countertransference is an inadequate descriptor for phenomena associated with spontaneous symbolism in clinical supervision, as supervisees are on the whole rather different from regressed clients. Rowan's (2002) concept of 'linking', together with concepts from Gestalt theory and quantum physics, allows us to begin to conceptualise the phenomena in terms of the linking of vibrating systems.

The willingness of the supervisor to enter into a state of embodied not-knowingness, to be fully present as both 'tuned-in' witness and experiencing self, appears to be key to the development of spontaneous symbolism during clinical supervision. I have written elsewhere (Meekums, 1998, 1999, 2000, 2002) about the importance of metaphor in conveying complexity and facilitating a deep understanding between client and therapist or between group members, allowing those individuals to provide the kind of silent 'not-knowing' (yet deeply understanding) witness that conveys far more than words, and also allowing for the transformative qualities of the metaphor to reveal themselves. If supervisors jump in too quickly with an opinion or interpretation, or stay with content, this may stunt the supervisee's growth and will not develop the kinds of processes from which profound insights can emerge. Only once a symbolic communication has been fully felt can the supervisee begin to make sense of and evaluate it using her or his own internalised supervisor and in dialogue with the embodied supervisor. Insights arising from this process may be experienced as deeply satisfying flow states.

The supervisory relationship, like the therapeutic relationship (Shaw, 2003), is affective and embodied. Both supervisor and supervisee need to feel willing to share material that may feel odd or even embarrassing. This kind of supervision may only be possible when a strong relationship of mutual trust has been developed. The supervisee's experience of the supervisor as benevolent witness is crucial, and may be more likely to occur when the supervisee is an experienced therapist who is not looking to the supervisor for guidance so much as for the holding of a reflective space.

Despite the obvious differences from clinical practice, the embodied nature of the supervisory relationship indicates the need for the supervisor to let go of uninvited material at the end of supervision sessions. The supervisor must also be mindful of her or his own lived body experience, present in the supervision room. Training in moment-to-moment awareness, as in focusing or meditation practice, can assist in determining the origins of experience. I would suggest that a physical warm-up at the beginning of movement supervision, followed by a process of 'emptying' of self (like the 'clearing a space' of focusing) and 'tuning in' to present experience (like Fulkerson's 'waiting without expectation') could be a useful preparation during the supervision session. A similar process involving 'tuning out' from the supervisee's material by the supervisor and re-tuning to oneself after the end of supervision is also recommended.

The phenomena associated with spontaneous (embodied) symbolism are undoubtedly present not solely in movement supervision, but also in more traditional verbal clinical supervision (Nolan, 2006, personal communication). My suggestions about tuning in and tuning out (or similar practices) may therefore have relevance beyond DMP and body psychotherapies, as indicated in some parts of the counselling literature (Cooper, 2001). I have used aspects of DMP in counsellor training since 2002. Harvey (2006, has researched the use of expressive therapies including authentic movement (AM) in counsellor training, and Payne (2001), personal communication) is unique in having offered AM to counselling trainees for 11 years. Dance movement might assist the trainee counsellor or psychotherapist to develop an awareness of the lived body, of subjectivity and intersubjectivity and of somatic intelligence including the felt sense (Gendlin, 1981). It may also assist in the development of the internalised supervisor (Casement, 1985; Payne, 2001) and assist the trainee in developing a capacity for creative 'not-knowing' and 'linking'. These propositions require testing through systematic research.

Conclusion

In asking the question 'what is going on here?' in relation to spontaneous symbolism within DMP supervision, I have rejected somatic countertransference as a theoretical construct in this context. Rowan's concept of 'linking' holds greater theoretical power while wave theory and field theory both offer explanatory mechanisms.

Bodywork and dance movement practices may be useful in developing the capacity of both supervisors and supervisees from other therapeutic orientations to open to the unpredictable nature of embodied insights, and they may also assist supervisor self-care. A willingness to open to experience, to merge consciousness, to risk exposure and to tolerate 'not-knowing' are all aspects of this form of supervision requiring a degree of maturity. These phenomena cannot be forced, but when they occur they are associated with feelings of well-being and even, as Adler (1999) suggests, love. At times, I would say that I have felt touched by Grace.

Notes

1 This chapter was previously published as 'Spontaneous symbolism in clinical supervision: moving beyond logic' by Bonnie Meekums in *Body Movement and Dance in Psychotherapy* (2007), vol. 2, no. 2, and is reprinted here by permission of the publisher of that journal (Taylor and Francis Ltd, <http:// www.informaworld.com/>.

2 For supervisees who have been working with me for some time, the supervisee's decision to move implies this tacit instruction.

3 I use the word 'witnessing' here to describe a certain attitude and role adopted by the supervisor. This is similar to the role adopted within authentic movement (AM) (Wyman-McGinty, 1998), but while my approach to movement supervision shares some similarities with AM the form is slightly different. One of these differences is that the supervisee may or may not have his or her eyes open, and either party may occasionally speak while the supervisee is moving. While I have some experience of AM, my own training in improvisatory movement and the wisdom of the body derives from my dance movement training during the 1970s with Mary Fulkerson (1982). I developed an experiential understanding of the power of witness through being witnessed by her, and much later I understood the concept also via my work with survivors of child sexual abuse, which I researched for my doctorate (Meekums, 1998, 1999, 2000).

4 My thanks to Tanya for her permission in using this case vignette. Her name has been changed.

5 Other writers refer to this phenomenon as identifying or concordant transference.

6 Space does not allow here for a full exposition of Gendlin's six movements of focusing. However, his work has been integrated into many person-centred counselling trainings, as it encourages trainee counsellors to become aware of their embodied experiencing. This is likely to assist congruence, and may also assist empathy. I would argue that DMT training could also benefit from the integration of focusing into its pedagogy.

7 I have meditated since the age of about 17. Since 1980, my spiritual practice has been largely located within the Religious Society of Friends (Quakers).

References

Adler, J. (1999) Who is the witness? In P. Pallaro (ed.) *Authentic Movement: A Collection of Essays by Mary Starks Whitehouse, Janet Adler and Joan Chodorow*. London: Jessica Kingsley.

Alexandris, A. and Vaslamatzis, G. (1993) Countertransferential bodily feelings and the containing function of the analyst. In A. Alexandris and G. Vaslamatzis (eds) *Countertransference: Theory, Technique and Teaching*. London: Karnac.

Beard, C. and Wilson, J.P. (2002) *The Power of Experiential Learning: A Handbook for Trainers and Educators*. London: Kogan Page.

Buber, M. (1937) *I and Thou*, trans. R.G. Smith. Edinburgh: T. & T. Clark.

Casement, P. (1985) *On Learning From the Patient*. London: Routledge.

Condon, W.S. and Sander, W.L. (1974) Neonate movement is synchronized with adult speech: interactional participation in language acquisition. *Science*, 183, 99–101.

Cooper, M. (2001) Embodied empathy. In S. Haugh and T. Merry (eds) *Empathy*. Ross-on-Wye: PCCS Books.

Cox, M. and Theilgaard, A. (1987) *Mutative Metaphors in Psychotherapy: The Aeolian Mode*. London: Tavistock.

Dosamantes-Alperson, E. (1984) Experiential movement psychotherapy. In P. Lewis (ed.) *Theoretical Approaches in Dance-movement Therapy*, Vol. 2. Dubuque, IA: Kendall-Hunt.

—— (1987) Transference and countertransference issues in movement psychotherapy. *The Arts in Psychotherapy*, 14, 3, 209–214.

Fulkerson, M. (1982) The move to stillness. *Dartington Theatre Papers*, 4th series, no. 10.

Gendlin, E. (1981) *Focusing*. London: Bantam.

Hackmann, A. (1998) Working with images in clinical psychology. In A.S. Bellack and M. Hersen (eds) *Comprehensive Clinical Psychology*, Vol. 6. Oxford: Pergamon.

Hawkins, P. and Shohet, R. (1989) *Supervision in the Helping Professions*. Buckingham: Open University Press.

Herman, J. (1992) *Trauma and Recovery*. New York: Basic Books.

Hosseini, K. (2004) *The Kite Runner*. London: Bloomsbury.

Lakoff, G. and Johnson, M. (1999) *Philosophy in the Flesh: The Embodied Mind and its Challenge to Western Thought*. New York: Basic Books.

Lewis, P. (1984) The somatic countertransference: the inner pas de deux. In P. Lewis (ed.) *Theoretical Approaches in Dance-movement Therapy*. Dubuque, IA: Kendall-Hunt.

Mattinson, J. (1975) *The Reflection Process in Casework Supervision*. London: Tavistock.

Meekums, B. (1993) Research as an act of creation. In H. Payne (ed.) *Handbook of Inquiry in the Arts Therapies: One River, Many Currents*. London: Jessica Kingsley.

—— (1998) Recovery from child sexual abuse trauma within an arts therapies programme for women. Unpublished Ph.D. thesis, University of Manchester.

—— (1999) A creative model for recovery from child sexual abuse trauma. *The Arts in Psychotherapy*, 26, 4, 247–259.

—— (2000) *Creative Group Therapy for Women Survivors of Child Sexual Abuse: Speaking the Unspeakable*. London: Jessica Kingsley.

—— (2002) *Dance Movement Therapy: A Creative Psychotherapeutic Approach*. London: Sage.

—— (2006) Embodiment in dance movement therapy training and practice. In H. Payne (ed.) *Dance Movement Therapy: Theory, Research and Practice*. Hove: Brunner-Routledge.

Ogden, T.H. (1993) The analytic management and interpretation of projective identification. In A. Alexandris and G. Vaslamatzis (eds) *Countertransference: Theory, Technique, Teaching*. London: Karnac.

Payne, H. (2001) Authentic movement and supervision. *E-motion, ADMT Newsletter*, 13, 4, 4–8.

Pearmain, R. (1999) What do we mean by developing empathy and intuition? *Counselling*, February, 45–48.

Polanyi, M. (1969) *Knowing and Being*. London: Routledge & Kegan Paul.

Ramseyer, F. (2006) Co-ordination of non-verbal behaviour in psychotherapy: synchrony as a marker of rapport? Paper presented to the 37th Annual Meeting of the Society for Psychotherapy Research, Edinburgh, 21–24 June.

Rizzolatti, G., Fadiga, L., Gallese, V. and Fogassi, L. (1996) Premotor cortex and the recognition of motor action. *Cognitive Brain Research*, 3, 131–141.

Ross, M. (2000) Body talk: somatic countertransference. *Psychodynamic Counselling* 6, 4, 451–467.

Rowan, J. (2002) Three levels of empathy. *Self and Society*, 30, 4, 20–27.

Rowan, J. and Jacobs, M. (2002) *The Therapist's Use of Self*. Buckingham: Open University Press.

Ryle, A. (1991) *Cognitive Analytic Therapy: Active Participation in Change*. Chichester: Wiley.

Samuels, A. (1985) *Jung and the Post-Jungians*. London: Routledge.

Scheflen, A. (1964) The significance of posture in communication systems. *Psychiatry*, 27, 316–324.

Schmid, P. (2001) Comprehension: the art of not knowing. Dialogical and ethical perspectives on empathy as dialogue in personal and person-centred relationships. In S. Haugh and T. Merry (eds) *Empathy*. Ross-on-Wye: PCCS Books.

Segal, H. (1993) Countertransference. In A. Alexandris and G. Vaslamatzis (eds) *Countertransference: Theory, Technique, Teaching*. London: Karnac.

Shaw, R. (2003) *The Embodied Psychotherapist: The Therapist's Body Story*. London: Brunner-Routledge.

Shlien, J. (2001) Empathy in psychotherapy: vital mechanism? Yes. Therapist's conceit? All too often. By itself enough? No. In S. Haugh and T. Merry (eds) *Empathy*. Ross-on-Wye: PCCS Books.

—— (c. 2004) A counter-theory of transference. Available online at <http://world.std.com/~mbr2/cct.counter-theory.html> (accessed 13 May 2007).

Staff and Departmental Development Unit (2002a) *Postgraduate Certificate in Learning and Teaching in Higher Education Route 1 Course Handbook 2002*. Leeds: University of Leeds.

Van der Kolk, B. (1994) The body keeps the score. Available online at <http://www.trauma-pages.com/a/vanderk4.php> (accessed 13 May 2007).

Winnicott, D.W. (1958) The capacity to be alone, reprinted in D.W. Winnicott (1965) *The Maturational Processes and the Facilitating Environment*. London: Hogarth Press.

—— (1960a) Counter-transference, reprinted in D.W. Winnicott (1965) *The Maturational Processes and the Facilitating Environment*. London: Hogarth Press.

—— (1960b) The theory of the parent–infant relationship, reprinted in D.W. Winnicott (1965) *The Maturational Processes and the Facilitating Environment*. London: Hogarth Press.

Wyman-McGinty, W. (1998) The body in analysis: authentic movement and witnessing in analytic practice. *Journal of Analytical Psychology*, 43, 239–260.

Zohar, D. (1990) *The Quantum Self*. London: Bloomsbury.

Chapter 3

The supervision process in training

Rosa Maria Govoni and Patrizia Pallaro

Introduction

Movement, words, imagination, creativity, self-reflection and analysis all contribute to awareness of the rich psychological interplay between therapist[1] and supervisor as well as of the parallel processes occurring between patient and therapist or therapist and supervisor. The complex task of supervision within a dance movement therapy (DMT) psychodynamic training programme involves linking specific theories to the clinical material presented, supporting specific methods of intervention to aid patients in the exploration of their experiences, developing the therapist's understanding of clinical issues and related therapeutic interventions, bringing to awareness transference and countertransference themes, individuating unconscious motivations and healing fantasies present in both patient and therapist, as well as aiding therapists in finding ways to creatively spark their patients' growth. All this needs to occur in an emotionally safe space in which both therapists and patients are respected for their hard work.

Art Therapy Italiana (ATI) integrates classic dance/movement therapy training with the study of object relations theory, as represented by the British Independent School (Kohon, 1992). The creative modalities used within the supervisory setting are: movement, gesture and dance. Body expression facilitates access to that *potential space* in which transformative events can take place at the threshold between internal and external reality, as indicated by Winnicott (1965, 1971).

The capacity to symbolise is fostered by allowing unconscious communication between patient and therapist (or therapist and supervisor) to surface, by engaging the therapist's creative process in response to such communication, developing movement- and body-based interventions, then verbalising the co-constructed experience, thereby facilitating the integration of body and psyche in both patient and therapist.

The specific movement instruments used to foster the therapist's understanding of the psychological process, as it relates to and informs body, expression and meaning, sustaining our students' learning throughout the course of ATI's dance/movement therapy training as well as in their clinical practice and during supervision, are:

- Laban movement analysis, integrated by Bartenieff Fundamentals (Laban, 1950; Bartenieff and Lewis, 1980).
- Kestenberg studies and movement profile (Kestenberg, 1973; Kestenberg and Sossin, 1979; Lewis and Loman, 1990; Kestenberg Amighi *et al.*, 1999).
- Authentic movement process (Adler, 1985, 2002; Chodorow, 1991; Wyman-McGinty, 1998, 2005; Pallaro, 2000, 2007).

Important theoretical concepts taught in ATI's training and emphasised in the supervisory process are:

- The study of the creative process, aesthetic experience and development of symbol formation, understanding of unconscious fantasies and their functions as well as analysis of the various developmental phases, each with their characteristics and specific roles (Klein, 1932, 1958, 1961; Segal, 1957; Milner, 1969; Kestenberg, 1973; Bollas, 1989; Chodorow, 1991; Alvarez, 1992).
- An understanding of the matrix of the body and its kinaesthetic nature, its unconscious reverberations and unmentalised experience (Schilder, 1950; Whitehouse, 1963; Chaiklin, 1975; Dosamantes-Alperson, 1980; Bernstein, 1984, 1986; Adler, 1985; Chodorow, 1991; Wyman-McGinty, 1998, 2005).
- An awareness of the functions that the *intermediate area* and *transitional object* play in the relationship between patient and therapist or between therapist and supervisor, as well as the understanding of the concept of psyche/soma (Winnicott, 1965, 1971; Milner, 1969; Bram and Gabbard, 2001; Thomas, 2005).
- The observation of both normal and pathological development as framed by the characteristic stages and phases of each (Klein, 1932; Erikson, 1950; Bick, 1964; Freud, 1965; Stern, 1985; Gaddini, 1987; Sowa, 1999).
- A deepening understanding of both transference and countertransference phenomena, particularly in their somatic manifestations, as well as an awareness of the embodied experience as it manifests in the patient (or patients), therapist and supervisor (Heimann, 1950; Racker, 1968; Ogden, 1982, 1997, 2005; Momigliano and Robutti, 1992; Scharff, 1992; Scharff and Scharff, 1998; Wyman-McGinty, 1998, 2005; Becker and Seibel, 2005; Pallaro, 2007).

This integrated curriculum was developed specifically to aid our students in comprehending movement expression as a form of primary organisation and codification of psychic experience in the pre-verbal phases of human development (Klein, 1932, 1958, 1961; Stern, 1985; Schore, 1999; Wyman-McGinty, 2005). Special attention is devoted to the understanding of how movement and embodied experience foster neurological as well as psychological growth (Winnicott, 1965; Stern, 1985; Berrol, 1992; Wyman-McGinty, 1998, 2005; Schore, 1999; Fonagy *et al.*, 2002).

Culture and ethnic background always frame these processes and imbue our experiences with different meanings (Foulks and Schwartz, 1982; Pallaro, 1993, 1997; Bonovitz, 2005). Therefore, awareness of culturally based stereotyping, ethnocentrisms and expectations, understanding of ethnically determined verbal as well as non-verbal communications, whether consciously or unconsciously expressed, are of vital importance in the therapeutic endeavour (Pallaro, 1997).

Our students are trained to provide their patients with a safe and secure environment, learning to pay close attention to their patients' needs, desires, longings, personal characteristics and potential growth capabilities, all in the service of fostering a secure sense of self. Students practise making conscious use of movement as an analytic tool, in order to grasp the complexity of what is exchanged between patient and therapist – the meaning embedded in a movement, in a body posture, in a sensation or in a word as relating to specific affective states in their own personal therapy, in their supervised practicums and experiential training. Students make conscious use of the body as a receptive instrument for kinaesthetic empathy, proprioceptive knowledge and imagination, as well as to discern crucial aspects of their somatic countertransferential experiences and to contain them (Pallaro, 2007).

Students are also expected to develop the ability to respect themselves and *the other*, each with their unique presence and original characteristics, to be able to open themselves to the unknown and withstand the ensuing tension, to enter the realm of potential space and transitional phenomena with neither judgement nor expectations, so that the creative process can unfold and manifest its complex interweaving relationships (Bion, 1970; Adler, 1985; Bram and Gabbard, 2001; Driver, 2002a; Thomas, 2005). Further, students are encouraged to delve into their personal psychological development to augment their capability to sustain and relate to their dissociated, disavowed, repressed, inhibited or split-off parts (Chodorow, 1991; Dosamantes, 1992) .

The supervision setting as a learning alliance

The supervision setting facilitates and supports a learning alliance, not a therapeutic relationship but one in which an open and receptive attitude towards deeper emotional intelligence is encouraged. The supervisory frame enables the development of the capacity to access preconscious and unconscious levels of experience and, most importantly, to take into account each supervisee's individuality, spontaneity and creativity (Meltzer, 1979; Resnik, 1995; Ferro, 1999; Driver, 2002a; Bolognini, 2003; Chasseguet-Smirgel, 2005; Martin, 2005; Ogden 2005; Thomas, 2005).

The concept of the supervisory frame or *holding* implies clear and definite boundaries about what a learning experience is as opposed to what a therapeutic intervention might be (Sarnat, 1992; Driver, 2002a). The supervisor's task is to hold everything which may surface during supervision (Godbout, 2004). Clinical sensitivity is therefore called upon to refer the supervisee to his/her own personal therapy in order to aid the student in further personal development while not succumbing to the temptation of providing therapy and thus crossing the teach/treat boundary (Sarnat, 1992; Stewart, 2002; Becker and Seibel, 2005).

Within the supervisory frame, the supervisees' learning styles, needs, capacities and deficits in relating to their patients may be revealed in the first paragraphs of a case presentation, its demographic data, in the discussion of issues regarding the therapeutic frame, the analysis of the material presented by the patients and the emotional and symbolic content of their movement expressions.

The act of a therapist-in-training presenting a clinical case in supervision may uncover problematic areas in the development of the student as a therapist as well as elicit specific questions aimed at deepening the relationship between patient and therapist. Using an analytical approach, supervisors help supervisees in presenting cases, in designing questions emerging from their work as they relate to technique, interpretation, transference and countertransference, as well as to the observation of their patients' movement patterns. It is crucial to a well-rounded development of the therapist-in-training to notice the multi-layered issues arising from reflection and analysis. For example, questions such as the the following may arise:

- What healing fantasies may underlie a particular intervention on the part of the supervisee?
- How does the supervisee deal with her desire to cure another person?
- How does the supervisee attempt to deal with those of her own life experiences which might interfere with or hinder treatment?
- Does the supervisee's unconscious longing to be healed motivate her interventions?
- How does the supervisee's present or past personal analysis or psychotherapy enter into the therapeutic, supervisory and learning process?
- What are the supervisee's own fantasies about what helps and what hinders treatment?
- How does the supervisee deal with her patient's transference towards her and, in turn, how does she deal with her own transference towards her supervisor and the institution within which they operate?

The therapist-in-training does not operate in a vacuum. The supervisee–supervisor dyad is a mutually affecting relationship, so the same questions apply to the supervisor (Ungar and Bush De Ahumada, 2001). ATI encourages supervisors to pose and reflect on the same issues and provides supervisors with group and individual consultations with the same themes in mind (Driver, 2002b). All levels of dyadic engagement (therapist/patient, supervisee/supervisor, supervisor/institution, supervisor/training programme, supervisee/institution, supervisee/training programme, supervisor/patient and all other possible combinations) are taken into account and, hopefully, processed (Yerushalmi, 1999).

Within the supervisory relationship, the learning alliance usually follows a developmental process (Driver, 2002a). The supervisor attunes to the supervisee's level of clinical experience, embraces the theories and modalities most familiar to the supervisee, and accepts the therapeutic contract as it is established in the clinical setting/organisation in which the supervisee works.

In the supervisory relationship, a synergy is established between supervisor and supervisee by sharing movements and their meaning as well as the words and thoughts connected to them, thus creating the deep understanding and self-knowledge that only body language can contain and manifest. The non-judgemental atmosphere held by the supervisor assures supervisees that whatever is revealed by their bodily expressions is part of the clinical work and will not be analysed in terms of the supervisee's life experiences or particular problems. Students are required to commit, throughout the course of the training, to acknowledgement of whatever may surface in supervision, that must then be faced in their personal therapy (and not avoided) in order to understand its clinical relevance for their patients' treatment.

No matter what modality is chosen to introduce a particular case, special attention is given to the non-verbal mode of communication with which supervisees share information regarding their engagement in the therapeutic relationship (Jacobs, 1994). Supervisors must be able to attune to their students' communication styles. They must also be willing to engage in their own self-reflections and analyses in order to understand the parallel processes operative within the patient–therapist dyad, the supervisor–supervisee dyad, the supervisor–training programme dyad, the therapist–agency dyad, and so on.

DMT, play and the creative arts therapies approach

Students' past experiences in dance and movement, DMT training, exposure to working with different clinical populations, personal therapy, practice with other art forms, as well as creative endeavours in general, shape the background knowledge from which a clinical case is presented. ATI's creative arts approach focuses on the supervisees' process of reporting their patients' movement phrases, significant postures, gestures, all expressed in role-playing enactments which evidentiate and pinpoint to the recognition of conscious and unconscious material as manifest through sensations, feelings and thoughts. Awareness of supervisees' own experience, as it manifests through their bodies, supports the process of tracing emotional and symbolic content as they relate to their patients' themes and dynamics.

Using dance, movement and gesture enables the supervisor to understand resistances, defences, projections and projective identifications as means of non-verbal communication (Jacobs, 1994; Becker and Seibel, 2005). Transference and countertransference, with special attention to somatic countertransference (Pallaro, 2007), are also addressed through dance, movement and gesture. All are elements of the therapeutic relationship that need to be examined for the benefit of the patient.

Creative, long-lasting learning occurs in play (Winnicott, 1971). Hawkins and Shohet (1989, p. 7) comment:

> In the supervision that we give we try and create a climate which avoids the sense of expert and student both studying the client 'out there' and instead create a 'play space' in which the dynamics and pressures of the work can be felt, explored and understood; and where new ways of working can be co-created by both supervisor and supervisees working together.

This is the atmosphere ATI supervisors strive to create with their supervisees.

The supervision process

In ATI's training, the supervisor's creativity finds its way in the interplay of primary and secondary processes, focusing with extremely detailed attention on movements, feelings, sensations and images, flowing amidst and shifting to and from the larger context in which different therapeutic processes and interventions (such as clinical history, clinical rationale for treatment, contract with the institution in which the supervised therapy is provided and a contract with ATI's training programme) take place.

Supervisors learn to shift their overall attention from outer realities impinging upon treatment to inner processes and phenomena, while paying attention to their own somatic countertransferential cues so as to aid their supervisees in mastering the art of providing psychotherapy.

Supervisors carefully monitor their tendencies to overstimulate and overfeed their supervisees. They focus on establishing a learning alliance by helping their supervisees to recognise psychological dynamics and movement themes, which may promote or obstruct their work with patients. Movement analysis is used to observe what the supervisee brings at a movement level, in the body. Verbal descriptions of sessions and session themes as well as dialogues between patient(s) and therapist are also scrutinised. If supervisees are not well aware of their own defences and personal issues, problematic dynamics may emerge from patients' conscious or unconscious material and communications. Movement is used in various ways to reveal these unconscious messages, often embedded in projective identifications, which are frequently disturbing to the supervisee. Moving through polarities, as Laban indicated in his effort-shape theory, using the Laban's 'cube' or Laban's 'drives' (Bartenieff and Lewis, 1980, p. 91), using specific exercises, called 'fundamentals' (Bartenieff and Lewis, 1980, p. 229) or improvising in relation to an image or feeling in order to work through countertransferential material, are all ways in which supervisors aid supervisees in opening their awareness and consciousness to deal therapeutically with the issue at hand. Whether it is a body image disturbance, a physical pain, difficulty in the expression of a developmental movement pattern or tension flow rhythm, the supervisor will initiate the movement work in the supervisory setting in order to help supervisees in the deconstruction of hidden communications, gentle dismantling of bodily defences and recognition of psychological obstacles or collusive relationships.

Training in authentic movement for the DMT supervisor supports development of further clinical sensitivity. It hones supervisors' skills to hold conflictual material, to discern transference and countertransferential cues as well as increasing their capacity to make choices which will benefit their supervisees' development and growth (Driver, 2002a; Becker and Seibel, 2005; Pallaro, 2007) as well as, of course, their supervisees' patients.

Instruments, techniques, methods and goals of supervision

The use of Laban's (1950) and Bartenieff's (Bartenieff and Lewis, 1980) techniques, which prepare for the engagement of perceptive attention and observation (Gendlin, 1978; Dosamantes-Alperson, 1980; Deikman, 1982; Aposhyan, 2004), ground supervisees in a deep experience of their bodies, allowing kinaesthetic sensations and feelings to arise in an environment of safety. Therapists-in-training become subtly aware of those deep connections. Becoming aware of those connections thus enables therapists to identify and then offer intervention strategies which may elicit profound psychological transformations in their patients, especially those who present as extremely regressed, severely ill or low functioning (Wyman-McGinty, 1998).

Sometimes it is useful to experiment with role-playing (La Barre, 2001) which allows students to access their patients' inner dynamics and manifestations in their patients' transference, as well as engages supervisees in examining their own countertransferential material towards understanding their own unconscious healing fantasies.

The practice of authentic movement (Adler, 1985, 2002; Chodorow, 1991; Wyman-McGinty, 1998, 2005; Pallaro, 2007) further enables students to open up to and yet be able to remain in that difficult emotional place of *not-knowing* (Bion, 1970; Adler, 1985; Yorke, 2005; Pallaro, 2007). Students develop the capacity to trust that an image aiding the therapeutic process may arise, that a sensation connecting their experiences to those of their patients may manifest, that a thought or insight rooted in their kinaesthetic experiences may elicit valid interpretations (McCall, 1986; Musicant, 1994, 2001; Pallaro, 2007).

ATI offers two different modalities of supervision, a group process and an individual one. Both are required in order to receive the final certification of completion of training. In both formats, authentic movement is often used along with role-playing structures, which vary depending upon the group modality. In the individual format, role-playing is usually done by the supervisee but the supervisor may also take an active part in it. In group supervision there is more space (physical, mental and emotional) to use different forms of creative exploration while role-playing.

Often therapists-in-training become conscious of their own personal desire to heal and to be healed in a group setting where cases are presented in a predetermined rotation schedule. Each member presents a clinical case. Along with the verbal information necessary to frame the issues and presenting problems, the supervisee is encouraged to play the parts of both patient and therapist at different times. Themes related to the healing patient/therapist couple will emerge, allowing the supervisor and the group to work as a *resonance body* (Nikolitsa, 2002) in a supporting yet differentiated manner, concentrating at times on specific issues in order to help supervisees become aware of their countertransference and discern personal material from projections and projective or introjective identifications. To be open and receptive to the group mind and resonance body allows therapists-in-training to discover new ways to promote reparative experiences and to offer appropriate creative interventions in the therapeutic work with their patients.

DMT training group and choreography

Akin to choreographic process, an example of a DMT group supervision session entails the components of the invisible dancer (patient) made visible in the body of the supervisee; the chorus (her fellow colleagues); and the supervisor. When positions and movements change in the dance, hunches and insights may occur. Supervisees may be able to shed light on their unconscious processes, thus gathering further thoughts or discovering other movements which may prove fruitful in the therapeutic endeavour with their patients.

The supervisee presenting the case is flanked by colleagues who, taking turns, choreograph different movement or body interventions in response to their bodily-felt experiences as they emerge from their own reactions to the material presented. Or, embodying the patient's themes, stance and movements, the chorus is made to move by the supervisee's directions and suggestions while the supervisee is engaged (through the so-called split attention process) in her own bodily-felt experience first and followed by that of her patient (Dosamantes-Alperson, 1980; Caldwell, 1997; Pallaro, 2007). The supervisor moves in and out, on and off the stage, sometimes offering her own bodily-felt experience as counterpoint, other times offering verbal suggestions, if deemed appropriate. At other moments, questions are formulated in order to discover the differences between two movement sequences and their induced reactions or to probe further about the supervisee's personal ideas, images, judgements, projections, blocks or emerging bodily-felt sensations.

In the final section of the dance, all supervisees pause in order to further process the material emerged and allow for the reintegration of new insights. All engage in enquiring into, for example, what the body feels it needs to do after this process and what the dance tells us about the patient, the therapist and ourselves. A composite picture of the patient–therapist-in-training dyad is thus created. Hopefully new ideas will surface from this dance which will in turn aid the supervisee in focusing on the next intervention needed to enable the therapeutic relationship to move forward.

Vignette *(extract from supervisee's notes)*[2]

> I remember the strange body feeling of much pain in my left arm and upper trunk, as if I were having a stroke, and a subtle rage experienced one day after one of my sessions with a borderline patient. In the supervision group in which I presented this material, the supervisor asked me to instruct two colleagues to play a bit of a typical scene occurring in therapy with that patient. They enacted the scene while I observed. At one point, the supervisor asked me to sit down and feel my trunk, feeling the shape/posture I was in, and then to release some of the tension by exhaling 'shape flow support breath'. This opening to shape flow support with breath allowed me to really feel what I was seeing. I saw the destructive behaviour of my colleague in the role of the patient and the masochistic conduct of the colleague in the role of the therapist. I felt a lot of anger, and at that moment, a personal memory surfaced while the sharp pain in my upper chest and left side disappeared. I realised then how much rage I was holding on behalf of my patient, seemingly spilling it into me and how difficult it was for me to be aware of it so that it could be properly contained and metabolised.
>
> Further work in my own therapy allowed me to work through my rage, which was blocking my clinical understanding. Through supervision, I realised I had identified with my patient's rage and was resonating with it, caught in a strong projective identification, holding feelings my patient could not feel at that moment. Later in treatment, my patient felt safe enough to disclose her constant fear that her mother would die of a stroke because of her incompetence. Further concomitant work in

supervision allowed me to search for and find better treatment interventions for my patient, who certainly needed more containment, and a therapist who could openly withstand her attacks and fear.

DMT training group and authentic movement

The training group, a protected and open territory of expression, offers an opportunity for students to move in a self-directed manner, to get in touch with both their conscious and unconscious motivations for movement. All supervisors in the programme have been trained in, and practise, authentic movement regularly. Authentic movement training is introduced in the third year of the four-year curriculum. Elements of authentic movement are used to increase knowledge and awareness of projective mechanisms.

Immediately after the group has moved for about 30 or 40 minutes in a self-directed manner, with no suggestions whatsoever coming from the leader of the group (supervisor), the supervisor asks students to select a movement phrase they have found to be particularly significant and to repeat it a number of times. Dyads are formed; one person takes the witness position, the other the mover. Both alternately move their movement phrases in the presence of each other. The therapist-in-training, who was the mover in each sequence, speaks first while the other offers her witnessing. Every dyad does this at the same time in different places in the room.

In this supervision structure, one objective is to deepen the consciousness of judgemental opinions and biases as these emerge from both the witnessing and the moving experiences in another's presence, be it the supervisor/supervisee dyad or the therapist/patient dyad. This practice invariably touches upon various transference and countertransference issues. Supervisees are asked to honestly respond to questions such as:

- Did your movement change when being witnessed by the other?
- How did it change?
- Did you notice anything changing in your body as you witnessed?
- What did you perceive (if anything): a body sensation, an urge to move, a feeling?
- Did you see an image in your mind's eye?
- How does this experience relate to the case presented?

Such focusing and awareness work helps students comprehend the ways in which they are likely to project upon others, the patterns they are accustomed to forge in relation to specific events or encounters. With this method, students also discover from inside themselves what kind of therapeutic strategies they feel comfortable implementing or challenged in executing.

Vignette *(extract from supervisee's notes)*

In my internship in a private institution. I saw a very disturbed 8-year-old child twice a week. He was driving me crazy, running all over me and spitting on me any time I would try to stop him, screaming and banging things against the radiators in order to make louder noises, throwing pencils and pens around, anything he could get his hands on.

Although I had organised the room in a special way just for him, emptying it of all the things he could break, placing cushions that could be thrown around without damaging anything or anybody, one day, this boy goes behind a curtain and finds a drinking glass (which unfortunately I had not noticed before) and breaks it right away. The glass splinters into a thousand pieces. Now we can really hurt ourselves. I scream 'stop' and really stare at him, feeling not at all like a therapist, afraid that we will hurt each other. I yell at him to stay really still until I finish cleaning the floor. He does remain still, clearing the floor takes me a long time. I feel despair. I do not want to work with him any more. I am not capable of this. The floor is finally clear yet I keep telling him to be still. Finally it is time for him to go.

In my supervision group, one day I presented this case and spoke of my countertransference and my feeling of utter despair in his presence. I was encouraged to move with my peers as witnesses and to wait for images to emerge which could/would help me in those moments of feeling lost and not knowing what to do next. I find myself back in the psychotherapy room, I'm sitting on the floor, silent, not responding to any word or sound the boy utters. Then an image comes of a strong, big guard, a soldier at the edge of a fort. As this image emerges, the fact that this child is always doing things he is not supposed to comes to my mind. I can picture now the psychotherapy room as that fort, as a space in which I can stand guard for his as well as my own safety. He can use this fort as a solid base to approach his non-violent self and recover his ability to play again as a soldier or a fighting boy, just beside me.

I embody that image and start moving it. I become that very strong soldier, that big, strong, bound, grounded guard, who steadily walks at the edge of the fort and by doing so defines a safe space with definite limits. I also begin to talk as that guard with a loud, strong and direct voice. I understand now what I need to do in order to help this boy be safe and develop impulse control.

Conclusion

Supervision in ATI psychodynamic-oriented training implies a profound, trusting, creative relationship between trainees and supervisors. The supervisor functions as a container for different layers of experiences lived by the supervisees, all of which must be seen, recognised, analysed and used to foster the therapist-in-training's learning and growth.

Body and movement are conceived as instruments allowing supervisees and supervisors to enter into contact with both manifest and latent elements and dynamics intrinsic to the therapist–patient relationship. These elements need to be recognised as communications of the inner world of the patient. The supervisor helps the therapist-in-training process and metabolises these communications so that, when decoded and transformed, they can foster patients' awareness, growth and recovery.

Movement, gesture and dance, imagination and self-reflection emerge as essential components in this creative process of supervision. ATI's direct method of learning makes use of supervisors' and supervisees' direct experience, allowing its therapists-in-training to integrate their theoretical, clinical and experiential knowledge.

Notes

1 'Supervisee', 'therapist' and 'therapist-in-training' are used interchangeably throughout.
2 The material is herein reproduced with the supervisees' informed consent. Identifying features have been changed to protect supervisees' and patients' confidentiality.

Acknowledgements

The authors wish to dedicate this chapter to the loving memory of Teresa Escobar. The authors also wish to thank and acknowledge the contributions of Teresa Escobar, Leonella Parteli and Marcia Plevin, faculty of Art Therapy Italiana (http://www.arttherapyit.org) to this writing.

References

Adler, J. (1985) Who is the witness? A description of authentic movement. In P. Pallaro (ed.) (2000) *Authentic Movement: Essays by Mary Starks Whitehouse, Janet Adler and Joan Chodorow* (2nd edn) (pp. 141–159). London: Jessica Kingsley.
—— (2002) *Offering from the Conscious Body: The Discipline of Authentic Movement.* Rochester, VT: Inner Traditions.
Alvarez, A. (1992) *Live Company: Psychoanalytic Therapy With Autistic, Abused and Borderline Psychotic Children.* London: Routledge.
Aposhyan, S. (2004) *Body–Mind Psychotherapy: Principles, Techniques, and Practical Applications.* New York: W.W. Norton.
Bartenieff, I. and Lewis, D. (1980) *Body Movement: Coping with the Environment.* New York: Gordon and Breach.
Becker, B. and Seibel, J. (2005) Becoming Better Supervisors. Proceedings from the 40th Annual ADTA Conference: American Rhythms/International Rhythms. *Dance/Movement Therapy Practice and Research.* Columbia, MD: ADTA.

Bernstein, P.L. (1984, 1986) *Theoretical Approaches in Dance Movement Therapy*, vols I and II. Dubuque, IA: Kendall/Hunt.

Berrol, C. (1992) The neurophysiologic basis of the mind–body connection in dance/movement therapy. *American Journal of Dance Therapy*, 14(1), 19–29.

Bick, E. (1964) Notes on infant observation in psycho-analytic training. *International Journal of Psycho-analysis*, 45, 558–566.

Bion, W.R. (1970) *Attention and Interpretation*. London: Tavistock Publications.

Bollas, C. (1989) *The Shadow of the Object: Psychoanalysis of the Unthought Unknown*. New York: Columbia University Press.

Bolognini, S. (2003) *Psychoanalytic Empathy*. London: Free Associations Books.

Bonovitz, C. (2005) Locating culture in the psychic field: transference and counter-transference as cultural products. *Contemporary Psychoanalysis*, 41(1), 55–75.

Bram, A.D. and Gabbard, G.O. (2001). Potential space and reflective functioning. *International Journal of Psycho-analysis*, 821, 685–699.

Caldwell, C. (1997) The moving cycle. In C. Caldwell (ed.) *Getting in Touch* (pp. 101–116). Wheaton, IL: Quest Books.

Chaiklin, H. (ed.) (1975) *Marian Chace: Her Papers*. Columbia, MD: ADTA.

Chasseguet-Smirgel, J. (2005) *The Body as Mirror of the World*. London: Free Associations Books.

Chodorow, J. (1991) *Dance Therapy and Depth Psychology: The Moving Imagination*. London: Routledge.

Deikman, A.J. (1982) *The Observing Self: Mysticism and Psychotherapy*. Boston, MA: Beacon Press.

Dosamantes, I. (1992) The intersubjective relationship between therapist and patient: a key to understanding denied and denigrated aspects of the patient's self. *The Arts in Psychotherapy*, 19, 359–365.

Dosamantes-Alperson, E. (1980) Contacting bodily-felt experiencing in psychotherapy. In J.E. Shorr, G.E. Sobel, P. Robin and J.A. Connella (eds) *Imagery: Its Many Dimensions and Applications* (pp. 223–250). New York: Plenum.

Driver, C. (2002a) The geography and topography of supervision in a group setting. In C. Driver and E. Martin (eds) *Supervising Psychotherapy* (pp. 85–96). London: Sage.

—— (2002b) Internal states in the supervisory relationship. In C. Driver and E. Martin (eds) *Supervising Psychotherapy* (pp. 51–63). London: Sage.

Erikson, E. (1950/1963) *Childhood and Society*. New York: Norton.

Ferro, A. (1999) *The Bi-personal Field*. London: Routledge.

Fonagy, P., Gergely, G., Jurist, E. and Target, M. (2002) *Affect Regulation, Mentalization, and the Development of Self*. New York: Other Press.

Foulks, E.F. and Schwartz, F. (1982) Self and object: psychoanalytical perspectives in cross-cultural fieldwork and interpretation. *Ethos*, 10(3), 254–278.

Freud, A. (1965) Normality and pathology in childhood: assessments of development. In *The Writings of Anna Freud* (Vol. 6). New York: International University Press.

Gaddini, R. (1987) Early care and the roots of internalization. *International Review of Psycho-analysis*, 1, 321–333.

Gendlin, E.T. (1978) *Focusing*. New York: Bantam Books.

Godbout, C. (2004) Reflections on Bion's 'elements of psychoanalysis' experience, thought and growth. *International Journal of Psycho-analysis*, 85, 1123–1236.

Hawkins, P. and Shohet, R. (1989) *Supervision in The Helping Professions*. Philadelphia, PA: Open University Press.

Heimann, P. (1950) On countertransference. *International Journal of Psycho-analysis*, 31, 81–84.

Jacobs, T.J. (1994) Nonverbal communications: some reflections on their role in the psychoanalytic process and psychoanalytic education. *Journal of the American Psychoanalytic Association*, 42, 741–762.

Kestenberg, J.S. (1973) *Children and Parents: Psychoanalytic Studies in Development*. New York: Aronson.

Kestenberg, J.S. and Sossin, K. (1979) *The Role of Movement Pattern in Development* (vols I and II). New York: Dance Notation Bureau.

Kestenberg Amighi, J., Loman, S., Lewis, P. and Sossin, M.K. (1999) *OPA – The Meaning of Movement: Developmental and Clinical Perspectives of the Kestenberg Movement Profile*. New York: Gordon and Breach.

Klein, M. (1932) *The Psycho-analysis of Children*. London: Hogarth Press.

—— (1958) On the development of mental functioning. *International Journal of Psycho-analysis*, 39, 84–90.

—— (1961) *Narrative of a Child Analysis*. London: Hogarth Press.

Kohon, G. (1992) *The British School of Psychoanalysis: The Independent Tradition*. London: Free Association Books.

La Barre, F. (2001) *On Moving and Being Moved*. Hillsdale, NJ: The Analytic Press.

Laban, R. (1950) *The Mastery of Movement*. London: MacDonald & Evans.

Lewis, P. and Loman, S. (1990) *The Kestenberg Movement Profile: Its Past, Present Applications and Future Directions*. New Hampshire: Antioch England Graduate School.

Martin, E. (2005) The unconscious in supervision. In C. Driver and E. Martin (eds) *Supervision and the Analytic Attitude* (pp. 3–33). London: Whurr Publications.

McCall, D. (1986) Personal communication.

Meltzer, D. (1979) *Sexual States of Mind*. London: Karnac Books.

Milner, M. (1969) *The Hands of the Living God: An Account of a Psychoanalytic Treatment*. London: Hogarth Press.

Momigliano, N.L. and Robutti, A. (1992) *Shared Experience: The Psychoanalytic Dialogue*. London: Karnac Books.

Musicant, S. (1994) Authentic movement in clinical work. In P. Pallaro (ed.) (2007) *Authentic Movement: Moving the Body, Moving the Self, Being Moved*. London: Jessica Kingsley.

—— (2001) Authentic movement: clinical and theoretical considerations. In P. Pallaro (ed.) (2007) *Authentic Movement: Moving the Body, Moving the Self, Being Moved*. London: Jessica Kingsley.

Nikolitsa, A. (2002) *Capturing and Utilising the Somatic Countertransferential Phenomena: An Heuristic Attempt*. Unpublished Master's thesis, Laban Centre, London.

Ogden, T. (1982) *Projective Identification and Psychotherapeutic Technique*. Northvale, NJ: Jason Aronson.

—— (1997) *Reverie and Interpretation: Sensing Something Human*. Northvale, NJ: Jason Aronson.

—— (2005) On psychoanalytic supervision. *International Journal of Psycho-analysis*, 86, 1265–1280.

Pallaro, P. (1993). Culture, self, and body-self: dance/movement therapy across cultures. In F.J. Bejjani (ed.) *Current Research in Arts Medicine* (pp. 287–291). Chicago, IL: a cappella books.

—— (1997) Culture, self and body-self: dance/movement therapy with Asian Americans. *The Arts in Psychotherapy*, 24(3), 227–241.

—— (ed.) (2000) *Authentic Movement: Essays by Mary Starks Whitehouse, Janet Adler and Joan Chodorow* (2nd edn). London: Jessica Kingsley.

—— (2007) Somatic countertransference: the therapist in relationship. In P. Pallaro (ed.) *Authentic Movement: Moving the Body, Moving the Self, Being Moved* (pp. 176–193). London: Jessica Kingsley.

Racker, H. (1968) *Transference and Countertransference*. New York: International Universities Press.

Resnik, S. (1995) *Mental Space*. London: Karnac Books.

Sarnat, J.E. (1992) Supervision in relationship: resolving the teach–treat controversy in psychoanalytic supervision. *Psychoanalytic Psychology*, 9, 387–403.

Scharff, J.S. (1992) *Projective and Introjective Identification and the Use of the Therapist's Self*. Northvale, NJ: Jason Aronson.

Scharff, J.S. and Scharff, D.E. (1998). The geography of transference and countertransference. In *Object Relations Individual Therapy* (pp. 241–281). Northvale, NJ: Jason Aronson.

Schilder, P.F. (1950) *The Image and Appearance of the Human Body*. London: Kegan Paul, Trench & Trubner.

Schore, A. (1999) *Affect Regulation and the Origin of the Self: The Neurobiology of Emotional Development*. New York: Lawrence Erlbaum Associates.

Segal, H. (1957) Notes on symbol formation. *International Journal of Psycho-analysis*, 38, 391–397.

Sowa, A. (1999) Observing the unobservable: the Tavistock Infant Observation Model and its relevance to clinical training. *Fort da*, 5(1). Retrieved from http://www.fortda.org/Spring_99/Observing.html.

Stern, D.N. (1985) *The Interpersonal World of the Infant*. New York: Basic Books.

Stewart, J. (2002) The interface between teaching and supervision. In C. Driver and E. Martin (eds) *Supervising Psychotherapy* (pp. 64–83). London: Sage.

Thomas, M. (2005) Through the looking glass: creativity in supervision. In C. Driver and E. Martin (eds) *Supervision and the Analytic Attitude* (pp. 115–129). London: Whurr Publications.

Ungar, V.R. and Bush De Ahumada, L. (2001) Supervision: a container–contained approach. *International Journal of Psycho-analysis*, 82, 71–81.

Whitehouse, M.S. (1963) Physical movement and personality. In P. Pallaro (ed.) (2000) *Authentic Movement: Essays by Mary Starks Whitehouse, Janet Adler and Joan Chodorow* (2nd edn) (pp. 51–57). London: Jessica Kingsley.

Winnicott, D. (1965) *The Maturational Processes and the Facilitating Environment*. New York: International University Press.

—— (1971) *Playing and Reality*. New York: Basic Books.

Wyman-McGinty, W. (1998) The body in analysis: authentic movement and witnessing in clinical practice. *Journal of Analytical Psychology*, 43(2), 239–261.

—— (2005) Growing a mind: the evolution of thought out of bodily experience. *Spring: A Journal of Archetype and Culture*, 72, 267–279.

Yerushalmi, H. (1999) The roles of group supervision of supervision. *Psychoanalytic Psychology*, 16, 426–447.

Yorke, V. (2005) Bion's vertex as a supervisory object. In C. Driver and E. Martin (eds) *Supervision and the Analytic Attitude* (pp. 34–49). London: Whurr Publications.

Chapter 4

Supervision in dance movement therapy

A proposed model for trainees

Dita Judith Federman and Lee Bennett Gaber

Introduction

According to *Webster's Dictionary* (1971), supervision is seen as 'the process or occupation of direction, inspection and critical evaluation' (p. 2296). *Webster's Dictionary* (2001) defines supervision as 'management by overseeing the performance or operation of a person or group'. Likewise, the *Oxford English Dictionary* (1993, p. 3151) defines supervision as:

> the action or function of supervising, general management, direction, or control; oversight, superintendence. The action of reading through for correction; revision by a superior authority. The direction and oversight of an undergraduate student's work by a tutor.

It is noteworthy that Yerushalmi (1991, 1996, 2000) compared supervision for individual psychotherapy with dyadic mother–child interaction in the course of development. He accentuates the importance of the 'maturational process'. This term he says 'refers to the evolution of the ego and of the self' (Winnicott, 1990, p. 85). This engenders a greater sense of self, develops a feeling of authenticity and sets in motion the underpinnings of true autonomy. It is not unlike Winnicott's (1965, p. 295) description of the development of the 'capacity to be alone'. The dialectical exchange wherein the self (personal identity) contributes to the other(s) and in turn, interaction with other(s) continually shapes and contributes to personal identity in an ongoing process, which is increasingly differentiated as development progress throughout the life span.

In the psychoanalytic psychotherapeutic approach supervision often refers to a situation where the psychoanalytic work, carried out by an inexperienced analyst-in-training, is done under the tutelage or surveillance of a senior analyst. The supervisor, as a member of a training institute, not only has the status of a supervisor, but also the power and responsibility to judge, evaluate and influence the status of the candidate, the trainee.

From a historical point of view, Berman (2004) points out that Freud never practised supervision in a structured, continual way, so that most early analysts were never supervised. Today, however, psychologists tend to take psychotherapy supervision for granted (Watkins, 1995) much like the student in an English class who was amazed to learn that he had been speaking prose all his life (Hess, 1987). Supervision in dance movement therapy is an integral part of the teaching process that students undergo during their training. From our experience both as therapists and supervisors the process of supervision is usually conducted using verbal methods, and the use of expressive methods is less common.

Watkins (1995) points out that despite psychotherapy supervision being considered relevant to professional practice and professional identity, 'psychotherapy-based' clinical supervision has changed negligibly during the past 25 years. Grater (1985), in an article discussing stages of psychotherapy supervision, delineated four hierarchical stages. The first stage concerns developing basic therapy skills and adopting the therapist's role. The second objective is the expansion of the range of therapy skills and roles to match the client's problems and role expectations. The third stage centres on developing the trainee's ability to assess the client's habitual and conflicting behaviour patterns, and in particular how these patterns are repeated in the therapy sessions. Likewise the selection of effective intervention methods is emphasised. The last stage helps the trainee learn to use the self in assessment and intervention. Grater says: 'In view of this, it is necessary for the supervisee to develop adequate mastery of each stage prior to moving on to the more demanding subsequent stages' (Grater, 1985, p. 607).

Despite theory, such as that of Grater, surrounding the usefulness of supervision, it is intriguing that the usefulness of supervision in general, and supervision which is used in all training and at all training institutions, is hardly questioned. Furthermore, the process of supervision (with a few exceptions) has not been systematically researched. For example, there is a dearth of research literature on the 'ill-effects' of supervision. There is minimal evidence that supervision changes trainees' actions or effects the outcome of therapy during or after supervision (Binder, 1993; Beutler *et al.*, 1997; Binder and Strupp, 1997; Reichelt and Skjerva, 2002). Most of the empirical investigations of supervision involve surveys of the satisfaction of the participants with the experience and with each other.

Nevertheless, it seems to be generally believed that the process of supervision is a very important part in the development of any therapist. It is not dissimilar to the process of therapy itself. Bernard and Goodyear (1993) stressed the 'supervision' of one of the participants in this dyadic relationship. It is the supervisor who has an overview of the process and therefore a range of perspectives. One may view supervision in terms of its constituent components taking place within a defined time/place (arena). Supervision, then, may be seen as a multi-dimensional process that ostensibly involves the two participants, yet covertly involves a host of internalised objects which enter a unique and creative dialogue. Supervision also often takes place within the format of a group.

The question proposed here is in what way does group supervision during training help to deepen understanding and make therapy more useful? The answer may well be found not in the actual theoretical knowledge under discussion within the supervision session (nor the *in vivo/in vitro* teaching), but perhaps in an increased understanding fostered by reducing conscious or unconscious anxiety that contaminates the therapist's functioning. In essence, supervision may afford an increased self-reflection and self-awareness of emotions and relationships.

Group supervision (much like group therapy) has certain unique advantages that are not readily available in individual work. When clinical material is presented to the group, there is often a multitude of associative links within each member and among the group members as a whole which act as catalysts in the exploration and understanding of the material. Moreover, the emotional as well as cognitive reactions of the group (including the group ambience) often enhance both emotional and intellectual insight into nuances of the clinical narrative.

When centring on the group experience in dance movement therapy (DMT), certain similarities between the group experience and group supervision readily appear. Scrutinising the prevalent models/paradigms of clinical training (field work/placement) in DMT, the supervisor often appears to be present (with the supervisee) during the sessions. Students in the training process are active participants; they take part in the clinical group session, not as co-therapists but as members of the group along with the clients. When the students gain more experience they may lead part of the session while the supervisor is part of the group (see a student's experience of this approach in Chapter 8). This may cause a complex relationship between supervisor and supervisee – mutual exposure exists. For the clients this is often an empowering experience enhancing a feeling of equality (all participants in the group are equal) while being exposed to a multitude of kinaesthetic associative expressions and interactions.

Various supervision orientations have been discussed in the clinical literature. The most prevalent of the approaches deals with the supervision of psychodynamic psychotherapy and/or psychoanalysis. Wallerstein (1981) as well as Rubinstein (1990) made the distinction between three general approaches to supervision. The 'patient-centred' approach is essentially a didactic approach (Rubinstein, 1990). 'Therapist centred supervision' (Rubinstein, 1990, p. 41), however, is a dynamic approach centring on countertransference as well as emotional material. 'Process-centred' supervision (Rubinstein, 1990, p. 41) with a dynamic orientation focuses on the processes, which essentially transcend the various contents of therapy. Kadushin (1992, p. 23) views the supervision process as a programme-centred process having an 'administrative', 'educational' or 'supportive' emphasis.

Theoretical orientation of proposed model of supervision

Both 'Chace' (Chaiklin *et al.*, 1993) and 'authentic movement' as found in Adler (1999), Chodorow (1999), Whitehouse (1999), and Payne (2004, 2006) approaches provide a theoretical basis not only for therapy but also for supervision in dance movement therapy. Both of these approaches to DMT deal with personal and emotional development that emanates as a result of group work in movement. Both theories accentuate the importance of movement with the 'other' or with 'others' for self-reflection as well as for the development of the individual. In supervision an understanding of these approaches enriches the possible usages of authentic movement as a phase of the supervision experience.

Authentic movement

This approach was originally called movement-in-depth by its founder Mary Starks Whitehouse (Chodorow, 1994). Authentic movement grew from Whitehouse's roots in dance, Jungian studies, and pioneering work in DMT. Building on Jung's method of active imagination, she saw symbolic meaning in physical action (Chodorow, 1994).

The concept of authentic movement refers to the movement of one person, the client/patient/supervisee, in the presence of another, the therapist/witness/ supervisor. Expression in movement in a safe space contributes to the feeling of security and openness. Authentic movement advocates group interaction in which individuals can co-participate in each other's imaginable realms, can project on each other and experience empathy from other members of the group (Payne, 2001, 2003, 2006).

Authentic movement facilitates bodily awareness in the mover. It reflects dominant functions of the personality (Adler, 1999) and encourages creative expression of inner life, thus offering a bridge between the conscious and the unconscious. It emphasises the awareness of the reactions to sensations, inner impulses and energies coming from the unconscious that are of significance. The reaction is important because it enables free association of movement. During the process of authentic movement, several meeting points between the mover and the other participants/witnesses are created in a sequence (Payne, 2001). Gradually, visible and conscious material emerges. Within the context of therapy supervision, the emphasis on authentic movement and its emotional resonance in the clinical arena (see Chapter 8 for an in-depth use of authentic movement as part of training supervision) is echoed in the work of Best (2003, p. 1):

> A relation is formed between the body of the client and body of the thera-pist and between the body of the therapist and body of the supervisor.

This mutual shaping is both active and passive and takes place in the spaces in between individuals and between individuals and contexts.

Verbal dialogue follows the movement experience. Both witnesses and participants describe what they have experienced and share their sensations and images. A level of perception of self and other is achieved that evokes deep respect and empathy.

The Chace approach

During the 1940s, Marian Chace pioneered the use of dance as therapy. Her principles and methods of practice serve as a model for group DMT (Chaiklin, 1975). Chace's basic concept is that dance is communication. There are four major classifications which encompass the basic principles that Chace used in therapy. Physical activity, symbolism, therapeutic movements and rhythmic group activity are used in dance and united into a special form of therapy. These principles enable the expression and communication of inner rhythms/ materials and empathic movement reflection. She argues that *physical activity* prepares the body for emotional and communicative expression. The 'warm-up' used at the beginning of the activity serves to create both atmosphere and body for the emotional voyage (Chaiklin, 1975).

Symbolism provides a medium for recalling, re-enacting and re-experiencing. Symbolism enables communication and expression of emotions in an indirect way: participants in the DMT group react symbolically to the symbols brought by other members and together they create a new story, a new symbolic interaction. The circle, so often used in group movement therapy, is a symbol of containment.

The concept of '*therapeutic movements*' (Bernstein, 1979) refers to the movement language. Chace (Bernstein, 1979) discovered how to establish a therapeutic relationship on a movement level. She expressed through movement that she knew how the client felt, thus establishing affective, empathic interactions.

'*Rhythmic movements*' (Bernstein, 1979) result from energetic activities which members of the group perform simultaneously, as in the 'warm-up' at the beginning of the group activity. A group moving together seems to have one breath and one pulse. When all members of the group perform the same energetic movement at the same time, a sense of power, organisation and trust arises (Chaiklin, 1975; Lewis, 1996).

It would appear that the interaction between authentic movement and the Chace approach to groups in a DMT group setting often facilitates a very basic and powerful 'being-with' experience. This reawakens archaic feelings and motifs within the individual and within the group (as an integrated whole) simultaneously.

Now that some of the major parameters as well as the central theoretical underpinnings of the DMT supervision process have been delineated and reviewed, supervision will be considered as an interrelational process.

Interrelational process

Supervision may be regarded as the crossroads of a matrix of relations of at least three individuals, each bringing his or her psychic reality into the dialogue/scene and thus creating a joint intersubjective milieu (Berman, 2000). These crossroads involve both conscious and unconscious expressions. The notion of intersubjectivity is rooted in psychoanalytic theory, and has implications for supervision (Berman, 2004). The concept of intersubjectivity attempts to integrate 'one-person psychology' studying intrapsychic processes, with 'two-person psychology' in which the study of interactions is the focal point.

Ogden (1994, 1999, 2001a) claims that there are two subjective realities and a dialectical process; my reality, your reality and the reality that is created and, further, the dialectic between the reality that was created to the other two realities. This common reality he calls 'the analytical third' (Ogden, 2001a, p. 255). In music, a melody is created, in words, a story or narrative comes into being, and in dance, a common dance is born.

Fairbairn (1952) and Sullivan (1953) made enormous contributions to the development of theoretical models that put the self–other relationship at centre stage. A creative reflective process (Lahad, 2000) is often used in supervision to develop understanding and insight of interpersonal relations between both therapist and patient, and therapist and supervisor. Best (2003) spoke about 'interactional shaping' (p. 29). This term was born as part of practical theory, designed to be useful in application, promoting active self-reflexivity. 'Interactional shaping' positions the therapist, not only as a movement observer, but includes the therapist's body alongside issues of power (Cecchin and Lane, 1994; Parker and Best, 2001). In the group, relations among members of the group may shed light on the relations between the supervisee/therapist and their patients (Lahad, 1999, 2000) in a parallel process.

Rationale of the proposed model

Based on our experience, verbal orientated supervision in DMT is frequently employed. In this way it is not dissimilar to the traditional verbal supervision often found in solely verbal psychotherapy. While DMT treatment can take place individually or in a group setting, using verbal as well as movement process techniques, we suggest that the supervision should follow in a parallel setting.

In this model of DMT supervision, movement is used as the major vehicle or, as the main language, to facilitate dialogue, symbols and metaphors allowing inner material to emerge. Movement as the major mode of expression is only supplemented, if necessary, by words (Ellis, 2001). The supervisees participate in a group within which (along with the supervisor and often the co-supervisor) they sit, listen and relate to the therapeutic situations recounted by a supervisee verbally. The group then elaborates the situation in both imagination and movement as well as reacting with words. While this method has been seemingly adopted from the verbal psychotherapies it transcends the verbal method in that it captures the unique nuances of the non-verbal elements in DMT.

The prevalent approaches, those using verbal supervision only, are usually, employed in DMT and often do not address the specific non-verbal and creative features of this therapeutic modality. In our model the nature and style of the treatment should necessarily influence the supervision process which is designed to be used in DMT. Movement is used to facilitate and/or elicit the pertinent inner content of the therapy, and as an aid in experiencing and then understanding the inner world of the patient as well as the supervisee–patient relationship. In both a metaphoric as well as actual sense, the supervisor often witnesses the unfolding of the therapy process of supervisees' patients through the movement of their supervisees. Likewise, the supervisor becomes a participant observer of the supervisee's work; gradually the roles change and the supervisee becomes participant and observer with the ability to experience, observe and understand the essence of his or her work with the client/patient.

As a participant observer in the group supervision format, the supervisor's inner world may well unfold in the presence of the group and, as such, may have his or her vulnerabilities exposed and elaborated upon within the group setting. This may well make him or her more susceptible to criticism (both professional and personal). Yet this same process may also afford a direct and unconditional modelling/learning experience for the trainee.

Proposed model for group supervision: the process

The two supervisors and supervisees (usually ranging from eight to twelve participants) gather in a group setting, sitting in a circle. In the first session the supervisor(s) explains the process of supervision, outlining the four-stage process.

Phase 1. Verbal focusing (30 minutes)

As the name suggests, the central purpose of Phase 1 is the selection of an issue, theme or situation which will be the focus of the supervisory session. At the outset, one participant presents a subject/issue with which he or she is occupied from his or her clinical work. The group helps to focus on the central issue (verbally). In response, each participant then shares verbally with the group his or her symbols, memories or thoughts regarding the central issue chosen by the supervisee.

Phase 2. Movement warm-up (15 minutes)

This is the transitional phase between the verbal mode of Phase 1 and the non-verbal kinaesthetic process. It begins with a guided movement warm-up by the supervisor. Music is played. The music is selected in accordance with the ambiance of the previous phase. Choosing the music can be akin to a voice or background singing, for example, to allow inner impulses to emerge. The guidelines are to enter the movement space and prepare the body for movement: pay attention to body parts, become acquainted with the space and with the other participants moving within it.

The group then moves to free association of movement, under the impression of the subject presented, the symbols that emerged, the music and the personal thoughts brought by the participants. Participants move in a free way, following their own inner impulses. The participants are influenced by the music but gradually move away from it. In the process of movement the group arrives at a common movement and rhythm. The focus is on inner reflection, an intrapsychic process rather than an interpersonal one.

Phase 3. Authentic movement (45 minutes)

In this phase the person who presented the subject/question for supervision invites some participants (about half of the group) to work in movement with him or her. The others sit in a circle around the individual – watching, being witnesses. Movement is suggested by the supervisor; eyes are closed. Usually no music is played. They are instructed to follow their inner impulses in terms of their own movement, their relations with the participant who presented the subject as well as their relations with each other. This, in essence, is a focused continuation of the previous section and is guided by content associations stemming from the clinical issue.

Phase 4. Sharing (30 minutes)

This phase aims at a verbal 'secondary working through' of the material experienced non-verbally and worked through via movement in the prior phase. The fourth phase brings the participants back to verbal interaction. The movement process is discussed. Both participants and witnesses share their inner materials, symbols and metaphors. The supervisee who presented the subject shares his or her insights. The supervisor summarises the process and the discussion in relation to the issue presented.

Clinical example

What follows is an example of the supervision process as outlined above. The supervision session to be described was centred on individual therapy with a child who hit/assaulted therapist B and then ran out of the treatment room. The young therapist B felt both frightened as well as hurt, since she believed that she was attentive to the child and was there to help him in any way possible.

Something about the way in which supervisee B related what had transpired seemed to be unclear. The way in which she retold what had happened was in a rigid, even perhaps frozen fashion which was discrepant with how she was previously perceived. Her movements always seemed to be congruent with the verbal material she presented. This time, however, she sat as if petrified and resembled a child who had received a parental punishment and could not comprehend the reason for such a punishment. The group experienced and responded with empathy towards B, understanding her feelings of rejection. I, as the supervisor and dance movement therapist, felt that I was in the position of a minority, since I saw the incident differently. Yet I felt that something was missing from the clinical vignette that was presented; I could not feel the presence of the child.

The main protagonist of the clinical vignette as described by supervisee therapist B was, indeed, the therapist herself. The supervision situation was somewhat unclear, as many essential points were missing. For example, what the child said was not included as well as the therapist's feelings in reaction to what was said. Likewise, there was a dearth of fantasy material – no associative linkages were spontaneously brought to mind.

I suggested that the session be replicated, upon which B invited a group member to act as the child in the therapeutic situation. The whole group was invited to imagine the therapy room with its furniture and in particular the character of the child; how he looked, how he was dressed, how he walked, how he sat down and so on, and finally, how he hit her.

B sat down on the floor and instructed her colleague, the chosen group member who acted the child, how to assume the role of the child, but gave her leeway to react spontaneously. The group member enacting the child sat on the floor at a distance and played, then left the game and came closer to the therapist in small and hesitant steps.

All of a sudden the colleague did not want to listen any more and independently began to move closer and closer to the therapist until she touched the therapist on the knee in what seemed either to be a rough caress or a knock. Then the colleague proceeded to quickly move away, with her eyes looking away in an almost humiliated fashion.

The process aroused a smile of understanding; everybody in the room, including therapist B who was presenting the case and myself, understood that there was a different way of interpreting the therapeutic situation. It was clear that the child could have been trying to approach the therapist in an awkward way and the therapist may have misunderstood the child's intention. The child did not want to assault but rather to come closer and touch her.

The group then discussed the implications (for the therapist, for the child as well as for the individual group members), which emanated from the experience. Moreover, members of the group who shared with each other their personal responses to the situation had an impact on the spontaneous movements of therapist B, and she became more fluid in the movement within the supervision session. In a later supervision session, B told the group that the child in question had changed his behaviour towards her, perhaps as a result of her greater understanding of his need for personal physical contact.

As may be seen from the aforementioned model and example of group supervision in DMT, the process is a multi-phased one. The process shifts from a verbal emphasis on selecting the pertinent issues upon which the supervision will be focused, to the warm-up phase which is movement centred. This allows for a bridge, a further shift to 'authentic' movement which is the heart of the non-verbal supervision experience. Shifting back to the verbal mode is the 'sharing' phase that allows for a further working through of the movement experience and for closure. The four-phase process contains an inherent movement of its own, shifting from verbal to non-verbal and then back to verbal mode.

Conclusion

Clinical supervision in DMT as described above is a creative process within which the verbal aspects of understanding and non-verbal aspects of insight are comprehended as an integrated whole. This is often a liberating experience which facilitates imagination and resourcefulness coupled with increased intellectual appreciation of the clinical process. Such liberation is the basis of a creative clinical practice as well as an underpinning of a sensitive, meaningful and insightful supervision encounter.

References

Adler, J. (1999) Who is the witness? A description of authentic movement. In P. Pallaro (ed.) *Authentic Movement: Essays by Mary Starks Whitehouse, Janet Adler and Joan Chodorow* (pp. 141–159). London: Jessica Kingsley.
—— (2004) *Impossible Training. A Relational View of Psychoanalytic Education.* London: The Analytic Press.
Bernard, J. and Goodyear, R. (1993) *Fundamentals of Clinical Supervision.* Boston, MA: Allyn & Bacon.
Bernstein, P.L. (1979) *Eight Theoretical Approaches In DMT.* New England: Kendal.

Best, P. (2003) Interactional shaping within therapeutic encounters: three dimensional dialogues. *The USA Body Psychotherapy Journal*, 2, 1, 26–44.

Beutler, L.E., Allstetter, N.S. and Robert, B. (1997) Research on supervisor variables in psychotherapy supervision. In C. Edward Watkins (ed.) *Handbook of Psychotherapy Supervision*. New York: John Wiley.

Binder, J.L. (1993) Is it time to improve psychotherapy training? *Clinical Psychology Review*, 13, 301–318.

Binder, J.L. and Strupp, H.H. (1997) Supervision of psychodynamic psychotherapies. In C. Edward Watkins (ed.) *Handbook of Psychotherapy Supervision* (pp. 44–62). New York: John Wiley.

Cecchin, G. and Lane, G. (1994) *Cybernetics of Prejudices in the Practice of Psychotherapy*. London: Karnac Books.

Chaiklin, S. (1975) Dance therapy. In E. Silvano (ed.) *The American Handbook of Psychiatry*, Vol. 5 (ch. 27). New York: Basic Books.

Chaiklin, S., Lohn, A. and Sandel, S. (1993) *Foundations of DMT: The Life and Work of Marian Chace*. Columbia, MD: The Marian Chace Memorial Fund of the American Dance Therapy Association.

Chodorow, J. (1994) *Dance Therapy and Depth Psychology: The Moving Imagination* (2nd edn). London: Routledge.

—— (1999) To move and be moved. In P. Pallaro (ed.) *Authentic Movement: Essays by Mary Starks Whitehouse, Janet Adler and Joan Chodorow*. London: Jessica Kingsley.

Ellis, M.V. (2001) Harmful supervision, a cause for alarm: Comment on L.A. Gray, *et al*. 'Psychotherapy trainees' experience of counterproductive events in supervision'. *Journal of Counseling Psychology*, 48, 4, 401–406.

Fairbairn, W.R.D. (1952) *Psychoanalytic Studies of the Personality*. London: Tavistock.

Grater, H.A. (1985) Stages in psychotherapy supervision: from therapy skills to skilled therapist. *Professional Psychology: Research and Practice*, 16 (5), 605–610.

Hess, A.K. (1987) Advances in psychotherapy supervision: Introduction. *Professional Psychology: Research and Therapy*, 18 (3), 187–188.

Kadushin, A. (1992) *Supervision in Social Work*. Columbia: University Press.

Lahad, M. (1999) Supervision of crisis intervention teams: the myth of the savior. In E. Tselikas-Portmann (ed.) *Supervision and Dramatherapy*. London: Jessica Kingsley.

—— (2000) *Creative Supervision; The Use of Expressive Arts Methods in Supervision and Self-supervision*. London: Jessica Kingsley.

Lewis, P. (1996) Authentic sound, movement, and drama: an interactional approach. In M. Robbins (ed.) *Body Oriented Psychotherapy*. Somerville, MA: Inter Scientific Community for Psycho-Corporal Therapies.

Ogden, T.H. (1994) *Subject of Analysis*. London: Karnac Books.

Ogden, T.H. (1999) The analytic third: an overwiew. In S. Mitchell and L. Aron (eds) *Relational Psychoanalysis: The Emergence of a Tradition*. Hillsdale, NJ: Analytic Press.

—— (2001a) *Conversations at the Frontier of Dreaming*. Northvale, NJ: Jason Aronson.

—— (2001b) Re-minding the body. *American Journal of Psychotherapy*, 55, 92–104.

Oxford English Dictionary (1993) *The Shorter Oxford English Dictionary, On Historical Principles*, Ed. L. Brown. Oxford: Clarendon Press (Vol. 2, p. 3151).

Parker, G. and Best, P. (2001) Moving reflections: the social creation of identities in communication. In L. Kossolapow, S. Scoble and D. Waller (eds) *Arts Therapies Communication: On the Way to a Communicative European Arts Therapies Conference Proceedings* (Vol. 1, pp. 142–148). (EcArte) Munster: I Verlag.

Payne, H.L. (2001) Authentic movement and supervision. *E-Motion, Association for Dance Movement Therapy*, 13, 4, 4–7.

—— (2003) Authentic movement, groups and psychotherapy. *Self and Society, Journal for Humanistic Psychology Practitioners*, 30, 7.

—— (2004) Becoming a client, becoming a practitioner: student narratives from a DMT group. *British Journal of Guidance and Counselling*, 32, 4, 511–532.

—— (2006) The body as expresser and container: authentic movement groups and the development of wellbeing in bodymindspirit. In J. Corrigall, H. Payne and H. Wilkinson (eds) *About a Body: Working with the Embodied Mind in Psychotherapy*. London: Routledge.

Reichelt, S. and Skjerva, J. (2002) Correspondence between supervisors and trainees in their perceptions of supervision events. *Journal of Clinical Psychology*, 58, 759–772.

Rubinstein, G. (1990) The bridge between therapy and supervision – a different view. *Sihot – Dialogue, Israel Journal of Psychotherapy*, Vol. V, no. 1 (in Hebrew).

Sullivan, H.S. (1953) *The Interpersonal Theory of Psychiatry*. New York: Norton.

Wallerstein, R.S. (1981) *Becoming a Psychoanalyst: A Study of Psychoanalytic Supervision*. New York: International University Press.

Watkins, C.E. Jr. (1995) Psychotherapy supervision in the 1990s: some observations and reflections. *American Journal of Psychotherapy*, 49 (4), 568–581.

Webster's Third New International Dictionary of English Language Unabridged (1971) Chicago: Encyclopaedia Britannica, p. 2296.

Webster's Dictionary (2001) http://www.webster-dictionary-online WordNet 1.7.1. Copyright © 2001 by Princeton University (accessed 23 June 2001).

Whitehouse, M.S. (1999) Creative expression on physical movement is language without words. In P. Pallaro (ed.) *Authentic Movement: Essays by Mary Starks Whitehouse, Janet Adler and Joan Chodorow*. London: Jessica Kingsley.

Winnicott, D.W. (1965) *The Maturational Process and the Facilitating Environment*. New York: International Universities Press.

—— (1990) *The Maturational Process and the Facilitating Environment: Studies in the Theory of Emotional Development*. London: Karnac Books.

Yerushalmi, H. (1991) On the need to be alone in supervision. *Sihot – Dialogue, Israeli Journal of Psychotherapy*, 5, 2 (in Hebrew).

—— (1996) Dynamic supervision. *Sihot – Dialogue, Israel Journal of Psychotherapy*, 10, n. 2 (in Hebrew).

—— (2000) Goals of the supervision on supervision group. *Sihot – Dialogue, Israel Journal of Psychotherapy*, 14, 3 (in Hebrew).

Chapter 5

Forgotten moments in supervision

The challenge for their recuperation

Heidrun Panhofer

Introduction

'What do you mean, how did I feel moving with *a man*?' the student asks me with eyes wide open. I look at her long blonde hair and slim limbs, insisting: 'Well, how did you as a woman experience dancing with this particular male client?' She still seems to struggle with my question, having reached a sticking point in her work with a young man from a psychiatric day unit. We decide to get up and kinaesthetically re-establish some of the session's movement material: I, as the supervisor, try to slip into the client's skin, enquiring about all his movement qualities and preferences, re-enacting some of his gestures and postures while the student remains in her role as the dance movement therapist trainee. When specifying physical closeness and visual contact, my student's eyes suddenly spark into life: 'Of course, he always stares at me as if I was a stranger, and whenever I look at him he avoids eye contact! I hate that, it makes me really nervous!' What seems an unimportant detail at the moment slowly develops into a complex construct of information, inter-woven by the student's personal background and the client's clinical history. As we keep moving and talking we encounter some more of the student's personal issues which the indirect advances from the young, bipolar client awaken for her.[1]

Ignored or forgotten information, such as that mentioned in the above example, offers a unique possibility in supervision. They can become mani-fest through student blank-outs, unfinished sentences, slips of the tongue or left aside aspects ('You mean, he is not just a patient, he is also a man?'). As in psychotherapy, supervision may offer a unique exploration into the unknown, in order to expand the domain of consciousness and enable the student to conduct his work with more awareness, freedom and choice.

This chapter invites the reader to an exploration of the supervision process on our Master's programme in dance movement therapy[2] based at the Autonomous University in Barcelona, Spain. The programme has been using both individual and group supervision sessions in order to facilitate students to gain more meaning from their clinical practice.[3] With large numbers of students (30) we had to consider new methods and procedures, engaging in an experiential, interactive, intersubjective learning process between students and supervisors. Our search brought us to investigate different ways of how to focus effectively the clinical work using creative processes within group dynamics; movement improvisation; psychodrama techniques; empathetic movement; and narrative. It is this approach which is described in this chapter.

The concept of forgetting in psychodynamic terms is reviewed and different ways of exploring and rediscovering forgotten material through movement is explored. Several specific issues around supervision within DMP training, such as power differentials, self-revelation, resistance, helplessness, parallel processes and assessment are then identified. These form a critical cocktail where overlapping roles and functions may cause double-bind messages and, as a consequence, painful conflicts. Several vignettes will be used to illustrate the different approaches we have been using in order to make sense of the clinical material in a DMP training setting. The last example combines narratives and movement processes within the dynamics of a supervision group and underlines the importance of creative processes when acknowledging and integrating forgotten clinical material.

Containing and exploring the unknown and all sorts of forgotten moments

> [T]he idea of consciousness is quite similar to that of attention. We are conscious of what we attend to and not conscious of what we do not attend to. We could become conscious of some things quite easily if we turned our attention to them.
>
> (Mollon, 2000, p. 7)

Having grown up in the Austrian mountains I remember, every now and then, especially in my early adolescent years, walking up one of the surrounding hills on my own, having a look over the valley and seeing my village from a different viewpoint. It was not so much about walking or escaping my home, but more about finding a place where, from a distance, I could overlook the scenery from a different place. All the conflicts and troubles down there would suddenly obtain a different meaning and I, slightly at a distance, would gain a new perspective. I was physically trying to '*super-videre*', in Latin meaning, 'overwatch', my teenage concerns down there in order to discover new aspects from a distance and, at times I felt I succeeded with this technique.

Metaphorically, in clinical supervision, we also leave the place of action and, alongside a supervisor and/or a peer group, try to reach a place from where what troubles us in our practice may be seen from above, watched from a different perspective and perceived in a new way. Aspects that cannot be identified 'from down below' may become tangible, and other neglected or forgotten facets may appear. This process of critical self-examination is seen as crucial to patients' progress because, according to Goldberg, it 'enables therapists to recognize how their own issues may be interfering with their reception and understanding of what their patients are reporting' (Goldberg, 1993, p. 159).

The psychoanalytic hypothesis of an unconscious motivation provides an explanation for the gaps and distortions in our awareness, such as are frequently found in the supervision process. Failures of memory, slips of the tongue or pen or other mistakes may therefore not only be accidental errors but unconsciously intended (Freud, 1915; Rycroft, 1995; Mollon, 2000). Mechanisms of defence, such as repression, projection, rationalisation or splitting, are important and common practices of 'lying' to oneself and can frequently be encountered in the supervision context in order to hide away the emotional truth from ourselves.

Forgetting the unbearable

A second-year student working in a residence with severely disabled adults brings a very concrete question to the supervision group. When dealing with a 30-year-old woman who suffers from Rett's syndrome she has a hard time keeping the client in the therapeutic space. Repeatedly she interrupts the sessions to leave the space, enhanced by the lack of a proper door to the room and a cleaner who keeps working outside when sessions take place. The student asks the group to think about interventions to make her client stay in the therapeutic space. We decide to explore the dynamics with a psychodramatic representation: the circle of the students' chairs is used to portray the therapy room. The student picks out a peer from the group to act as the cleaner and another one to represent herself as a therapist. She chooses to take on the role of the client and after having given some further descriptions the psychodrama starts. The dynamic consists in the therapist bringing the client to the therapy room, sitting down in a particular space and starting the verbal check-in. However, soon after arrival, the client, enacted by the student, gets up and leaves the room while her peer, the therapist, remains in the room, feeling annoyed and incapable. The cleaner, outside of the circle, keeps making little noises to state her presence and enhances the therapist trainee's countertransference of not being able to look after the client properly. It seems as though the patient, fed up with listening to instructions and orders from the residence staff, uses the therapeutic space to do what she truly would like to do – leave! – and places all her feelings of impotence and frustration within the therapist. Following this, the group reflects on possible ways of containing these difficult feelings of helplessness and dissatisfaction and suggests verbalising them to make them more tangible for the client, and in this way, giving some insight and command back to this 30-year-old female patient.

This example illustrates how certain aspects of the clinical experience can be too raw or distressing and need to be hidden away from awareness. The student forgets about her own countertransferencial observations and tries to focus on mere interventions. The impotence and frustration of the client seem too great to bear, and only the psychodrama activity brings further insight into her own, and the client's, issues.

Material from the 'descriptively unconscious' (Rycroft, 1995) or 'pre-conscious' (Freud, 1915) can be easily accessed if only we turn our attention to them, as in the case of this student an invitation to connect with the emotional pain around the relapse is sufficient to link up with the lived experience. The so-called 'dynamically unconscious processes' also refer to material that is too painful or disturbing, but has therefore been actively repressed and is harder to access. They conform mostly to primary processes of thought, while pre-conscious and conscious processes conform to the secondary processes (Rycroft, 1995). Here is another vignette to illustrate the point.

Forgetting the context

A female student on a placement in a special needs school presents the case of a boy with a mental disability whom she sees in individual DMT sessions. Originating from a southern region of Spain where close physical proximity is generally much more common than in the Catalonia region, she talks about her difficulty of how to handle issues around touch and closeness. With her personal cultural background she feels comfortable greeting the boy with two kisses, hugging him or holding him during the sessions, especially since he has been deprived of physical holding in infancy. At the same time, she doubts as to how far this may be culturally acceptable in Barcelona (Catalonia) or whether it may be an adequate intervention within the DMT setting. The students in the supervision group quickly integrate into a long cultural debate, a very topical subject in an autonomous region such as Catalonia, with its fight for its own cultural identity and more independence. Group members not only come from many different regions in Spain, but also from South America and Central Europe, and passionately exchange opinions about the matter. It is only after some time that the attention returns to the client and to the DMT setting. Students become interested in what actually happens in the sessions concerning touch and proximity, when suddenly somebody enquires: 'How old again did you say the boy was?' The supervisee stumbles, seems to reflect on something completely forgotten, holds her breath for a moment and then, slightly blushing, answers: 'Sixteen.' The fact that she is dealing with an adolescent young man, rather than with a little boy, gradually occurs to her and, together with the group, she begins to reflect how she has ignored the arising issues about puberty and sexuality.

The above example illustrates the rather complex structure of dynamically unconscious processes: perceiving a 16-year-old retarded young man as an individual with sexual needs and fantasies, rather than a little boy, seemed too overwhelming and anxiety-provoking in the context of individual DMT sessions where touch and physical proximity are constant issues. The entire peer group falls into the same trap of repression, not expressing any interest in the actual age of the boy but rather discussing more concrete and accessible matters such as their own cultural differences and how these may colour the subject of touch.

Sometimes it is specifically difficult to enter these non-verbal areas of experience, as we have not been able to generate words or any other form of mental representation for them. The so-called 'presymbolic unconscious' belongs to areas of which we cannot be properly conscious (Rycroft, 1995) as they belong to non- or pre-verbal material. However, in DMP, where 'body and mind are in constant reciprocal interaction' (Schoop, 1974, p. 44), the moving dialogue between the conscious and unconscious mind allows for a deeper embodied consciousness even into non- and pre-verbal processes (Hartley, 2004). The awareness of unconscious contents and their integration is probably the primary psychotherapeutic benefit in DMT (Stanton-Jones, 1992). Movement, just like dreams or other psychological phenomena, evidences unconscious processes (Davis, 1974; Stanton-Jones, 1992) and may therefore be helpful in supervision where group processes in dance, play and movement may be valuable techniques for bringing repressed material to light in clinical practice.

Investigation through movement

At the beginning of the academic year, as students are still experiencing for the first time what a supervision group may offer them, different practical concerns about the placement are verbalised by the participants. Some placement contracts have not arrived; a few details about the exact number of clinical hours still need to be clarified; several concerns about client observation are voiced. A particular student who has chosen to work in an oncological hospital complains about the difficulties of arranging an interview with the on-site placement tutor and worries about the complications of trying to enter into the hospital dynamics. She starts to cry, imploring the group to help her: 'It is so hard to get in, I am not sure if I will be able to do it! My own father died of cancer, sometimes I wonder if this is really the place I want to work!' The group allows some time for the shared emotion to die down. Since the difficulty of 'getting into the placement' seems to be a common theme of this young supervision group, I suggest a simple movement dynamic. The students are asked to look for a place within the room that may represent best how they feel right now with regard to beginning their clinical practice. Students visualise their placement in the middle of the room, and then take different positions and body postures, trying to embody their inner attitude. Some stand immediately next to the centre, upright, with open chests and arms, looking straight ahead as if they were expecting something particular.

Others move around, and dip their feet into the interior as if checking something with their toes. The student in the oncological clinic crouches outside the circle that is being formed, remaining down below and glancing sometimes inside, then again outwards. More movement occurs, places are swapped in an exploratory manner, some outer body parts connect slightly and a swaying rhythm appears. The student on the ground seems to take interest in this rhythm, picks it up in her torso and head, still looking in and outside. Her peers have formed a clear circle now and, as their shoulders and arms join up, they open up a place for her. Gradually she relates to the group and eventually links up with the circle, joining in their rocking rhythm and maintaining eye contact within the group.

The delicate issues concerning personal disclosure within a clinical training are discussed at a later point in this chapter. This particular movement activity allowed some acknowledgement of the student's powerful emotional response to her choice of clinical placement. None the less, its primary goal focused more on a communal reflection regarding the group's difficulties and resistance to getting into client work. Logistical matters are often put forward in order not to enter into clinical material in training supervision. Trying to embody their inner attitudes and improvise with the group in movement allowed for some different questions to become apparent. For example: Is it possible to remain physically outside, crouching down in fear? Can I just stand and wait, with my arms wide open, and see what happens? How deep can I dip my toe into this unknown water? Can I change places with somebody else, step into their shoes and understand what it feels like where they are at? Who is there to help me and with whom can I join? Will the group be able to rock and calm me when fear appears? These unasked questions seem to have been represented metaphorically in a short movement improvisation that starts from a place of fear and resistence.

> The metaphor in DMT facilitates a complex interplay between the embodied experience of movement, associated sensor-motor 'body' memory, projected symbolism . . ., affect and verbalisation. As such, it involves integration of the intuitive, affective right-brain functions and the logical, linguistic left-brain functions.
>
> (Meekums, 2002, p. 25)

The use of movement, our primary tool in DMT, and the creative process, may allow for new insights to emerge within the supervision context.

Stepping stones in training supervision: the challenge

Jasper and Jumaa (2005) define clinical supervision as a formal process of professional support which enables practitioners to develop competence and knowledge, assume responsibility for their own practice and enhance patient protection and safety. But supervision is also, as described by Itzhaky and Ribner (1998), a learning process which requires involvement of the whole self, a process that tends to be personal and directed towards self-awareness. It involves reflection as an individual and professional, but also confrontation, change and integration, and may therefore give rise to many difficult feelings and consequent adaptive responses.

Dosamantes (1992) portrays the task of the therapist as striving to be in touch with subjective experience, including somatic, imagistic and private thoughts – a quite complex and difficult task for any dance movement therapist, especially students in training. They may experience difficulties in separating their personal and professional roles and responses, and as they may often find themselves in a place of 'not knowing' they may need to review issues around self-esteem and identity. This challenging process may provoke anxieties, feelings of insecurity, resentment and anger (Edward and Daveson, 2004).

In the context of clinical training it is important to note the distinct power differential between the supervisor and student in training, for example:

> The student is aware that the supervisor is assessing their work, the supervisor is obliged to maintain standards within the profession and within the workplace so it is necessary to give feedback where student behaviour does not meet standards, and the student in learner role may experience feelings of helplessness, 'not knowing' and confusion that have not yet been integrated for use as part of professional therapeutic contact with clients.
>
> (Edward and Daveson, 2004, p. 68)

Power differentials, peer rivalry and fear of assessment add to the complexity of the supervisory relationship and may enhance resistance in the training context. These difficulties may lead to a lack of presentation of clinical material or a forgetting of certain concerns around the case in the form of conscious and unconscious editing. Forgetting may include lying; that is, deliberately or non-deliberately misrepresenting or withholding case material in supervision may be an attempt to protect the self from the disruption of the narcissistic equilibrium. This process may be linked with fantasies of either confronting or being damaged by the supervisor (Hantoot, 2000). Dithrich (1991) suggests that lying may offer protection from painful effects associated with failing to meet internal standards, and it can serve as a defiant attack, explicitly (or inexplicitly) belittling the importance of the course's values and objectives.

Struggling to meet the course requirements

In this illustration a student struggling with economical matters has organised several part-time jobs alongside her clinical internship. As she cannot manage to meet the timetable requirements of her assigned placement she decides to look for a different arrangement by herself in order to accomplish the clinical practice requirements. Several weeks of frustrating searches follow until she finally manages to get started in a different organisation that matches her busy schedule. In the meantime, most of her peers have already begun to see clients and bring their first clinical material to the supervision sessions. Soon after, the student too shares her first steps of her DMT process with an adult suffering from a mental disability and seems to have engaged satisfactorily in her clinical work. Two months later she suddenly presents a new case which she finds quite challenging. She expresses concerns about the high degree of aggression and reveals her personal resistance in working with this case. The group's first reaction addresses the violent and hostile behaviour of the client, searching for a possible meaning of the attacks. Her attention is drawn to why a referral by the institution had been made so late during the academic year. Only then the student reveals that she herself had required such a referral, and that the client she had been assigned was the only available person left in the centre. 'It's because one of my clients died,' she said, 'and in order to complete my placement hours I needed to take on somebody new.' In my countertransference as a supervisor, I connect with the sheer shock and listen half numbed to the group's questions around the death of the patient. It seems impossible to believe that the anxiety of not satisfying the course requirements has led the student to withhold such important information as the death of a client. Through the empathic reactions of peers and supervisors the student is finally able to recall the experience of the loss of her patient, how she had learned about his illness (severe pneumonia), and how he had finally died. We take some time to remember the DMT process the student had shared with the client, and she is then able to emotionally connect with the anguish and sorrow of the sudden event. She even recalls an image of having seen the client for the last time, already ill with pneumonia and unable to come to the session, and thinking that he looked 'half dead' and in some way anticipating what was going to happen.

The strict course requirement of the completion of a certain number of direct client contact hours comes into conflict with the student's need to juggle work and studies – which is, generally speaking, a very common issue in Spain. The student finds herself almost in a double-bind situation, where ends cannot be met; that is, when at work there is enough money for the training, but when working there is not enough time for the training; a very stressful starting point for students. Somehow this student manages to combine both activities, fitting in all the necessary direct client contact hours during her spare time. The sudden decease of a client unbalances her entire arrangement and, yet again, she fails both her inner and outer requirements. The supervisor is perceived by the students as not only supportive through the therapeutic process, but also as a representation of the course requirements. In this case, the painful aspects around the loss of the client need to be hidden in supervision; resulting solely in the presentation of her preoccupation of how to manage to fulfil the required hours.

Many debates have taken place (see e.g., Spiegel and Grunebaum, 1977) around how far the supervision should enter into the students' personal dynamics and serve as an exploration for the supervisee's countertransference, or merely limit itself to looking at the patient's diagnosis and treatment. Matters as delicate as self-revelation may be especially critical in the context of a clinical training, where assessments and power differences may condition the spontaneous reactions of the student. Nevertheless, if emotional responses are not being addressed by the supervisor, the student may feel that such information is irrelevant. An overt explanation to students on the difference between psychotherapy and supervision may be needed in order to keep the focus on the client and not on the student (Hutto, 2001).

Stepping stones: parallel processes in clinical work and private circumstances

An international student has left an important position in her home country to study for the Master's programme. Coming from a position of power and knowledge she struggles with her new place as a first-year student, feeling helpless in her placement and looking desperately for guidelines as to how to behave correctly as a DMT trainee. Finding the position of 'not-knowing' unbearable, she starts challenging the supervisors with confrontational questions, demands and requests, and attacks the group's value, arriving late or answering the phone during the group supervision sessions. Some of the issues of her loss of professional identity, the struggle for cultural adaptation and the helplessness as a young DMT professional can be addressed in supervision, as they are shared to some extent by peers; others have to be directed towards tutorials and the personal therapeutic process.

The fact that this particular student has chosen to work with children severely affected with cerebral palsy seems important. Not only does she herself experience impotence and helplessness in her situation as a DMT trainee, but she also finds herself confronted with the very same dynamics in this specific client group. In the course of meetings with the various professionals involved in the supervision of this student, a perception of emotional numbness is shared. Whereas the student makes a tremendous academic effort designing movement profiles and treatment plans for the clients, she seems to remain emotionally distant in her clinical work. Both in group and individual supervision the student no longer brings clinical material concerning the therapeutic relationship, but ponders on logistical details and superficial comments around the treatment itself. The fact that the various different supervisors share an experience of feeling left out and numbed helps us to understand an important parallel process which is taking place. The developing similarities between the supervised case and the supervision of the case (Arlow, 1963) – numbness, emotional distance, feelings of exclusion – indicate something else than mere resistance but important parallel processes. Searles (1955) coined the term 'reflection processes' and stated that the 'processes at work currently in the relationship between patient and therapist are often reflected in the relationship between therapist and supervisor' (ibid., p. 135). Searles believed that the emotion or reflection experienced by the supervisor was the same emotion felt by the therapist in the therapeutic relationship (Sumerel, 1994) and was later also described as being bidirectional (Doehrman, 1976). The specific and non-specific parallel processes found throughout the course of supervision are an important means of expression for the perceptions and ideas that the supervisee takes from the supervisor. When identifying the parallel process in supervision, an important starting point for change in our international student can be noted. She is able to gain some awareness of the many unconscious facets around her clinical work and starts to understand better both her professional and her personal responses to the clients' material.

A creative enquiry into the forgotten

> Truth becomes manifest through art.
>
> (Heidegger, 1971/1976, p. 678)

On many occasions, solely mental processes cannot bring about deeper insight. Pure verbal reflection may not be able to get us in touch with profound unconscious material. In these cases the use of artwork such as expressive movement, drawing, writing, acting and so on are extremely helpful for the supervision process, as illustrated in the following example.

Mending the opposites

A very dedicated first-year student laments a certain division she perceives in a group of two autistic adults which she has been conducting for a couple of months. One of them seems to do all the moving, initiating and repeating, whereas the other appears to be all passive, slow and compliant. She struggles to unite the divided group and we use our individual supervision time to reflect on movement interventions that may foment group unity and bilateral exchange between the two members. At a later stage, she identifies a similar issue in another group which she leads, and wonders if this leitmotiv[4] connects more with her than with the clients. As the session is almost coming to an end I suggest she takes some time apart to write a poem, or create a dance or a song to reflect on the presenting polarity and what it means to her. A week later, she brings the product of her process of investigation to her supervision group. A sombre requiem accompanies the first text which she reads out to the group:

Deep, deep inside me incrusted, on the bottom of the abyss, fear.
Running, very slowly. Long, dark abyss. Cold. An island of loneliness.
Up there there are people, they talk and speak about strange things.
Where to hold on when falling in the well?
A melody that hurts. No, be quiet! I speak without words. I exhale
   syllables into this emptiness, without air, tense space, chewable. Dark,
   dark.
Paralysed with sorrow, believing that some of the drops that fell down
   were human beings.
Walking in this space, where to?
Without understanding the reason to be alone in this loneliness, wishing
   death, sometimes.
It weighs this coldness, this heat, it does not matter, it drowns and
   captures me. There are no hands or bodies to rock the loneliness.
Deeper every time, in the crevice, walking more inside, enjoying,
   enjoying, I don't want to come out any more. I couldn't even if
   I wanted to.
The air does not move, stagnant, caught in the edges.
And black walls falling down, an ongoing refrain.

And black walls falling down, an ongoing refrain.
The air does not move, stagnant, caught in the edges.
Deeper every time, in the crevice, walking more inside, enjoying,
   enjoying, I don't want to come out any more. I couldn't even if
   I wanted to.
It weighs this coldness, this heat, it does not matter, it drowns and
   captures me. There are no hands or bodies to rock the loneliness.
Without understanding the reason to be alone in this loneliness, wishing
   death, sometimes.
Walking in this space, where to?
Paralysed with sorrow believing that some of the drops that fell down
   were human beings.
A melody that hurts. No, be quiet! I speak without words. I exhale
   syllables into this emptiness, without air, tense space, chewable. Dark,
   dark.
Where to hold on when falling in the well?
Up there there are people, they talk and speak about strange things.
Deep, deep inside me incrusted, on the bottom of the abyss, fear.
Running, very slowly. Long, dark abyss. Cold. An island of loneliness.[5]

She changes the music to a fusion between Bach and African traditional rhythms and presents the second text to the students (unfortunately too long to be presented in this chapter), a narrative that contrasts to the scenery of the previous account: between sunset and sunrise colourful images of thunder, wind, leaves, trees, bodies, water, sun and moon connect through movement; there are dances, jumps, swirls and touch, transmitting a fresh, alive interplay of life and death, submerged into the light of magic. Both the music and the text create a completely different atmosphere to the first presentation, filling the room with strong, colourful images, assaulting the senses, interweaving yearning and pleasure, madness and sanity, day and night. The opposites exist alongside, nourishing and complementing each other.

As the student finishes the presentation, her peers offer associations triggered by the two different texts. They, as listeners, reflect or echo back the two stories with their own words and in their own style (Reason and Hawkins, 1988). Some are struck by how well the opposites are portrayed as if it was a story about life and death, a seed of the contrary, one tale about a strong, fibrous, black child and another one about a pallid, ill, white child. What does it feel like to work with such different clients in a group? Everybody is keen to hear about the therapy in process. The student talks about the lively client with its active, repetitive structure and about the passive, slow patient that shows no initiative at all. 'In fact,' she says, 'when writing the two different texts I thought a lot about them, but also became aware of how numbed and deadened the lively client feels sometimes, and how much life there is in the second.' She states that for her there is sometimes a lot more life in a flower in the desert than in an entire garden full of flowers. Two students, who in the initial check-in had not demanded any time, share issues around a similar conflict and about how hard it sometimes is to unite the opposites, but how close they are in many other ways. Following on from this, my colleague and co-supervisor suggests a game called 'Eternal pairs'. He labels the two ends of the room using different, opposing pairs: man–woman, life–death, cold–hot, Catalan speaker–non-speaker of Catalan, dance movement therapist–dance teacher, and so on. He then invites the students to move around in the space and to locate themselves according to where they feel they belong. Even though at first students place themselves in clear static spots within the continuum, soon, with some encouragement, they start to move around more freely within the same theme. They play with being completely a woman, or incorporating some male aspects. They seem to enjoy exploring the different possibilities within the continuum. When looking at the activity from the outside our personal tendency of placing people in overdetermined positions becomes evident. Students comment on their inclination to do this, especially when anxious or frightened. To finish, my colleague suggests an activity which encourages the students to reflect on the process of working with clients under supervision. He proposes six different words that might best describe how they view the work they are doing (experimenting, integrating, baring, surviving, curing, tolerating) and asks them to place this list in order of priority. Students share their ratings and note with surprise the variety of different angles from which they have perceived the dynamics of their work and how much their priorities have changed over time.

Two texts that metaphorically try to capture the challenging dynamics of a DMT group with autistic adults echo related themes in every single member of the group and serve to help each member comprehend and acknowledge their own clinical material in different ways. The wide range of possibilities within every human being seems to be a forgotten part for the student who responds to the difficulties of joining two autistic adults by fixing them in her mind as complete opposites. She splits them into two contrary parts, simplifying the complexity of the nature of every single one of them. Feeling trapped in her perception and unable to unite them, the creative enquiry through narratives enables her to gain new insight into the occurrence: 'The process of composition – and indeed the textual product itself – is an important mode of analysis of its own right' (Coffey and Atkinson, 1996, p. 122).

The writing process finally allows for new insights. Already after having created the different texts, she understands how she has been rigidly putting the clients into two opposite corners, neglecting the inner reality of two complex human beings. The feedback from her peers and what arose from the movement game illustrate further the ongoing dynamics and allow for an embodied experience and a greater understanding of a wider process.

Conclusion

This chapter has explained the concept of forgetting and looked at different ways of exploring and rediscovering forgotten material through the creative process. Illustrated with case vignettes, important specific issues around supervision within DMP training have been addressed. Before concluding, I would like to relate a little anecdote to show that forgetting not only happens to students in their clinical practice, but also to supervisors. When collecting material for this chapter, one of the examples that came to mind was the above-mentioned story of the student who had chosen a placement in an oncological hospital. For some reason, though, I could only remember the beginning and end of the process, and searched through my notes to find more on the issue. There was nothing I could find that could give me more clues, and I decided to ask my colleague co-supervisor for help. Together we were able to uncover some more parts of the story, but still we could not rediscover the entire episode – some important fragments remained lost. At this point I chose to speak to the student herself and surprisingly enough she, too, had some important gaps in her memory. In fact, she was quite surprised that she had not taken down more notes in her diary, since the event had been very significant for her and helped her to process both her role as a clinician, as well as triggering some fundamental issues in her personal work. She wrote me a little account of what she remembered and this is how the above described vignette was finally put together. Somehow, I suspect that this general forgetting is linked to some very personal material that has been exposed, and yet that could not be attended to fully in clinical supervision. As described above, issues around self-disclosure may be critical in the setting of training supervision, where power differentials and the evaluation process condition the relationship between supervisor and supervisee in a very specific way. Neither could we, as supervisors, contain and process the painful loss of her father and nor could the student find a safe place in her training supervision to work it through. Forgetting, in this case and certainly in many others, also appears to make reference to uncontainable issues that reveal our limitations as supervisors and supervisees.

Notes

1 All identifying features of both the client and the student have been removed from the entire clinical material. Case examples have been collected through clinical notes of the supervisor or notes from the student. For the latter, approval to use the case material has been given by the student.
2 At the date of publication Spain keeps using the term 'dance movement therapy' (DMT) which has been changed to 'dance movement psychotherapy' (DMP) in the UK. This chapter will use both expressions, the Spanish term DMT and the UK idiom DMP.
3 Whereas most of the supervision groups have been co-led by my colleague Peter Zelaskowski, a group analyst, and myself, the individual supervision sessions have been led by different dance movement therapists registered as supervisors within the Spanish Association for DMT (ADMTE).
4 A *leitmotiv* (German, literally meaning 'leading motif') makes reference to any sort of recurring theme, whether in music, literature, life or fictional characters or individuals. Originally coming from music it can be associated within a particular piece of music with a particular person, place or idea, and is not being used for any recurring theme or subject in a broader sense.
5 Translation from the Spanish by Heidrun Panhofer; approval for publication given by the student.

References

Arlow, J.A. (1963) The supervisory situation. *Journal of the American Psychoanalytic Association*, 2: 576–594.

Coffey, A. and Atkinson, P. (1996) *Making Sense of Qualitative Data: Complementary Research Strategies*. Thousand Oaks, CA: Sage.

Davis, M. (1974) Movement patterns of process. *Main Currents in Modern Thought*, 31: 18–22.

Dithrich, C.W. (1991) Pseudologia fantastica, dissociation, and potential space in child treatment. *International Journal of Psychoanalysis*, 72: 657–667.

Doehrman, M.J. (1976) Parallel processes in supervision and psychotherapy. *Bulletin of the Menninger Clinic*, 40: 1–104.

Dosamantes, I. (1992) The intersubjective relationship between therapist and patient. *The Arts in Psychotherapy*, 19: 359–365.

Edward, J. and Daveson, B. (2004) Music therapy student supervision: considering aspects of resistance and parallel processes in the supervisory relationship with students in final clinical placement. *The Arts in Psychotherapy*, 31: 67–76.

Freud, S. (1915) 'The unconscious'. *Standard Edition of the Complete Psychological Works of Sigmund Freud*, Vol. XIV. London: Hogarth Press.

Goldberg, C. (1993) The unexplored in self analysis. *Psychotherapy*, 30 (1): 159–161.

Hantoot, M.S. (2000) Lying in psychotherapy supervision: why residents say one thing and do another. *Academic Psychiatry*, 24: 179–187.

Hartley, L. (2004) *Somatic Psychology: Body, Mind and Meaning*. London: Whurr Publishers.

Heidegger, M. (1971/1976) Poetry, language, thought. In A. Hofstädter and R. Kuhns (eds), *Philosophies of Art and Beauty* (pp. 647–708). Chicago: The University of Chicago Press.

Hutto, B. (2001) Some lessons best learned from psychotherapy supervision. *Psychiatric Times*, 18 (7).

Itzhaky, H. and Ribner, D. (1998) Resistance as a phenomenon in clinical and student social work supervision. *Australian Social Work*, 51 (3): 25–29.

Jasper, M. and Jumaa, M. (eds) (2005) *Effective Healthcare Leadership*. Oxford: Blackwell.

Meekums, B. (2002) *Dance Movement Therapy. Creative Therapies in Practice*. London: Sage.

Mollon, P. (2000) *Ideas in Psychoanalysis: The Unconscious*. Cambridge: Icon Books.

Reason, P. and Hawkins, P. (1988) Storytelling as inquiry. In P. Reason (ed.), *Human Inquiry in Action* (pp. 79–101). Thousand Oaks, CA: Sage.

Rycroft, C. (1995) *A Critical Dictionary of Psychoanalysis*. London: Penguin Books (2nd edn).

Schoop, T. (1974) *Won't You Join the Dance? A Dancer's Essay into the Treatment of Psychosis*. California: Mayfield.

Searles, H.F. (1955) The informational value of the supervisor's emotional experience. *Psychiatry*, 18: 135–146.

Spiegel, D. and Grunebaum, H. (1977) Training versus treating the psychiatric resident. *American Journal of Psychotherapy*, 31 (4): 618–625.

Stanton-Jones, K. (1992) *An Introduction to Dance Movement Therapy in Psychiatry*. London/New York: Routledge.

Sumerel, M. (1994) Parallel process in supervision. ERIC Clearinghouse on Counseling and Student Services, Greensboro, NC. Available online at http://www.ericdigests.org/1995-1/process.htm (accessed 20 June 2006).

Chapter 6

From here and elsewhere

Transcultural issues in supervision

Isabel Figueira

Introduction

I will present several considerations from my own DMT experience of transcultural encounters, clashes or misunderstandings. This chapter comprises three main sections and a final theoretical reflection. I organised these sections according to my own position in the situations I will recall: (1) as a student in a training group, (2) as a student therapist in a clinical placement and (3) as a supervisor on a training course. Alongside the change of status from student to supervisor there was a change of country since I trained as a dance movement therapist in London and now practise and teach DMT at a university in Lisbon, Portugal. I have chosen this approach because I would like to emphasise the dynamic aspect of supervison – we *become* supervisors. This is a multi-layered process, involving the present relationship with the student in front of us, the recent past of the therapeutic experience the student chooses to reflect on with us and the distant past of our own experiences that we use to relate to what is being told. There is also a future dimension when we combine all these aspects and imagine or suggest alternative approaches, opening new pathways both to the student and to ourselves.

This chapter designed itself through the recollection of my own experiences in DMT and in analysing the transcultural situations from different perspectives. It invites each of us to imagine ourselves in at least three different positions related to DMT training and practice. DMT practitioners can be particularly prepared to develop what Bakthine calls the 'dialogical communication' (Bakthine, 1970, p. 129), which is the capacity of being in dialogue with another, of being able to see ourselves through the eyes of the 'Other'. It implies a dual capacity of being aware of our own values and perspectives and at the same time being aware how the Other can perceive us, with his or her own values.

This internal movement in the dialogical relationship can have an obvious correlation to the movement (physical and metaphorical) in the therapeutic space. Dance therapists can easily train this dialogical attitude; we actually have always done it – changing body shape, positions, levels, directions and movement effort qualities are just some of the possibilities. Through the body we can pick up signals about how the Other 'talks', about the best way of getting into dialogue with the person facing us. With good movement observation skills we can make our bodies replace, where possible, their 'language or accent', which are our favourite gestures and shadow movements and adopt the language of the Other, picking up their postures, gestures or gaze. However, sometimes we cannot nullify the real distance between personal experiences, we cannot cross the transcultural gap and it is better to acknowledge that there is a difference than trying to ignore it. The acknowledgement of this difference is the main idea for this chapter and it will demonstrate that to accept each other's differences can be the best way to honour and reach the Other.

As a student in a training group

Our second academic year was starting and this was another dance movement therapy training group, with a leading teacher/therapist new to the course. Sitting on the floor, we started by introducing ourselves. I mentioned my anxiety about being in such a group, as in the previous year concepts of personal space, closeness and physical touch were a strong issue with some of my English colleagues. I explained, in my odd accent, that I was Portuguese, born in Angola, where I had lived for 14 years and that the cold weather in England made me feel uneasy in my body. It was even more difficult, I added, as my need for physical closeness was so strongly questioned by some of my colleagues. To my amazement, I got a reply, in a perfect English accent, that I was understood, continuing to point out that in 'civilised' countries people do not touch as much as in the 'other' countries.

Was she honestly trying to understand? Was she unaware of the split vision of the world she was giving us, clearly suggesting that she belonged to a 'civilised' country whereas I came from an 'uncivilised' one just because I had mentioned a different approach to touch? Because this was a training group I was even more hurt, as I would have expected a model for a good therapeutic attitude. Instead of containing my normal anxiety in the beginning of a new group she had actually emphasised my sense of marginality. The difference I had expressed about myself had not been acknowledged. She had instead tried to nullify the difference with her claim that she could understand me. By doing that, not only had she showed her dichotomic, old, imperialistic concepts but she transformed what I had presented as part of my identity into something that made me inferior to her, creating a division between civilised and uncivilised countries, very strange concepts to me.

Trying honestly to reach me, she pushed me away. She had related my words such as 'touch' or 'Angola' to her very personal set of values from which I was excluded, even though I could perceive myself as belonging to a same world, a white person and also a member of what was then known as the European Community. Facing this gap between 'civilised' and 'uncivilised' countries I wondered which of us was in fact showing less civility. I remembered all the description of others who had faced cultural prejudices, as I was having a similar range of feelings. Our course had students from many different countries such as Mexico, Malta, Israel, Denmark, Sweden, Japan, Switzerland, Austria, Australia, Hungary, Greece. We were used to daily cultural exchanges and many of our teachers had showed sensitivity on working with our class. This new teacher had introduced the cultural prejudice through an authoritative figure and I could understand how damaging this could be.

I realised that we, as therapists, needed to be aware that our personal views of the world leak through our clinical practice and that it can interfere with the therapeutic relationship. Now, as a course coordinator and supervisor I insist on a conscious phrasing of our interventions, and on a good verbal psychotherapeutic training as demanding as the training in movement observation and non-verbal technical skills. I am now more aware that sometimes we cannot understand or reach the Other, that sometimes the difference does exist and needs to be honoured instead of denied.

As a student therapist in a clinical placement

I was offered the possibility to do my final DMT placement in a primary school, as part of a project supported by the Portuguese Consulate. It aimed to help the social integration of Portuguese immigrant children and to improve their school results. I would do dance therapy but initially had to observe the children in all classes, assess those previously indicated to me, and finally decide, talking with the teachers and my supervisor, which ones I would take in therapy.

The first week immediately stirred in me a lot of projections and countertransferences. Working so close to Portuguese immigrants made me rethink my own position in the host society and also my position in my own country. Some of the immigrant families I talked with showed me a different reality about my own country. I lived near Hampstead Heath, and to travel to Stockwell (from a rich, quiet and traditional English area to a poor, busy and multicultural area) meant an even greater cultural gap because it also meant I had to travel backwards and forwards in the concepts I had about myself, my sense of social belonging, and my cultural references. I became suddenly aware that I was reproducing towards these other Portuguese (a reality I ignored while living comfortably in Portugal) a similar hierarchical attitude to that of my teacher towards me. I perceived all my ambiguities – the pleasure of discovering Portuguese coffee shops and restaurants in the area, of tasting again Portuguese cakes – were in conflict with not wanting to be identified with immigrants whose Portuguese accent sometimes I could not even understand. To be able to embrace the crude reality of these families made me more humble and more prepared to work, once I came back, with immigrants who continued to come to Portugal from Brazil, China, Eastern Europe or African countries.

While observing a class I saw many cultural misunderstandings and could better understand the daily struggles of the children who had only recently arrived and did not exactly know why they were in this new country. Their parents did not discuss all these changes with them, and they were trying to cope with a school system where sometimes they could not even understand the language. Their teachers wondered how much they knew and kept asking if they could understand or even talk in Portuguese, as some of these children seemed to show selective mutism.

However, the problems were mostly emotional or psychological. For example:

> I was observing a class of 5- and 6-year-old children attending a lesson based on the theme of transport. After a clear explanation the teacher told them to draw a map of their route from home to school and the transport they used to come to school. As the teacher and I wandered between the tables, we saw some maps with cars and buses and some of the children where smiling mischievously because they had understood that they were not supposed to draw any transport, since they lived nearby and walked from home. Standing near a Portuguese boy I will call João, the teacher made an impatient gesture, looking at me as if to emphasise what he had told me earlier – that he had the feeling that João had a learning difficulty as he failed most of the tasks in class. I approached João's table and saw some clouds and a plane drawn care-fully on the middle of the paper. The teacher told João that he had certainly not come to school that morning in a plane. I sat down next to João and asked him in Portuguese if he had understood what he had been asked to do. João then told me in a shy, weak voice that he had understood, and told me he heard the teacher say to draw the transport he had used to come to school from his home. He had thought a lot about this and had decided that the place where he lived nearby was not a home, just a house, so he drew a plane similar to the one he had been on a year before. 'My home is in Portugal, I had to show the way from home to school.'

The teacher had concentrated on the cognitive aspect of the lesson, João on the emotional. The gap between them was still wide after one year because the long trip that João had made to arrive at that school had not yet been acknowledged. The school was insisting that he be just the same as other boys without first giving him the right to be different. Part of him was frozen in that part of his personal story he so badly wanted his teachers to recognise that he kept relating his tasks and lessons to the experiences he had left behind. I was touched by the emotional tone in his voice and the dilemma he had obviously lived with while deciding where his home really was. He missed home so badly that he was not intellectually available for a simple school lesson, which he had very easily understood but made him face the more existential dilemma of his own roots and his sense of belonging. Marie Rose Moro (2003) explains how this confrontation with school can be a crucial moment for self-reorganisation and social integration or the moment of a lost opportunity if the child's dilemma is not overcome:

> Some live this moment as a necessary but impossible choice between two worlds. They then suspend their words, their thoughts, their own beings. They hide their creative potential under the masque of inhibition, behavior problems, lack of interest, etc.
>
> (Moro, 2003, p. 173)[1]

In supervision I remind students to carefully separate what is told to them about their patients from what they discover and feel about them at first hand. They need to trust what they feel in spite of what teachers and parents tell them. However, they also need to take such reports into account and make parents and children feel heard while defining a clear boundary and protecting their therapeutic work, not only from others but also from their own projections.

I learned that I had to contain and process my own countertransferences while getting in touch with these children's world. A world so far from mine, I thought. Until my anger and sadness made me realise that these immigrants, unrooted children, made me face the frightened teenager I once was when leaving Angola, running away from bombings and violence and having to adjust to Portugal, a country I could hardly accept as my own. Now as a supervisor I work with trainees on their previous ideas and perceptions about their patients, trying to clear internal space for the unexpected, helping them to face their own shadows before they could deal with the patients' fears.

I took João and two other boys into individual sessions of half an hour each and also created a group of five lively girls of 5 years old. In supervision I had discussed how these girls seemed to have coped better with the immigration process. Their worries about beauty and clothes also made them more interested in the world around them, which they were eager to imitate. The boys seemed more isolated and difficult to reach, so we had decided on individual sessions, as they seemed already to be vulnerable children. Vulnerability depends on individual characterisitcs but is also related to life events and risk factors. Under the severe conditions of the immigration process their psychological fragility was impairing their development:

> Vulnerability is then a dynamic notion; it affects a process in development. The psychic functioning of a vulnerable child is such that a minimal

variation, internal or external, brings up an important disfunctioning, often a tragic suffering, a pause, an inhibition or a minimal development of his potential.

(Moro, 2003, p. 172)[2]

João seemed paused in time, suspended between two worlds, trapped between two homes. The group process was very girlish. Initially they loved to use the props I brought to dress up and put on 'fashion shows', after which they started taking turns being a 'class teacher', a role they were eager to dramatise for several sessions, as they all wanted to behave as a 'grown-up'. I was turned into a child and they had fun bossing me around. They tried to confuse me by giving contradictory orders or telling me how stupid I was for not understanding them. After several interpretations about their need to make me live what they had experienced in their classes, they wanted to be a 'therapist', and their way of communicating with each other changed, becoming more articulate. They had so far reproduced the rude or careless way their families used to address them, or they had been as severe and demanding as their teachers. As 'therapists' they were discovering another way of relating, accepting that they did not need to scream, turn aggressive or scornful to get what they needed. Months later other needs started to appear. They walked on all fours along the floor, pretending to be little cats, each of them making soft noises to get 'mummy's' attention. They were still competing but their movements became slower, more flexible and indulgent, and finally they called themselves little babies – some of the babies, they said, had lost mummy, she had had to go away to work in another country. I knew this had been the story of a few girls who had been left in Portugal with their grandparents until they could join their immigrant parents in London. These girls were re-enacting early traumas, a necessary stage in their recovery. Even if they seemed to be coping well, their experience needed to be told in therapeutic play, in little dramatisations they made during the final sessions. In this way they could integrate their split experience of being big and powerful like the teacher or small and lost like an abandoned baby.

A similar re-enactment took place in all the other sessions. Filipe, 5 years old, re-created the scene at the airport, a place where he found himself suffocated in the arms of a crying grandmother without understanding what was going on. His mother pulled him by one arm while his grandmother was still holding on to him, complaining hysterically that she would lose him for ever. This was quite traumatic for Filipe, who asked me to repeat the grandmother's complaints and to grasp his arm while he explained to me that he had to leave and go on the plane. I still see his body showing this emotional split in such an obvious mimic, pulled by me/grandmother: part of his body was leaning to the right while the other half stretched to the left, in the direction of his mother. Filipe needed to do this over and over again and then added a bit more to this scene which went something like this:

F: Now we are in the plane and it is cold, very, very cold. The plane is above the clouds.

I: Where are we going? I asked, shivering and holding my arms to my chest just like him.

F: I don't know, but it is so cold, this is so big and cold. And grandmother is still crying down there.

I: Do you miss her?

F: Yes, but mother needs me, she is sad too. . . . Oh, I am so cold in this plane.

After reliving this scene several times it seemed that what was frightening to Filipe was not to be told what was really going on. He had been pulled away and carried along with a vague sense that he had to go, as he carefully explained to me/grandmother several times, but not knowing why or what for. He had managed to make me feel his fears and fragmentation. Just offering interpretations would not be useful for this child, so frightened still that he clung to me on the way to and from the therapy session. He even clung to me one day when I was about to change a music tape in the middle of a session, saying 'don't go, don't go'. I explained that I would not leave the room, just cross it and put on another cassette, but he continued to cling to me. He was in panic and told me in Portuguese that if I left him he felt he would fall out of the window and die. The sessions took place on a third floor, an unusual place for Filipe, whose class was on the ground floor, but the windows were barred and it was quite safe. He was telling me about his incapacity to change (of levels, countries), about his lack of limits between inside and outside, about his feeling of not being held and contained, a situation that was actually happening in his real life. A week previously, the police had reported to his school that he had been found at 11 p.m. standing by his drunk, sleeping mother. Again the cold. This time it was the freezing cold of a winter night in London, standing next to a mother who lived off prostitution. Filipe was another very vulnerable child, considered by my supervisor at the Tavistock Clinic as already showing symptoms of psychosis.

Therapeutic interpretations were not a good approach for this child. Filipe needed a more basic intervention, with physical handling and emotional holding. He needed to find refuge in my body, taking the initiative to sit on my lap while I explained to him that the cold in the plane was the air-conditioning, his first experience of such technology, and we relived that moment with a different, less frightened attitude. I showed him where Portugal and England were in the maps he chose from the forgotten bookshelf in the corner of the therapy room. He asked me to count with our fingers, 'saying numbers' endless times in Portuguese and English until we started travelling together around the room, repeating in both languages the names of the objects he indicated. Walking next to me, pointing at things and ordering me to name them, it seemed that Filipe was starting to re-create his world. But he was still too fragmented and lost, a child at risk (Moro, 2003, p. 171), and more work would be necessary over the years.

João, the boy already mentioned at the beginning of this session, created his own repetitive scene:

> João built a house with plastic mats and told me that I had to build another house for myself near his. He told me that I should go into my house and that he would do the same. 'Then you will see what happens', he told me. . . . Once there I asked him what I was supposed to do – 'you eat, you sleep and you just wait', he said. I did as I was ordered, while Filipe seemed to be doing the same in his house. Suddenly I heard a noise and understood that João's house had imploded – 'Big explosion, my house exploded, I have no house any more, can I come to your house?' Filipe took refuge in my house, his body shaking in pretend and real fear. We were both curled up inside while he explained that he had no house, no place to stay. João was obsessed with the explosion and needed to make sure that he would not 'stay ouside', that I had a house waiting for him.
>
> This became a ritual play at the beginning of many sessions, with significative changes which enabled Filipe to own and integrate the past events that inspired this game. By the end of the academic year he already had a house that could stand. A house which he could get into and out of as he chose, around where he made a garden, a safe transitional space to explore the world outside and to relate to me/the neighbour next door.

Both Filipe and João needed to narrate in more or less symbolic ways their previous traumatic experiences, as Rosseau points out:

> [T]he individual intervention, centered around a verbalisation of the premigratory experience in a therapeutic context, takes a central place for victims of violence and extreme stress.
>
> (Rosseau, 2003b, p. 152)[3]

For young children lost between two idioms, verbalisation can be replaced, as we tried to show, by creative movement and dramatic play. Dance movement therapy, giving a relevant place to the body where the traumatic experience is still held, can be very useful for transcultural therapeutic interventions with young children. In this way perhaps we can bring to a flowing present the children arrested in a frozen past. Such was João, who became absent minded during classes:

> [T]he balance between silence and different spaces of enunciation, between various universes of meaning and non-meaning, between belonging and strangeness, allows the reintroduction of a movement which

makes it possible to leave behind the suspended time, the immobile time that suits the trauma.

(Rousseau, 2003b, p. 154)[4]

As a supervisor on a training course

Rita was a DMT student placed in a primary school on the outskirts of Lisbon, an area mostly occupied by immigrants. The school population largely comprised children descended from African people who came from the ex-Portuguese colonies (Mozambique, Angola, Guiné and Cabo Verde) but there were also Indian descendants. Born in Portugal, they spoke Portuguese and also the idiom used at home. After a few days of observation in class Rita accepted most of the teacher's suggestions and pressures and ended up with a group of two girls and four boys of 5 years old. Maria and Poonam, the African and Indian girls, set themselves apart from the beginning, having their own favourite corner of the room where they played throughout the session, apart from the aggressive games of Pedro, Marco and Rui, the three African boys. Miguel, a caucasian, also stayed apart and aloof the whole time, climbing the wood structure on the wall, claiming that he would like to fly and threatening to jump.

Rita brought her despair and frustation to the supervision sessions at not being able to deal with such a demanding situation. She could perceive the group split between genders, as girls and boys did not like to engage with each other and preferred activities with very different movement qualities. She understood that her desire to please the teachers had created what she now called an 'impossible group'. How would she deal with such different attitudes and behaviours, especially if she needed to stay most of the time near the child who was threatening to jump? She described sessions where she left the girls quietly playing their secretive, giggling games while she spoke from a distance to the ruthless boys, almost shouting and reminding them not the use the gymnastic apparatus and not to hurt each other. At the same time she hardly moved, as she felt she had to 'protect' Miguel, a quiet and shy child, in spite of his desire to jump.

This example shows the usual problems we often meet in supervision – how to choose the members of a group, how to deal with the students' early enthusiasm when they believe they can do almost everything and are not yet willing to take into account our advice. How far can we let them try on their own, or interfere in the therapeutic process and their experience? How to negotiate with the school which children to take in therapy and to arrange a suitable room for therapy, since this gymnasium contained apparatus that could be dangerous for the children? However, this group is also a very inter-esting example of a rich transcultural situation – more important than the split between boys and girls was the split between the boys, and the students' incapacity to face it. Rita described session after session where she seemed overwhelmed and frozen, staying most of the time near Miguel, because he seemed frightened and lost, because he set himself apart and was the only one alone, as the others had peers to play with. I soon realised the importance of Rita's countertransferences towards Miguel.

Miguel's father had left when he was born and he lived alone with his mother who was very protective of him, just as Rita was. His family was also isolated in the social area where they lived as they were part of the small white minority living in an area largely occupied by African-Portuguese families. The school formed part of a social and educational charity project run by nuns, who were very dedicated and proud of their work in the area. This school was a centre of social integration and promotion of equality and moral values, where children of many origins and skin colour started studying together from an early age.

Being a single child, Miguel had difficulties in joining with others in rough activities and sat alone in school much of the time. His desire to climb during therapy sessions could be seen, at the same time, as a wish to be apart from the confusion the other boys were creating and a way of calling their attention by also doing a 'risky' thing. It was also a very effective way of getting the therapist's full attention. As all this was interpreted, Miguel started climbing less and less until he started gradually to touch the ground. He began exploring a limited area near him, always protected by the presence of the therapist, already aware of her many projections towards this child but still unable to detach from him. One day Miguel covered himself with the therapist's blue lycra cloth and wandered around the room making frightening sounds and saying that he was a 'white ghost'.

I understood that the theme of being white or black would have to be addressed, as Miguel did not join the other boys because he felt he was different. In a school where the majority of students had black skins, Miguel was showing concern, not about racism, but about identity. He knew he was different, but he was not quite sure in what way, and he was telling us that, among the others, he was a 'ghost'. When I suggested that the student should address this fact during the session she showed great resistance – would she not be introducing a notion of racism and establishing a difference that did not seem to be meaningful for these children, who were used to growing up together? As I tried to understand her resistance I realised that she saw in Miguel an image of her own little boy of 6 years old, who had also recently started school. I also discovered that the student had to make, at the beginning of the academic year, the choice between putting her child in an official school or in a private school. She lived in a place between a poor area with social problems (where the official school was frequented mostly by black children) and a rich area with a private school where she knew that her child would get a different level of education, among a more homogeneous social background. Because the student had had an engaged past with political awareness and moral values she refused the idea of racism and experienced a real dilemma when choosing a school for her child. Theoretically she would have liked her child to study in the official school but she chose instead the private school in order to spare her child any violence and to give him a better education. She was still feeling guilty and confused about this choice, as she felt that all children should have a similar opportunity.

Rita's worry about proving that she was not racist was actually preventing her from facing the real difference that existed between these boys. She needed so badly to refuse such a difference that she was actually unable to address the 'white ghost' that kept wandering around the room, advancing towards the other children but unable to join them, separated by his cloth, his symbolic white skin. The supervision work had to be done at two different levels, by analysing and interpreting Miguel's movements and his desire to meet the others but also Rita's resistance and feelings. Rita was finally able, in the third term, to make interpretations where the skin colour differences were recognised and, as Miguel heard his difference verbalised and accepted, he also found himself more capable of playing with the others, who eagerly integrated him into an improved band of rap. Their final sessions were spent dancing and making up songs, whose words, in indirect and symbolic ways, talked about being isolated or being part of a group, of being different and yet accepted. The isolated white ghost, once his difference was recognised, could finally have a more incarnated presence, assuming a body that had been hiding under a cloth and becoming a peer among peers – just like the others, he could sing rap.

Final reflection

As training courses all over Europe become more open to students from different cultures and nationalities, we need to introduce a coherent transcultural discourse both in the staff's attitude and in the students' awareness and practice. This is even more urgent as our students will feel the transcultural challenges that some of us are already facing in our practice. Client populations can be quite diverse in origins, values and cultural backgrounds. Institutional pressures can create demanding situations, asking specific questions of different individuals or including in the same group people from varied cultural backgrounds.

We need to learn how to avoid having an attitude towards the Other centred in ourselves, but also to accept that sometimes we cannot avoid that possibility. It is better for everyone if we honestly become aware of our own stereotypes, our thoughts and fantasies and communicate these when meeting the strange. The stereotyped perception is very often dichotomic, dealing with pairs of opposites (Sturm, 2004, p. 274) but reality can be rather more complex. Sometimes things can be easily detectable if we see a clear dichotomy, such as civilised/uncivilised, as in the example given in the first section of this chapter, but it can become more complex than that. The example of my student's attitude was exactly the one of wanting to avoid stereotypes; therefore she could not accept that addressing the skin colour issue was not about racism but about identity. Rita's over-concern about being politically correct and her avoidance of her own guilt in choosing a better school for her son were also difficulties experienced in the therapeutic process.

As Sturm says,

[T]he simple absence of racist convictions in the therapist is not enough for avoiding that stereotyped representations get in the therapeutic relationship, mainly those used in a defensive way to control the anxieties provoked by the meeting with the other.

(Sturm, 2004, p. 274)[5]

A good transcultural training and clinical practice would require a supervisor with transcultural experience and a willingness, both from a therapist and supervisor perspective, to see things from a different cultural and social viewpoint. Only by being able to accept the difference in the Other can we open the possibility for dialogue, the basis of any therapeutic encounter.[6]

Notes

All extracts quoted in this chapter are from French texts which have been translated by me from the following original publications.

1 Certains vivent ce moment comme un choix nécessaire mais impossible entre deux mondes. Alors, ils suspendent leur parole, leur pensée, leur être-même. Ils cachent leur potenciel créateur sous le masque de l'inhibition, des troubles du comportement, du désintérêt, etc.
2 La vulnérabilité est donc une notion dynamique; elle affect un processus en développement. Le fonctionnement physique de l'enfant vulnérable est tel qu'une variation minime, interne ou externe, entraîne un dysfonctionnement important, une souffrance souvent tragique, un arrêt, une inhibition ou un dévelopement a minima de son potenciel.
3 [L]'intervention individuelle, centrée autour d'une verbalisation de l'experience prémigratoire dans un contexte thérapeutique, occupe donc une place centrale pour les personnes victimes de violence et de stress extrême.
4 Le jeu entre plusieurs espaces d'énonciation et de silence, entre plusieurs univers de sens et de non-sens, entre l'appartenance et l'étrangeté, permet de réintroduire un mouvement que permet de sortir du temps suspendu, du temps imobile qui suit le traumatisme.
5 La simple absence des convictions racistes chez le thérapeute ne suffit pas pour éviter que des représentations stéréotypées entrent dans la relation thérapeutique, notamment les stéréotypes utilisés de façon défensive pour contoler les angoisses provoquées par le rencontre avec l'autre.
6 All names and identifying details have been changed to preserve confidentiality.

References

Bakthine, M. (1970) *La Poétique de Dostoievski*. Paris: Éditions du Seuil.

Baubet, T. and Moro, M.R. (2003) *Psychiatrie et Migrations*. Paris: Masson.

Moro, M.R. (2002a) *Enfants d'Ici venus d'Ailleurs. Naître et Grandir en France*. Paris: La découvert.

—— (2002b) *Parents en Exil. Psicopathologie et Migrations*. Paris: Presses Universitaires de France.

—— (2003) Parents-enfants en situation migratoire: une nouvelle clinique des métissages, in: T. Baubet and M.R. Moro, *Psychiatrie et Migration* (pp.155–178). Paris: Masson.

Rousseau, C. and Nadeau, L. (2003a) Migration, Exil et Santé Mentale, in: T. Baubet and M.R. Moro, *Psychiatrie et Migration* (pp. 126–136). Paris: Masson.

—— (2003b) Violence organisée et traumatismes, in: T. Baubet and M.R. Moro, *Psychiatrie et Migration* (pp. 148–154). Paris: Masson.

Sturm, G. (2004) Le racism et l'exclusion, in: M.R. Moro, Q. De la Noe and Y. Mouchenick (eds), *Manuel de Psychiatrie Transculturelle. Travail clinique, Travail Social* (pp. 265–278). Paris: La Pensée Sauvage.

Chapter 7

The contribution of authentic movement in supervising dance movement therapists[1]

Wendy Wyman-McGinty

Introduction

In the past 40 years, as dance movement therapists have received additional training in counselling, social work, psychology and psychoanalysis, many have begun to integrate principles of dance movement therapy (DMT) within these disciplines. Recent advances include the recognition of the kinaesthetic dimension of attunement and empathy in the context of the therapeutic relationship (Pallaro, 1996; Wyman-McGinty, 1998, 2006), the personal and archetypal aspects of the somatic unconscious (Chodorow, 1999), the role of the affects in the development of the imagination (Chodorow, 1991, 2000, in press), and the influence of somatic experience in the development of symbol formation, including the capacity for transforming unmentalised experience into thought (Wyman-McGinty, 1998, 2006). Parallel to this has been a developing interest in the body and bodily based experience within the fields of psychology and psychoanalysis. For example: the role of affect regulation in managing unbearable states of mind (Schore, 1994; Wilkinson, 2006); the concept of psychic skin (Bick, 1968; Feldman, 2004); the importance of somatic attunement in determining attachment styles (Fonagy, 2001; Holmes, 2001); an understanding of somatic countertransference as a means of identifying with and differentiating from a patient's internal intersubjective state (Samuels, 1985; Bollas, 1987), and the development of symbolic thought as an inherently body-based experience (Winnicott, 1967; McDougall, 1989; Mitrani, 1996; Aron, 1998; Wrye, 1998).

As a profession, dance movement therapists are in a unique position to add to our understanding of the role of the body in psychotherapy. Regardless of the clinical population with which we work, certain core concepts inform our practice in DMT. These include an awareness of and ability to differentiate between internal feeling states at a somatic level, a finely developed sense of kinaesthetic empathy and attunement, the capacity to tolerate a range of affective material in a non-defensive and containing manner, and an awareness of somatic countertransference.

The authentic movement group as a supervisory experience

I would like to suggest that participation in an authentic movement group, as both a mover and a witness, allows the therapist/supervisee to become familiar with her own unconscious process at a somatic level, including primitive mental states. I have found that therapists who are unfamiliar or uncomfortable in relating to states of mind in themselves, tend to inhibit their expression in their patients, or fail to contain them adequately. In terms of learning to witness others, the therapist/supervisee focuses on somatic countertransference, noting what kinds of feelings evoke her own complexes and defences.

In authentic movement, the person who is moving is asked to focus inward, attending to any bodily sensations, images and feelings, and to allow these to serve as the impetus for self-directed movement. In the process of focusing inward on one's bodily felt experience, images, somatic memory and the accompanying feelings which arise are then available to be explored as a communication from the mover's unconscious. The quiet, focused attention of the witness helps to create a secure containing environment in which the person moving can experience a sense of feeling held and seen. It is this sense of containment which allows the mover to begin to make contact with the somatic unconscious, the unconscious as it is experienced and expressed in the body.

In a long-term study conducted with DMTs who had participated in authentic movement training groups of several years' duration, Lucchi (1998) evaluated authentic movement as a training modality. Each movement therapist whom she[2] interviewed had experience working with psychiatric patients as well as more neurotic patients in a private practice setting (most were also trained in verbal psychotherapy). In reflecting about the influence of authentic movement on their work with patients in a more traditional verbal psychotherapy practice, these therapists consistently reported a heightened sensitivity to and awareness of their patients' somatic experiences, as well as their own somatic countertransference. Lucchi found that those therapists who appeared to be well acquainted with their own primitive mental states and defences tended to be less likely to project their material on to their patients, to have clear boundaries, and more empathy for their patients' mental suffering. During the course of her interviews, participants consistently reported that authentic movement helped them identify and discriminate between internal feeling states on a somatic level, which in turn led to the capacity for self–other differentiation. Lucchi suggested that the ability to discriminate between internal states of mind at a somatic level served to reduce the therapist's tendency to overly identify with patients' projections. Finally, she noted that authentic movement seemed to facilitate the capacity for symbolisation within clinicians. By supporting them in developing a relationship to their own symbolic content, she believed that this awareness would make clinicians more sensitive in understanding the ways in which one begins to shift from a more concrete towards a more symbolic way of relating to unconscious material. For example, a therapist who had experience in authentic movement in dealing with her own primitive mental states, such as feelings of helplessness, dependency, fear of falling to pieces, would hopefully become more sensitive to and aware of these feelings in her patients. In terms of supervision, she would then be able to refer to those experiences in herself as a way of developing empathy, compassion, and ways of thinking about these difficult states of mind. Similarly, experience with witnessing the movements of others can teach the supervisee about tracking the emotional, subjective state of her patients.

Like the mother who learns to attune herself to her infant who communicates through movement, touch and vocalisation, the DMT learns to develop kinaesthetic empathy and kinaesthetic attunement to better understand the affective experience of the mover. In this way, the function of the witness is very similar to that of the mother who is able to help the infant transform beta elements (emotions which are yet not able to be verbalised) into thoughts (alpha function) (Bion, 1967). Kinaesthetic attunement refers to the ability to recognise emerging feeling states at a somatic level, while kinaesthetic empathy refers to the therapist's capacity to understand at a bodily felt level her patient's lived experience. This means that the DMT is constantly working to track her patients in terms of what is being communicated overtly and covertly, as well as any personal reactions she may have to her patient's material. This includes becoming conscious of one's attitude towards the patient's material in terms of what it is being stimulated in the therapist's psyche. As part of this process, the DMT utilises her somatic countertransference, the feelings, images and associations which are evoked in response to observing the movement. Some witnesses find it helpful to physically mirror the movement in an abbreviated way, in order to get a better 'feel' for the mover's experience. For training purposes I ask the witness to take notes, which may include their own feeling reactions, a description of the movement, and any associations. When the mover has finished, she is the first to speak. The role of the witness is to listen for the underlying effect and associations of the mover, with an emphasis on reflection rather than interpretation of the mover's experience. The sense of trust, safety and mutuality which characterises the relationship between mover and witness is essential in creating a safe environment in which to explore unconscious processes.

Learning to witness requires an awareness of the therapist's unconscious dynamics, including primitive mental states, self–other differentiation (an ability to distinguish between their own and the patient's internal states of mind), and the capacity to work symbolically (to reflect on the material rather than become identified with it). The experience of feeling understood in such a primary way creates a sense of containment, which over time can begin to be internalised by the mover (Adler, 1999). It is from this place of containment that one can begin to develop the emotional capacity to see another. In order to create a safe space for one's patients to begin to experience and explore their feelings through movement, the therapist must also have an understanding of her own relationship to a range of affective experience at a bodily level. The development of empathy is related to one's capacity to have a sense of compassion and curiosity about these often infantile states of mind, rather than getting rid of them through defence mechanisms such as projection, projective identification, dissociation, devaluation or sublimation.

The relationship between mover and witness in the development of thought

The ability to identify one's feelings, and to communicate them symbolically through movement or words, leads to the development of a reflective function, what Fogany (2001) called 'mentalisation'. In the mother–infant dyad this happens by the end of the first year, and depends greatly on the mother's capacity to accurately attune to the non-verbal experience of her infant. The gap between that which the child experiences and that which the mother recognises is the origin of the process of symbolic representation (Fonagy, 2001). The mother's ability to subjectively recognise her infant's psychological state, and to reflect about it through words, mirroring and kinaesthetic attunement allows the infant to experience itself as a subject in the mother's mind (Giannoni and Corradi, 2006). The development of a symbolic attitude is thus considered to be a relational process (Bovensiepen, 2002). Fogany suggests that it is the experience of attachment which allows the child to create an interpersonal space in which mental subjective phenomena can develop (Giannoni and Corradi, 2006). This is very similar to Winnicott's intermediate area of experiencing (Winnicott, 1951), a transitional space between the inner and outer world in which image and effect are linked, and which in turn gives rise to fantasy and imagination.

In verbal therapy, the therapist's ability to attune to the non-verbal bodily experience of the patient is critical in establishing a sense of empathy and containment. What is unique about DMT is the emphasis on the primacy of the body in communicating about affective states. Witnessing involves the development of the kinaesthetic aspect of attunement and empathy, as well as an awareness of the somatic countertransference. Training in witnessing can help the DMT learn to track the moment-to-moment evolution of an embodied symbolic expression of unconscious material. In the process of witnessing, the DMT is able to develop a reflective function which allows her to think about what is emerging in the movement, and to mirror this back to the mover, either verbally or in movement. Segal (1991) noted that symbols govern the capacity to communicate not only with others, but with one's internal world, and they form the basis of verbal thinking. In DMT, the movement offers an opportunity to observe the emergence of a symbolic process before it is verbally articulated, and before defensive structures have been enacted.

Structure of the authentic movement supervision group

For supervision purposes a group of eight to ten is ideal. A weekly meeting of two to two-and-a-half hours for a minimum of two years allows individuals enough time to develop a relationship to their somatic unconscious, as well as learn to witness others. Most people find it helpful to be in concurrent psychotherapy or analysis, as personal issues invariably arise which may require greater attention than is possible within the constraints of this form of training group.

The group generally begins seated in a circle, with a brief verbal check-in, followed by a movement warm-up such as stretching, working with movement polarities and moving through space with different energy qualities. The focus gradually becomes more introspective as the movers are asked to begin to close their eyes and focus on their breath or any bodily sensations they are observing. If the group is experienced in authentic movement, the warm-up is generally less directed, with the leader only cueing a time of inward focusing, breath awareness, and a quiet waiting until each person feels ready to begin.

If the group leader wishes to introduce themes or images as starting points for self-directed movement, these need to be open-ended enough so that each person has the opportunity to follow her own associations to the material. If possible, I will try to incorporate issues that group members have brought up, which pertain to them personally or to their clinical work. For example, using the broader idea of body image, I might ask participants to imagine taking an imaginary journey through the interior of their body, noting the skeletal system, muscles and organs, observing the images, feelings and associations that they might have. One suggestion would be to notice the physical and emotional ways in which they experience holding themselves together, then to work with the movement polarities of coagulating and dissolving. Another idea would be to revisit any surgeries, medical procedures or difficulties with a part of the body as an impetus for movement.

Once group members become more familiar with authentic movement they can begin to work in dyads, alternating between being a mover and a witness. After the movement is complete, the mover speaks first. As the witness listens, she takes time to reflect, linking up what she is hearing with her own experience while observing the movement. It is important that she is able to differentiate her own projections and fantasies about the meaning of the movement from the mover's perspective.

In the following example, a witness reflects about her experience:

R seems to be seeking the wall, as if for comfort. She cannot stay in one place for long, seems restless. I feel agitated, like I want to get out of the room. I'm hungry and thirsty, though I just had lunch. I have the image of milk, do I want to mother her? I'm feeling faint, wish the session would end soon. R seems to be settling down. I wish I could rock or comfort her. Her body feels brittle and fragile. I feel protective, angry . . . and sad.

Afterwards, when the mover began to describe her experience, she reported an image of being in a desert filled with dead cows. Her association was to a dead internal mother who wanted to kill off her aliveness and creativity, as though her life were being sucked out of her. R's frantic attempt to self-soothe paralleled the witness's somatic countertransference response of emptiness, hunger and a desire to escape. As feelings of longing and desire for her unavailable mother began to surface, the mover began to weep quietly. In the process of trying to hold the mover's feelings in her mind, the witness noted her own defence mechanisms including a desire to numb out, end the session and vacate her body. She noted her tendency to 'space out' during the time R was moving through the desert, and was able to associate this with her difficulty in dealing with patients who were very dependent on her. As a therapist/witness, she was concerned about being taken over, or not being enough. As the witness was able to work with these feelings in her own movement process, she became more aware of a latent depression and her manic defences against this feeling. In the ensuing months as she was able to carry her depression more actively, she noted that she was having an easier time staying present when working with her more depressed patients.

In the dyadic work described above, it is expected that the affective experience of the mover will impact upon the witness. In a long-term group where there is ample time for each person in a dyad to move and to witness, a sense of intimacy and trust develops between group members as they hold the container for one another. I believe it is this constant experience of truly seeing and being seen that changes one as a therapist. An atmosphere of acceptance, curiosity, non-defensiveness and openness to one another translates into a sense of authenticity in the consulting room.

Self–other differentiation

When working with the chronically mentally ill, borderline or narcissistic patients, the therapist's ego can be taxed in terms of dealing with the intensity of the affects that she is being asked to metabolise. It is only by becoming more conscious of the ways in which our patients stimulate a feeling response in us that we can learn to begin the process of sorting out our internal world from theirs. This kind of reflection is characteristic of a psychodynamic approach which relies on the transference/countertransference relationship as a means of understanding underlying dynamics.

For example, one supervisee had a borderline patient in individual psycho-therapy who placed extraordinary demands on her. She would upset the magazines on the table in the waiting room if the therapist did not open the door at what she deemed to be the proper time, and threatened to destroy the office. The only way she could deal with her out-of-control feelings was to erupt in fits of rage. Needless to say, she had been through several therapists. In terms of her countertransference response, the supervisee felt intimidated, overwhelmed, frustrated and angry. This therapist, who had also had extensive training in authentic movement, was familiar with her own rage and the fear that this patient had engendered in her. The therapist worked with it in the movement supervision group. The experience of being able to express her feelings in movement and to have them held and contained by different witnesses over several months allowed her to begin to confront this difficult and threatening patient. Although this therapist was exceptionally compassionate and sensitive, she also had a tough side, which she allowed to come out more in her movement. In supervision she continued to address the difficulty of setting boundaries, but with an increased awareness and understanding of the affects which this patient generated in her. The patient, sensing that the therapist had developed a new 'edge', gradually backed down, and her acting-out decreased.

The body self, the interpersonal self and the intra-psychic self

With reference to observing movement, I would like to suggest a theoretical model based on three aspects of the self, which I have called the body self, the interpersonal self and the intra-psychic self. In the context of an authentic movement supervision group, the model can serve as a template for the therapist to find her own relationship to these aspects of the self, so that she may in turn translate this to her clinical work with patients. These concepts reflect an individual's relationship to their body, to others and to inner states of mind (Wyman-McGinty, 2005). From a developmental perspective, each aspect of the self is viewed along a continuum, from a literal concrete response towards a more symbolic stance. For example, a regressed patient may be unable to identify feelings as her own, and so takes refuge in splitting and projective identification. The movement may appear literal, almost mimed. Another patient may be able to identify her feelings but feels flooded by them, and unable to think clearly (movement may appear cathartic and disorganised), while a third patient can tolerate the tension of her feelings and be able to reflect and find meaning in them (the movement reflects a sense of integration, as the feelings, images and underlying associations are in active relationship to one another).

The body self

The body self describes the individual's relationship to her body. This includes a sense of body ego, self-agency, body boundaries, an awareness of effective states and body image. On the most primitive level, this can be expressed as '*I exist*'. Winnicott's (1967) belief that it is in the mirroring relationship between infant and mother that the infant comes to recognise his/her own emotional state has been borne out by current infant research (Knox, 2003). The ability of the mother (therapist) to contain, reflect and communicate a range of effective experience to her infant is instrumental in helping the infant (or patient) develop a mind which includes the capacity to form a relationship to rather than be taken over by these often painful states of being (Wyman-McGinty, 2005, 2006).

In terms of supervision, some of the areas that the dance movement therapist would be asked to assess include the extent to which individual patients are able to express affective states, identifying feelings that patients may find difficult to tolerate, the kinds of defensive mechanisms that are employed, such as anxiety, depersonalisation, dissociation, an awareness of a sense of appropriate boundary between self and other, and any issues related to a patient's sense of their body image.

Consequently, supervision would need to enable the therapist to reflect on what these issues evoke in her in terms of her own psychology (such as the kinds of feelings she is more or less comfortable dealing with, or whether there are any issues with body image or boundaries). The therapist who is familiar with a somatic understanding and containment of her own primitive mental states is far more likely to recognise, empathise and tolerate these painful states of mind in her own patients. This sense of feeling held and contained by a therapist who can make sense of and metabolise these early states of mind contribute to the development of a secure ego, rooted in somatic experience.

The interpersonal self

The interpersonal self describes the individual's relationship to others. Some examples would be the capacity for attunement, empathy, self/other differentiation, the ability to distinguish between internal and external states of mind, the development of interpersonal relationships, and the ability to communicate. Developmentally, this marks a shift away from self-involvement to a sense that '*I exist in relationship to something outside of myself*' such as to another person, one's family, community, to humanity as a whole. The ability to tolerate differences between oneself and others in an empathic and thoughtful way, to manage feelings of separation and reunion, dependency and desire, particularly within the transference, are indicative of the development of an interpersonal self.

With reference to group supervision, the dance movement therapist might be asked to assess an individual patient's capacity for empathy towards other group members, such as a sense of camaraderie, a willingness to initiate, and a sense of trust in the group. The therapist in her clinical setting would also observe which individual patient group members were able to attune to one another in terms of changes in mood, movement quality, use of personal space, and ability to mirror one another's movement in a way which is congruent emotionally as well as physically. For example, when working with a patient who tends to take over or dominate the group, the supervisor might ask the therapist to reflect if this is a familiar pattern, such as a projection, a response to a particular feeling, a need for attention, or some combination. The therapist would also be asked by the supervisor to consider her own feelings towards this patient, and to explore these first in movement, noting, for example, if she felt intimidated, angry, passive or competitive as a means of exploring her own unconscious dynamics. Examining the defences of projection and projective identification like this is another way of learning to differentiate a patient's internal world from one's own.

The intra-psychic self

The intra-psychic self describes the development of a reflective function, such that the individual can reflect and communicate about inner states of mind verbally as well as non-verbally. This includes an awareness and understanding of how one defends against certain painful feelings, such as splitting, projection and projective identification. It also includes the ability to utilise symbolic expression, including working with productions of the unconscious such as dreams or active imagination (Wyman-McGinty, 2006). Psychologically, this would translate to '*I exist in relationship to something larger than myself*', such as one's relationship to nature, to God, art, music, literature and so on. The intra-psychic self is concerned with making meaning out of human experience. Clinically this would translate to one's ability to form symbolic representations as a means of reflecting and communicating about one's inner experience.

In group supervision, the therapist might be invited by the supervisor to reflect about the degree to which individual patients are able to use metaphor and symbol to communicate about feeling states. For example, with a depressed patient whose movement was sluggish, the therapist/supervisee introduced the movement qualities of sluggishness and inertia, then encouraged the patient to notice her associations and images. Through mirroring her patient's movement and reflecting about the underlying feelings, the therapist began a dialogue in which her patient could begin to give voice to the events which led to her hospitalisation. This is different from a psychotic's use of metaphor as a form of symbolic equation in which they might imagine they are actually the object of fantasy. An example would be a patient who thought he was Christ. In this case, the supervisee/therapist was able to work with this by reflecting on the suffering this patient had endured and the burden that he felt he carried. This kind of mirroring and containment on the part of the therapist led to an acknowledgement by the patient of the enormity of the task he felt he faced. Although in the ensuing weeks he continued to talk about Christ in terms of his qualities as a man, his need to identify himself as Christ began to shift. Through the relational aspect of the transference, what was previously experienced as a symbolic equation ('I am Christ') had moved towards a more symbolic representation of an inner experience ('I share qualities of Christ').

Clinical examples: body self, interpersonal self, intra-psychic self

Whether in a hospital group or a private practice setting, in group supervision the therapist is encouraged to observe individual patients in terms of their relationship to these three aspects of the self. I want to stress that this is a dynamic process, in that certain experiences may heighten our awareness of a patient's difficulty in a specific area. For example, a supervisee brought to supervision a session in which one male psychiatric in-patient responded with concern about her safety. He asked if she was married, then, noting the ring on her finger, went on to comment that if she were his wife he wouldn't let her out of the house as she was sure to be raped if she went outside. She noted that he seemed upset and agitated. She felt that he wanted to protect her, and so reassured him, although he did not seem comforted. This left her feeling that perhaps she had missed something, so she brought the material to supervision. In the clinical session, which focused on mirroring, the patient had been an active participant, and very connected to her, almost aggressively so. Upon reflection, she had felt drawn to him, thinking that he seemed exciting, and not at all like a patient. As a beginning therapist, she was appreciative of his participation, as it made her feel that the group was going well. She hadn't thought much about her impact upon him, for example, that he might have felt aroused, vulnerable, or even angry. He seemed unable to reflect about his own state of mind (intra-psychic self), and experienced difficulty distinguishing between internal and external states of mind (interpersonal self). He was unclear as to what his own feelings were (body self), although he was aware that he did not want the therapist to get hurt. The only way he could imagine protecting her was to prevent her from going out into what he perceived to be a dangerous world, a concrete and literal response to his own state of mind (e.g. feelings of love and hate, desire and fear of rejection). In supervision, this therapist allowed herself to reflect about his possible attraction to her, and the ways in which she deflected these feelings consciously and unconsciously. She was able to work with her fear of him in movement, and to face her own agitation at dealing with aggression, both his and hers. She recognised that her sense of independence and self-sufficiency served to protect her from her own feelings of anxiety and loneliness. As these parts of herself became more available to her, she found herself more able to respond to such remarks in a more reflective and authentic way.

In contrast to the previous example, a male patient in a private practice setting frequently complained of somatic symptoms, primarily a fear of having cancer or injuring himself. As the therapy progressed, the therapist recognised that these symptoms tended to occur more intensively after holidays or breaks. Working with the body more symbolically through imagery revealed a fear of falling apart and not being able to coagulate. Because the therapist was familiar with this in terms of her own history, she felt able to contain him. A more difficult issue was allowing herself to experience the fragmenting aspect of anger when it was directed towards herself. She worked on this for some time. Simultaneously, as this patient's anger at the therapist for leaving him became more conscious, his physical symptoms gradually lessened. This patient, although very high functioning, dealt with psychic pain by somatising feelings he could not hold in his mind (McDougall, 1989).

In working with these issues in supervision, the therapist needed to find a relationship to her own experiences of disintegration and fragmentation. Not surprisingly, these were activated when she allowed herself to experience the intensity of someone's anger directed at her. Exploring these issues more fully allowed her to stay in relationship to these parts of her patient's psyche, and to begin to make links between his rage, his fear and his somatic symptoms.

In comparison to the first patient who was very concrete, this man was able to communicate more directly about his psychic pain. During this time he had a dream of venturing north into Eskimo territory. One of his images that he worked with in movement was of an 'ice boy'. As he began to associate to some of the ways in which he had felt frozen, he held his arms stiffly at his sides, and felt unable to make contact with others. This led to a realisation of the ways in which he froze over intense feelings out of a fear of being taken over by other people. Because he was unclear as to what his own feelings were (body self), he would often project uncomfortable feelings on to others and then feel in danger that others could take him over (interpersonal self). He experienced his feelings as something that 'came at him from the outside' rather than being part of himself. Initially his movement was somewhat enacted and concrete, with the imagery reflecting the ways in which he felt helpless and humiliated.

In supervision, the therapist often experienced feeling flooded with feelings when she was in the room with him. Initially she treated these as her own somatic countertransference without realising that there was a projective identification process occurring, in that she often experienced feelings of which he was not conscious. At times he became quite angry with her; for example, if she didn't match him perfectly. Any disturbances to the field between them felt like abandonment. Although she did her best to reflect his feelings accurately, she could not be perfect. As she was able to talk with him about the pain of there being two people in the room, with two different minds, he would respond with grief and frustration that she couldn't be an extension of him. As she worked with this material on her own, she was able to find a more conscious relationship to her own desire for fusion. This seemed to shift something in the transference, as he became increasingly aware of his projections and underlying feelings of anger, longing, shame and desire. This was reflected in his movement, which became more expressive. As he became increasingly able to recognise his own feelings and to experience them on a bodily level, including feelings of longing and desire (body self), his ability to distinguish between internal states of mind and outer reality became more differentiated (interpersonal self). His growing capacity to reflect about his internal state of mind (intra-psychic self) led to a sense of integration. No longer relegated to the realm of the unthought known (Bollas, 1987), this patient became increasingly able to hold his feelings in both his mind and body. Consequently his need to somatise lessened significantly. More importantly, when somatic symptoms did appear, for example, under stress, he was able to link their appearance to feelings that were difficult to experience, but which clearly belonged to him.

Conclusion

One of the primary goals of dance movement therapy is to help patients find a relationship to their body, to others and to internal states of mind. To be effective, the dance movement therapist needs to be able to differentiate between internal feeling states in herself and her patients. In addition, she must be able to contain and metabolise a range and depth of effective experience while maintaining an empathic connection to her patients, without becoming overly identified with, or defended against, their psychological material. Participation in an authentic movement supervision group is an effective way to further develop such skills for practice. This approach, which focuses on the supervisee's/therapist's own movement process as well as developing the capacity to witness others, can help the therapist become more conscious of her own somatic experience, as well as learning to track the somatic aspect of the countertransference in increasingly specific ways. By finding a relationship to our own internal states of mind, including an awareness of how we carry these feeling states in our bodies, perhaps we can develop a sensitivity to allow these often painful states of being to be more fully alive in ourselves and in our patients.

Notes

1 After teaching in a university graduate programme in dance movement therapy, I worked with a group of dance therapists (many of whom were also trained as

verbal therapists) who wanted to learn more about authentic movement and witnessing. We met weekly for approximately ten years. I would like to dedicate this chapter to these extraordinary women who are gifted clinicians in their own right, and who were the inspiration for this writing.

2 Although it is typical to use the pronoun 'he', I have chosen to use 'she', since the majority of dance movement therapists are women.

References

Adler, J. (1999) Who is the witness? A description of authentic movement. In P. Pallaro (ed.) *Authentic Movement: A Collection of Essays by Mary Starks Whitehouse, Janet Adler and Joan Chodorow*. London and Philadelphia: Jessica Kingsley Publishers, pp. 141–159.

Aron, L. (1998) The clinical body and the reflexive mind. In L. Aron and F. Anderson (eds) *Relational Perspectives on the Body*. Hillsdale, NJ, and London: The Analytic Press, pp. 3–37.

Bick, E. (1968) The experience of skin in early object-relations. *International Journal of Psychoanalysis*, 49, 484–486.

Bion, W. (1967) A theory of thinking. In *Second Thoughts*. London: Maresfield Library, pp. 110–119.

Bollas, C. (1987) *The Shadow of the Object: The Psychoanalysis of the Unthought Known*. New York: Columbia University Press.

Bovensiepen, G. (2002) Symbolic attitude and reverie: problems of symbolization in children and adolescents. *Journal of Analytical Psychology*, 47(2), 241–257.

Chodorow, J. (1991) *Dance Therapy and Depth Psychology: The Moving Imagination*. New York: Routledge.

—— (1999) To move and be moved. In P. Pallaro (ed.) *Authentic Movement: A Collection of Essays by Mary Starks Whitehouse, Janet Adler and Joan Chodorow*. London and Philadelphia: Jessica Kingsley Publishers, pp. 267–278.

—— (2000) The Marion Chace Foundation Annual Lecture: The Moving Imagination. *American Journal of Dance Therapy*, 22(1), 5–27.

Feldman, B. (2004) A skin for the imaginal. *Journal of Analytical Psychology*, 49(3), 285–311.

Fonagy, P. (2001) *Attachment Theory and Psychoanalysis*. New York: Other Press.

Giannoni, M. and Corradi, M. (2006) How the mind understands other minds: cognitive psychology, attachment and reflective function. *Journal of Analytical Psychology*, 51(2), 271–284.

Holmes, J. (2001) *The Search for the Secure Base*. Hove, East Sussex: Brunner-Routledge.

Knox, J. (2003) *Archetype, Attachment, Analysis: Jungian Psychology and the Emergent Mind*. Hove, East Sussex: Brunner-Routledge.

Lucchi, B. (1998) *Authentic Movement as a Training Modality for Private Practice Clinicians*. Unpublished doctoral dissertation, California Graduate Institute, Los Angeles.

McDougall, J. (1989) *Theaters of the Body*. New York: W.W. Norton.

Mitrani, J. (1996) *A Framework for the Imaginary: Clinical Explorations in Primitive Mental States of Being*. Northvale, NJ: Jason Aronson.

Pallaro, P. (1996) Somatic countertransference: the therapist in relationship. In

Conference Proceedings, Third European Arts Therapies Conference, Vol. 1, The Arts Therapist. Hatfield: School of Art and Design, University of Hertfordshire.

Samuels, A. (1985) Countertransference, the mundud imaginalis and a research project. *Journal of Analytical Psychology*, 30, 47–71.

Schore, A.N. (1994) *Affect Regulation and the Origin of the Self: The Neurobiology of Emotional Development*. Hillsdale, NJ: Erlbaum.

Segal, H. (1991) *Dream, Phantasy, and Art*. London: Routledge.

Symmington, J. and Symmington, N. (1996). Container/contained. In *The Clinical Thinking of Wilfred Bion*. London and New York: Routledge, pp. 50–58.

Wilkinson, M. (2006) *Coming into Mind: The Mind–Brain Relationship: A Jungian Perspective*. London and New York: Routledge.

Winnicott, D.W. (1951) Transitional objects and transitional phenomena. In *Playing and Reality*. New York: Basic Books, 1971, pp. 1–25.

—— (1967) Mirror-role of mother and family in child development. In *Playing and Reality*, New York: Basic Books, 1971, pp. 111–118.

Wrye, H.K. (1998) The embodiment of desire: relinking the bodymind within the analytic dyad. In L. Aron and F. Anderson (eds) *Relational Perspectives on the Body*. Hillsdale, NJ, and London: The Analytic Press, pp. 97–116.

Wyman-McGinty, W. (1998) The body in analysis: authentic movement and witnessing in clinical practice. *Journal of Analytical Psychology*, 43, 239–260.

—— (2005) Growing a mind: the evolution of thought out of bodily experience. *Spring: A Journal of Archetype and Culture*, 72, 267–279.

—— (2006) Merging and differentiating. In P. Pallaro (ed.) *Authentic Movement Vol. II*. London and Philadelphia: Jessica Kingsley Publishers.

Chapter 8

We could dance at the opera house

A novice practitioner's experience of in-session supervision in training

Maggie Young

Introduction

This chapter is an account of my learning experiences while under supervision as a trainee in my DMT Certificate practicum. As a student I chose to work at a dance and DMT training institution in Sydney, Australia with a group of physically and intellectually disabled clients because it was closer to my home in Newcastle than the placements near the Melbourne training course.

Not only will I recount the learning experiences and a heightened awareness of DMT interventions that occurred, but I will trace my journey from anxiety to confidence complete with a renewed sense of wholeness of personality. Throughout the chapter I will map a parallel journey in italicised inserts of my thoughts, fears and anxieties.

Initially I was worried about my lack of dance training, being criticised for my mistakes and fearful of failure in a new (to me) discipline. Being a mature student added to my list of anxieties.

Suddenly, after years of experience facilitating drama workshops, I was an apprentice again with my work about to be monitored. I identified with Elizur's (1990) observation that there is a very real fear and high level of anxiety with the unprecedented degree of exposure and constant monitoring of a trainee's work. Trainees, Elizur warned, could even experience persecution fantasies if they felt they were relegated to the status of apprentices. I was anxious too that being supervised would bring up old wounds from childhood authority figures of a critical teacher wielding power and knowledge in an unequal relationship. Phil Mollen's (1997, p. 24) statement resonated with me:

> Trainees of an authoritarian disposition, or an authoritarian professional background (such as nursing) frequently have difficulty in conceiving of any other function of the supervision that is not to do with authority.

I soon realised that Marcia Leventhal's observation 'That a change in movement expression will result in a change in personality or behavioural change' (Leventhal, 1987 p. 10) applied just as much to me as to the client group with whom I would work.

Beginning the placement

So here I am at the Institute in Sydney on a Monday morning, having travelled three hours (this is 'close by' in Australia!) to get here from the northern city of Newcastle. I have caught an early morning train to Sydney Central, hardly noticing the picturesque Hawkesbury River on the journey. Outside Central I wait for the infrequent 501 bus to take me to the Institute.

Euna,[1] my supervisor, welcomes me into the tiny dance studio. She is a vivacious, Japanese-born, Korean Australian and a lecturer in disability and dance therapy at the Institute. She moves with grace and ease as she introduces me to Emily and Jane, two other DMT trainees.

I am thinking how much like dancers they look. On my way here I had seen the dancers training in the studio next door to Euna's studio – young girls in leotards, hair pulled back, Alice bands, lithe bodies, and those little skirts attached to tights. Am I too old for this?

I am to spend eight in-session DMT sessions with Euna and my fellow trainees. Euna explains that the clients travel to the Institute once a week from community centres and the hour spent with her is the only contact she has with them. Euna gives me information sheets outlining the course. There are four client objectives for the supervisees to consider. First, the clients' fine and gross motor skills are to be developed by expanding the range of movement stimulated by creative movement, props and music. Second, social skills can be developed by interacting and cooperating in pairs and groups and by using mirroring and reflective movements. Third, personal skills will be learned with body awareness, trust, and awareness of space, relaxation and stillness. Finally, communication skills will be fostered by focusing on eye contact and the following of instructions. While Euna writes the session's activities from warm-up through to theme and closure on the whiteboard she explains our roles in the session. Euna explains that after each DMT session we will have time for debriefing to discuss, give feedback and verbally evaluate all that we have learned. We collect mats, check the CD player and I learn the key code to unlock the props cupboard.

'How are you? How are you? It's good to see you!' Chris says as he bursts into the tiny dance studio, his face beaming. He is followed by nine other adult clients with mixed disabilities. The disabilities cover a wide spectrum, from Chris[2] who has only a mild intellectual disability, to James, Arnold and Warren who are severely physically and intellectually disabled and are in wheelchairs being pushed by their carers. All three have only some mobility in their hands and can move their heads slightly but with little or no mobility in their legs.

Sharon, Joanne and Martin have Downs' syndrome. They have heavy, slow movements, indirect space and bound flow. Joanne looks at me sideways, acknowledging this new person in the room. Grinning broadly, she lunges unsteadily towards me and, with a body almost twice my size and weight, totally envelops me in a warm bear hug.

I thought I already knew so much about running workshops but realise I have so much more to learn. The eight sessions I am to spend with this group will be a new challenge as I have not worked with disabled clients before.

David enters now with sudden, jerky movements, a light weight, indirect space and a bound flow, and in his mouth are two linked straws which will stay there throughout the session. He is clutching a bunch of twigs tightly to his chest.

Tony enters – a slight man with a stooped posture who needs huge built-up shoes so that he can walk. His effort is light weight in spite of the shoes, bound flow, sustained time and indirect space.

I worried about whether the ideas and strategies I knew would still work with this group. I was used to running things in my own way and I had previously never really questioned in depth why things had worked or even why they had not.

Brian lurches into the room now. He has a large body with bound flow of a tight rocking forward-and-back movement as he propels himself diagonally in a straight line across the room. He uses a strong weight effort and direct space. His huge chest is out of proportion to the rest of his body. For a moment he stands still at the door as if appearing to plot a course and then, without looking where he is going, rocks his large body in a forward direction with a swinging movement of his arms.

The session begins with the ritual name welcoming in the circle, 'Brian is here! Brian is here! Brian is here!' everybody chants loudly in unison while clapping the rhythm, and Brian bows and grins his pleasure as he rocks backwards and forwards on the spot. 'Joanne is here! Joanne is here! Joanne is here!' Joanne smiles and bows. She sees me, and again grasps me tightly smothering me in a warm hug.

The men in the wheelchairs have a sunken body shape and Brian's and Joanne's postures depict the other extreme of an overly inflated body shape. There are obsessive movements here – Brian's continued rocking, Joanne's sudden lunges, David's vacant ambling, David's and Tony's shuffling movements. Sharon's movements are generally unpredictable – either dancing frantically or flopping into an unmovable heap.

I worry that I am unprepared for this disparity when it is my turn to lead a session. Will I be able to keep the same caring, respectful control that Euna has? Nothing I have done before seems to have prepared me for this.

Euna has asked me to lead the entire session the following week and I tell her my plans to run the session with a theme on birds using masks and muslin wings. She looks at me worriedly and asks me to include plenty of strong movements among all the light, flowing movements.

Learning more about DMT

Theories

I realised then that we were talking about Laban Movement Analysis (LMA). The continuum of weight effort could be stuck in light and I make a note to have eagles swooping and heavy swamp birds wading through mud, to encourage the other end of the continuum for balance. Although I studied LMA in my course, it is here, with Euna's insight, that I can fully put it into practice, and I am pleased to have a common language in which to relate to her.

Euna takes the group in 'follow the leader' and now that I am aware of the new (to me) system of LMA I can see how the combinations of weight, time, space and flow provide the dynamics for all movement. Even such a simple activity as 'follow the leader' focuses on all these combinations and I see that the four objectives of the DMT sessions are met with this one activity. By following Euna's movements as we progress in a circle, motor skills are being developed, body awareness is heightened, movement range is expanded and social skills of cooperation are taking place. When Euna asks for volunteers to take her place as a leader, she is giving the clients space to develop their own creativity and improvisational skills.

Being presented here in this group with so many different aspects of the use of effort and space in the human body, I could see more clearly the need for a system to analyse and interpret these movements. I became aware of LMA as a system for evaluating by predicting future behaviour, measuring progress and building on new observations. At one debriefing session we all commented on Warren's new extended arm movements when Emily threw a thick balloon to him and he punched it away from him in a strong weight effort and direct flow. Being familiar with the LMA terms meant we knew what to look for in terms of expanding Warren's movement range. We decided to work on this activity even more, using similar props in the next session.

From reading the session's aims and my first impressions of Euna's teaching approach, I believe that the humanistic model of psychotherapy is underlying the DMT sessions. The teaching style that Euna models for us appears to be defined by Frick's (1971) definition of the humanistic model of psychotherapy as 'a greater measure of freedom to concentrate on significant human problems and concerns that can take man's full range of inner experiences into account' (Frick, 1971, p. 11).

Euna models for us a client-centred approach where 'the therapist is non-directive and reflective and does not interpret or advise except to encourage or clarify points' (Reber and Reber, 1985, p. 126). The clients are encouraged to enact their own inner capacity for change in a safe, non-judgemental environment. 'That's wonderful Joanne! Can you show everybody?' Euna says, and Joanne laughs as she shows us her bird walk. Everyone claps delightedly.

Later Euna tells us to look for every little sign of change in a client's movements and to comment positively throughout the session. When it was my turn to lead the welcoming circle ritual Carl Rogers' words took on a greater meaning for me:

> [I]t seems that my inner spirit has reached out and touched the inner spirit of the other. Our relationship transcends itself and becomes part of something larger. Profound growth and healing and energy are present.
>
> (Rogers, 1980, p. 12)

Initially I planned to tap out the rhythm with brightly patterned clapping sticks from Arnhem Land instead of beginning with the usual hand clapping. As I began to tell the story of the totem pattern Sharon interrupted, speaking rapidly and excitedly miming clapping with the sticks. I stopped speaking and spontaneously gave her the sticks. Sharon immediately clapped out her own rhythm with them and everyone joined in enthusiastically. 'Sharon is here! Sharon is here! Sharon is here!'

As soon as I relinquished the sticks I knew that I had relinquished my own planned control. I believed I was connecting to the group dynamics here and that the clients wanted to have some control over this activity. They had some ownership now of a familiar activity and had the opportunity to extend their movements.

Sharon spontaneously handed the sticks to the person beside her so that each client tapped out their own rhythm and everyone joined in.

I felt strongly that by letting go of my need to control the situation we had tapped into something greater than all of us and thus opened up opportunities for the clients' self-empowerment.

I walked around the circle trying to keep up. I realised I was no longer in charge. I looked across at Euna and she smiled and nodded her approval.

When Euna smiled I felt that she was sending me a clear message that going with the needs of the client, even at the expense of modifying an existing plan, was a most important lesson. I was aware now that empathy, attunement and especially letting go of the need to control were present in this moment.

Something magical and greater than all of us had happened.

Rhythm, ritual and repetition

Euna encourages us to use the 3 Rs of movement – rhythm, ritual and repetition – in each session to help achieve the four course objectives. The morning greeting ritual provides a transition from the rest of the clients' lives as soon as they enter the studio and is an immediate focus for their attention. This form of introduction consists of the power of the rhythm in name-calling and the familiar repetition of the clients' names, causing them to smile or bow their pleasure. There appears to be a sense of familiarity and belonging to the group. Even in this introductory activity the four DMT goals are being met. As each client confidently interacts, acknowledges others and uses eye contact I observe that social and communication skills are taking place. Standing in a circle and clapping is encouraging motor skills and personal skills of trust and body awareness. The clients are familiar too with the ritual at the end of the session when they will lie down, stretched out with eyes closed on the blue gym mats, giving them even more awareness of their bodies by encouraging stillness and relaxation.

Schott-Billmann (1992) writes of the healing power of dance using the anthropological approach or 'Primitive Expression'. She argues that freed from the magical and religious connotations the holistic power of traditional dance with its emphasis on rhythm, repetition and ritual can be culturally transferred: 'everyone can personally attach his or her own myth to the ordered, rhythmic, repetitive archetypal activities proposed' (Schott-Billmann, 1992, p. 108).

The same holistic power of dance I had witnessed in Arnhem Land corroborees was present in the studio with the disabled clients when they began and ended their DMT sessions with ritual, rhythm and repetition.

Mirroring

Mirroring is an activity I found that children loved; it was often a way to create a rapport, build up observation and concentration skills or as a body-awareness exercise which sometimes led into creating a play. Here in this supervised therapy session with adults, I could observe a greater depth to mirroring, knowing that staying with the clients, joining in their rhythms, repeating them and enlarging them could reach a point where an original movement pattern was changed. I watched Sharon laughing and talking to Jane who was mirroring Sharon's movements, and considered that here was a good example of clients learning interaction and social skills through mirroring. 'You are very good dancers,' Chris tells Emily and myself as we mirror his movements of such free flow. He expresses such joy in his dance. 'You could dance at the opera house' he tells us. 'Only with you', I reply.

Here Chris would seem to be seeing a mirror image of a self that he really loved and admired and I felt that his comment about being a very good dancer really applied to himself. He knew he was a good dancer in spite of whatever else was happening in his life. I believe I was reflecting back and acknowledging that I had a glimpse of his inner life too through his dance. I must admit I was just a little flattered by his comment!

I mirror David's movements of shuffling his legs from side to side as his hands are firmly clutching a bunch of twigs to his chest. Suddenly the shuffling movements turn to lifting his legs into a sideways kick and David laughs with delight at this change in his movement pattern. Then he stops perfectly still. He looks at his bunch of twigs, and slowly and carefully divides them into two bunches and thrusts one bunch into my hand.

I was deeply touched when David offered his gift to me. Because I had been echoing his movements it was almost as if he was acknowledging that I was understanding his inner self. Mirroring may have evoked a feeling of gratitude too. I felt tearful when I accepted the gift because to me it meant that through a shared movement experience we had recognised each other. I held his gift in my hand throughout the rest of the session and hoped he noticed how much the exchange had meant to me.

Groups

Euna informs us that a group of clients with such diverse needs and abilities may not have the skills to form a circle, to stop on cue or to work with a partner. To encourage the clients to form a circle each one holds part of a long length of lycra stitched into a circle. The very stretchy nature of the lycra encourages stretching, pushing, pulling, winding, twisting and a range of completely uncharacteristic movements. Euna models, giving clear instructions before starting this activity, and always praises and comments positively throughout.

I worry about changing the activities too quickly in a group. Can I read the group dynamics well enough? Am I giving everyone enough time to thoroughly explore an activity?

Emily, when it is her turn to lead the group, writes the heading 'Mexican Wave' on the whiteboard for her fellow trainees before the session begins. 'Think of flowing movements,' Emily writes, 'Fast and slow, in and out of the circle. Pass the movement around the circle.'

This looks so ambitious and complicated written down and I wonder how she will convey these directions helped by Jane changing the rhythms on a drum.

However, it works. Everyone can participate at their own level of ability from Warren with limited movement in his wheelchair, to Chris who loves to extend his movement range to take up as much space as possible. The Mexican Wave is a great success and later Euna praises Emily for her clear and simple instructions.

Clear and simple. I need to remember this.

In one memorable session four people held a long piece of blue velvet fabric stretched across the length of the room and clients were encouraged to explore endless movement possibilities around, under and beside the cloth. This gave them many opportunities to explore relationships with their own and other people's body shape, and the space around them. I noticed that Brian in particular was moving in an unaccustomed way with indirect space and free flow as he dodged the other clients' indirect movements. Such an exercise as this was a wonderful opportunity to achieve the first three DMT course objectives of developing fine and gross motor skills, social skills and personal skills. The theme of the session was 'waves', and when the whole group held and moved the blue velvet, Euna spoke of being on the beach on a sunny day. Soon clients were joining in telling stories of picnics. When Euna shook the length of velvet vigorously and yelled that a storm was coming, everyone screamed on cue and moved faster. The fourth course objective of fostering communication skills was achieved by reacting and responding to individual comments and feeling motivated to continue the story. Such a creative exercise encouraged the clients to use their imagination, improvise, move in unfamiliar ways, and to extend their movement range.

I admired how Euna could sense the dynamics of the group and knew when to change the rhythms and when to bring the activity to a close. Euna always acknowledged each individual's contribution while still maintaining the group as a whole. I thought that this was something I could only learn from paying close attention to a professional practitioner and assimilating her methods.

Levine considers that observing and absorbing the work of an experienced practitioner supervisor is one of the most important ways a trainee can learn to be an expressive arts therapist. Working in this way means, 'This is like the system of apprenticeship in order to learn a trade' (in Knill *et al.*, 2005, p. 238).

Props

Recalling the group activity with the blue velvet fabric, I saw that a prop could be a focus for an entire group to weave their bodies and stories around. Along with the fabrics in the props cupboard there are colourful balls of differing sizes and textures, thick balloons, rainbow-coloured ribbon sticks, elastics, lycra pieces sewn into a circle, a parachute, percussion instruments and scarves.

Emily gives the clients funny hats to wear and Euna later warns that as a disabled group they may be held up to ridicule.

I felt nervous at first about having to disagree with Euna on this point because she had many years of experience working with disabled clients. Even though I was absorbing everything Euna was teaching me, she was also encouraging me to draw on any previous experiences and gave me space to voice an opinion or concern. Here I expressed the view that there was a universal appeal of clowning with all its funny hats, red noses, silly walks and ill-fitting costumes, and it was worth exploring as a medium of expression for disabled clients.

Observing the way Joanne rushed to put on the hat before Emily had a chance to distribute them to the group, and later, when Sharon and Joanne piled juggling scarves on their heads as funny hats and created 'silly walks', I felt reassured that clowning was an appropriate medium of expression for them. After all, clowning concerns play, pleasure, relishing the chaos and a freedom to express an inner need as well as enjoying living in the present moment.

There is a sense of self-discovery through the manipulation of an object. Wearing a scarf, a hat, a mask, a cloak or even muslin bird wings can give the wearer another sense of himself; he can act out 'as if' in spite of his limitations. When Warren, dressed in brightly painted bird wings, was wheeled around by his carer in the middle of the circle to demonstrate flying, he flapped his arms and grinned with pleasure. His eyes were shining as if for a moment he really was flying!

To me there was a marked difference between this incident in a DMT session compared to a similar incident occurring in a drama workshop because here I was focused entirely on the force, time and space dynamic of movement. My aim in this instance was for Warren to respond to the prop with bodily movement by heightening his awareness of his arms and extending his range of movement. He usually sat rigidly with a sunken body shape and bound flow, his arms folded tightly in front of his chest, often yelling loudly that he wanted to go home. But once Warren's arms were fitted into the muslin wings the power of imagination took over and he stretched his arms out, imitating a flying bird. Warren lengthened his arms into a light weight and a free flow thus providing a different movement path for him to express his inner life.

Trudi Schoop (1974) writes of using props to further her aims of giving psychiatric patients a bodily sense of the centre of themselves. Schoop's intentions are summed up beautifully in her words: 'I use every available means to give the body back to the owner' (Schoop, 1974, p. 100).

Authenticity and unpredictability

This would be the first time I had been supervised since training as a teacher in the 1960s, so I was anxious about the process, remembering how hard it was to be observed and still face a class of pupils.

I worried about just how authentic I could be when I knew I was being observed. I was always aware when Euna jotted down some notes. What has she written? Have I made a mistake? I feel uncertainty. I fear failure, of being criticised. This might be my last chance to make it perfect.

The journey back home in the train is a good place for writing and reflection, and I write in my notebook:

It is as if Euna is holding the space for me. As if this is a dyad between us and she is observing and witnessing my movements. If I can be as authentic as possible then there is no right or wrong way and I need not be so anxious about doing DMT perfectly.

Later I am reassured by reading Christine Brems' (2001) advice that a successful therapist or counsellor is one who is authentic and genuine and therefore able to express their own humanity.

Janet Adler writes of a conscious witness emerging within the mind of the mover and an unconscious activity within the witness. Then, 'Increasingly like the mediator, both mover and witness carry the tension and the union between these polarities within themselves' (Adler, 1987, p. 24). So thinking of my supervisor as a witness changes any fears about authority and criticism that I may still have.

I observe how Euna deals with unpredictable behaviour such as sudden conflict when Chris conflicts with his carer and begins to yell loudly. Euna steps in between them with the basket of percussion instruments and distracts him, asking him to give out the instruments to others in the circle. When Joanne slumps in a chair or refuses to get up from the floor Euna respects that choice and does not coerce her into joining in. Eventually Joanne moves when she is ready. Confidence and respect appear to be the key in these situations of conflict.

I decide to use hoops when asked to take a warm-up during one session. I think we can have a lot of climbing through, spinning, working in pairs, leaping in and out. My mind is racing with ideas. Oh no! Clients in wheelchairs! I had forgotten! Sharon saves the day by throwing a hoop over my head and then everyone, particularly the wheelchair occupants, enjoy throwing hoops over me. A human quoit! Although I managed to turn this mistake to my advantage, I was not so fortunate when I asked a carer if he would like to stand in the centre so we could move around him. He flatly refused.

I was embarrassed by this mistake especially as Euna, rightly, brought up the incident in the debriefing session advising us about the carers' role. I made a note to be more careful of my demands in future and not to assume that everyone loves attention.

I spent a lot of time and energy trying to be perfect during the supervision. Wolman (2005) recognises this in the supervisee's striving for perfection and suggests instead to look on our mistakes as an opportunity to make meaning. She believes that supervisees should be enabled to develop an independent system of internal supervision and I can see now how this could happen (see Chapter 2, Bonnie Meekums). Spinelli, in an interview with Sullivan, also believes that there is a positive side to mistake-making in training: 'it's not the less you make mistakes, it's that you are more able to utilize the mistakes you make for the therapeutic purposes and value they have' (Sullivan, 2005, p. 62).

Completing the placement

It is my last day at the Institute and I say goodbye to the clients at the end of the session.

I feel very sad to have ended this placement as I would have liked to continue working with the clients and observing their progressive movement changes. As if Joanne senses my feelings she gives me a sideways look and lumbers over to envelop me in a warm hug.

I appreciate the clients' exuberance and their sheer joy in moving. They encapsulate Trudi Schoop's (1974) observations: 'But there are no words to impart the marvelous sense of joy, the love of life, the enchantment with existence that envelops the dancing human' (Schoop, 1974, p. 157).

Chris is the last to leave the dance studio. 'Goodbye! Goodbye! Very good dancing. Thankyou! Thankyou very much! See you next week!' he says, bending his body into a sweeping bow and looking up with his whole face alight with joy.

Reflections

On recovering a sense of wholeness and containing fears

Since my supervisor encouraged and acknowledged any innovations from my drama background, this placement experience gave me the sense of integration and wholeness to which Warren Lett refers:

> Using the arts in therapy helps us to uncover an unimagined storehouse of inner richness – packages from life put away into the spare room of disconnectedness, until an experiential imperative arises that drives us into our neglected selves.
>
> (Lett, 1993, p. 16)

Chodorow's term, 'wholeness of personality' (Chodorow, 1991, p. 93), sums up how I feel after eight weeks of my placement in-session supervision. I feel now that I have gained a sense of integration and a renewed confidence in myself.

Anxieties about being inadequate and fears of failure had dissipated by my last session. When Chodorow (1991) writes that fear is expressed and transformed through ritual, I realise that the ritual procedure of these sessions has helped me as well.

Different models of supervision

I did not really question the process, methods or arrangements offered to me. When I realised that there were other models on offer such as individual in-session and after-session group supervision, I began to see the advantages of the in-session supervision with a small group of trainees. I gained insights from observing the other trainees and stimulation from their input in the debriefing sessions. It meant there was a variety of approaches and ideas and I had access to the way DMT was undertaken in a different institution. Later on I was fortunate enough to experience the individual supervision in-session model during a two-week placement in a hospital with two pre-school boys with delayed learning.

From the beginning of the individual in-session supervision I felt a more personal connection with Bronwyn, my supervisor. I felt comfortable in a one-on-one situation and already had a rapport with Bronwyn because she had been my DMT tutor throughout the year. When I was entrusted with the clients' case histories before my first session, I felt I was being treated more like a colleague than a beginning student.

One-on-one supervision was not as formal as the group in-session supervision format and I felt that I was able to focus more directly on the clients because there were only two of them.

Debriefing

After this model of supervision there was more time for informal reflection and debriefing. We even continued our discussions while eating a picnic lunch in the hospital grounds overlooking the ocean. I could relate more easily with Bronwyn on DMT issues having gained more confidence and knowledge because of my group in-session supervision experience.

However, the debriefing sessions with Euna were more formal. For example, the four of us would arrange the chairs in a circle and take turns to discuss our observations and feelings. I was prepared for this verbal evaluation but what if we had pushed the chairs to one side and used the space to *dance* instead? Then I would have felt as though I was sharing my true feelings with my supervisor and peers through movement.

I remembered the delight I felt one day when I arrived at the studio early to find it unlocked and the red velvet curtain covering the mirrored wall had been drawn aside. I felt prompted to dance around the entire space and practise at the barre, recalling ballerina fantasies from childhood.

Wadeson and colleagues suggest a model of supervising art therapy trainees that applies 'the essence of art therapy' so that art-making is exchanged between supervisor and supervisee instead of an emphasis on a verbal exchange. They concluded that the mutual intensive learning that took place was a powerful and enriching experience for both, and that 'it is a natural progression to include art making and other self-expressive tools to process our experiences as art therapists in more depth' (Wadeson *et al.*, 1989, p. 432).

Luckily, I was able to process my practicum experiences in two other ways. First, I could share those experiences through dance, drawing and discussion with my lecturers and fellow students on my return to the Melbourne DMT course. Then, since 20 hours of dyads with a partner as mover and witness were a requirement of the course, I could recall my own authentic experience in movement with a dyad partner as witness.

By including drawing, movement and dramatic re-enactment in the debriefing sessions as a means of reflection, the experience would be enhanced in my view. Ellen Levine writes of the benefits to trainees of this kind of supervisory approach including the art form itself and notes that 'because it is done through the arts it has a more exploratory quality than a linear discussion might have' (Knill *et al.*, 2005, p. 247).

I remember the delight I felt dancing in that space and would have dearly loved to have shared it with Emily, Jane and Euna at the time.

Summary

Now that I have completed the DMT Certificate course I have begun facilitating dance therapy sessions with a variety of clients ranging from intellectually and physically disabled groups in a hospital setting to mature-aged women in a community centre. I am very grateful for the supervision received in training because it gave me the tools to become my own internal supervisor. Carroll and Gilbert's (2006) statement about the final 'internal supervisor' stage resonates with me: 'At this stage you will digest what you have learned and you will change or retain individual elements that suit your style as a person and a professional' (Carroll and Gilbert, 2006, p. 47).

When I run my own dance movement sessions now I have become aware that my supervision experience was just as Ellen Levine had wished for when she wrote that 'a major goal of supervision is to encourage the students to continue to tune themselves as instruments for therapeutic practice' (Knill *et al.*, 2005, p. 254).

I was given the space to observe, absorb and reflect on the discipline of DMT by working directly with experienced DMT practitioners in the group sessions as well as the individual sessions. I was able to learn so much about the healing power of movement by working with clients and observing the clients' sheer joy and enthusiasm for movement. I learned about the effort/shape changes that took place both in clients and in myself during the sessions.

Through supervision I was given opportunities to overcome any fears and anxieties about being monitored, not having a dance background or failing, and recovered a sense of wholeness, and I believe this was partly due to the enthusiastic and generous responses of the clients as well as the management skills and encouragement Euna gave to me, especially by encouraging me to use aspects from my drama experiences.

The incident with Sharon and the clapping sticks reminded me to trust my own intuition and to discover, as Datillio (2006) had discovered, that letting go and being patient were integral to finding one's way in therapy.

Now I see supervision as a necessary and important part of my ongoing professional development and I have arranged to meet a DMT supervisor fortnightly for after-session individual supervision. My practicum experience taught me that including dance and drawing as well as journal-keeping and verbal discussion are important to me to give a greater depth and understanding to my work. My first objective is to document 70 more hours of supervision (as well as a minimum of 250 hours of practice) as one of the requirements of becoming a professional member of the Dance Movement Therapy Association of Australia. After that I am considering studying for a Diploma in DMT with the aim towards further professional development gaining more experience and insights. I would like to learn and experience as much as possible about dance movement therapy. Knowing this, and realising that I love this work very much, I am now open to all possibilities.

Notes

1 Names and all identifying features have been changed throughout the chapter.
2 See above for all the following clients.

References

Adler, J. (1987) Who is the witness? A description of authentic movement. *Contact Quarterly*, winter, pp. 20–29.

Brems, C. (2001) *Basic Skills in Psychotherapy and Counselling*. Brooks/Cole, Pacific Grove, CA: Thomson Learning.

Carroll, M. and Gilbert, M. (2006) *On Being a Supervisee. Creating Learning Partnerships*. Kew, Victoria: PsychOz Publications.

Chodorow, J. (1991) *Dance Therapy and Depth Psychology. The Moving Imagination*. London/New York: Routledge.

Dattilio, F. (2006) In consultation. Throwing away the script: helping trainees trust their gut. *Psychotherapy Networker*, 30(2), pp. 27–29.

Elizur, J. (1990) 'Stuckness' in live supervision. Expanding the therapist's style. *Journal of Family Therapy*, 12, pp. 267–280.

Frick, W. (1971) *Humanistic Psychology: Interview with Maslow, Murphy and Rogers*. Columbus. OH: Charles E. Merrill.

Knill, P., Levine, E. and Levine, S. (2005) *Principles and Practice of Expressive Arts Therapy: Towards a Therapeutic Aesthetics*. London: Jessica Kingsley.

Lett, W. (ed.) (1993) *How the Arts Make a Difference in Therapy*. Victoria, Australia: Australian Dance Council (AUSDANCE).

Leventhal, M. (1987) *The Ancient Healing Art of Dance. Keynote Speech*, First Annual Dance Therapy Conference. Melbourne, Australia.

Mollen, P. (1997) *Supervision as a Space for Thinking*. In G. Shipton (ed.) *Supervision of Psychotherapy and Counselling: Making a Place To Think*. Philadelphia, PA: Open University Press.

Reber, A. and Reber, E. (1985) *The Penguin Dictionary of Psychology*. London: Penguin Books.

Rogers, C. (1980) *A Way of Being*. Boston, MA: Houghton Mifflin.

Schoop, T. with Mitchell, P. (1974) *Won't You Join The Dance? A Dancer's Essay into the Treatment of Psychosis*. Palo Alto, CA: Mayfield Publishing.

Schott-Billmann, F. (1992) Primitive expression: an anthropological dance therapy method. *The Arts in Psychotherapy*, 19, pp. 105–109.

Sullivan, B. (2005) Becoming a therapist: challenging the role of training – an interview with Ernesto Spinelli. *Psychotherapy in Australia*, 11(3), pp. 60–64.

Wadeson, H., Durkin, J. and Perach, D. (eds) (1989) *Advances in Arts Therapy*. New York: John Wiley and Sons.

Wolman, W. (2005) Internal and external supervision of boundary mistakes: a mistake evidence system for new therapists. *Australasian Journal of Psychotherapy*, 24(2), pp. 107–123.

Chapter 9

The Balint group model applied to dance/movement therapy supervision

Imke A. Fiedler

Introduction

The author will introduce a concept of supervision for dance/movement therapists developed from the structure of psychoanalytically oriented Balint (1957) supervision groups. This concept moves beyond Balint's ideas; it is a modification of the classical verbal setting while incorporating kinaesthetic and movement aspects into the method and process of supervision for dance/ movement therapists.

After a brief historical review of supervision in Germany, two case examples will be outlined to illustrate the author's theoretical ideas on supervision. The developed concept of group supervision for dance/movement therapists will be conceptualised in seven stages, integrating kinaesthetic empathy, authentic movement and somatic countertransference. They are known as effective tools of dance/movement therapists and here they will be introduced additionally as useful methods within the supervision process. The basic ideas of Balint groups will be incorporated to make the original roots apparent. In addition, the concept of transference and countertransference will be presented to stress the 'mirror phenomenon' which is a core concept of psychoanalytic supervision. Finally, the chapter will address the necessity to work with more than one programme in supervision. The hypothesis is that dance/ movement therapists need to reflect not only on a psychoanalytic perspective of the client–therapist relationship, but also on their professional role in teams, and to understand institutional structures in order to be more fully supported by the supervision process.

Historical background

In Germany the roots of supervision stem from three different approaches.

Around 1920 the 'Berlin Institut of Psychoanalysis' started to offer control analysis for their trainees (Pühl, 1990). Psychoanalysts in training discussed their cases with experienced psychoanalytic clinicians to get professional feedback. This form of supervision still exists today in various schools of therapeutic training (called control analysis) and is one strong root of supervision.

A second root (and the term itself) originated in the USA at the end of the nineteenth century, when 'paid agents' were installed for administrative and later educational supervision for teams or groups within large social welfare organisations. This form of supervision is more administrative with a focus on teaching, monitoring and controlling social work practitioners. In Germany this approach was modified. External clinical supervisors were hired for team and group supervision with a focus on case work, on professional roles of the individual, and on group interactions, neglecting the administrative aspect.

A third approach was developed by Michael Balint, a Hungarian MD and psychoanalyst. His way of doing case work in groups with a special focus on the 'doctor–patient relationship' has influenced general practitioners, psychoanalysts, psychotherapists, social workers, and other health professionals throughout the world.

In Germany various settings and approaches for supervision have been developed from these basic ideas. Regarding the setting there is individual supervision, group and team supervision, and supervision for organisations. The various approaches relate to different psychotherapeutic schools and their theoretical backgrounds: for example, psychoanalytically oriented supervision (Oberhoff and Beumer, 2001), group dynamic oriented supervision (Foulkes, 1974), systemically oriented supervision (Brandau, 1991). There are as many definitions of supervision as there are approaches (Lippenmeier, 1984; Fatzer and Eck, 1990; Pühl, 1990; Schreyögg, 1991; Pallasch et al., 1992). In this chapter supervision will be defined as a form of clinical supervision to improve professional competence through a process of self-reflection.

An integrative approach by Rappe-Giesecke (2003) looks at the necessity of having access to different 'programmes' regarding the needs of the supervision process. She differentiates between the programmes of: case work, role exploration, self-experiential processing regarding the professional function and setting, and analysis of the institution. The last section will look at the advantage of making use of different programmes to support the supervisee in gaining a broader understanding of their professional situation.

Supervision for dance/movement therapists in Germany is offered by experienced practitioners. Most of them are trainers approved by the national dance therapy association 'Berufsverband der TanztherapeutInnen Deutschland' (BTD).[1] Since 2005 specific standards for supervisors have been outlined by the association, requiring own supervision hours, participation in workshops on supervision, and continuing advanced training in the field.

The following two case examples will give a first impression of supervision in groups for dance/movement therapists.[2]

Case examples

These cases were presented in one of my supervision groups which has met every three weeks for the past two years, with five experienced dance/movement therapists. I will mark the phases of each supervision process in parenthesis and will outline these phases later. Special terms like 'mirror phenomenon' and 'concordant and complementary countertransference reaction' will be defined later.

I always encourage supervisees to present the introductory session with new clients in supervision because, generally, in the first session everything is there but not clear.

Case example I

Eileen, a psychotherapist in private practice and a dance/movement therapist, presented the following introductory session to the group.

- *Verbal case presentation:* Connie, a 34-year-old freelance graphic designer, was seeking individual therapy because for weeks she had been experiencing feelings of exhaustion, fatigue, depression and difficulties falling asleep. In addition, she described an acute conflict with her female colleague at work. She mentioned that she and her colleague were currently consulting a coach for ten sessions to clarify their professional relationship and also that they were seeking professional help from a financial supervisor regarding their business issues for a total of six sessions.

    Eileen mentioned how puzzled she was to hear about these various 'helpers'. She had the impression that this 'support system' would rather scatter the client's focus and it could make it difficult for Connie to really engage in a therapeutic relationship. At this point in the session she invited the client to engage in a brief movement sequence to express her current situation.
- *Embodiment:* In the supervision group I asked Eileen to show Connie's movements the way she remembered them. Eileen used her right and left arm for horizontal movements sideways and across, with sudden and gentle pre-efforts, in the middle-reach kinaesphere. She used bound flow during the initiation, continued with neutral flow (more wooden-like), and ended the movement with passive weight in the arms, bringing them downward.
- *Verbal case presentation:* Eileen described that she was trying to focus on the various issues (the professional relationship, the financial problems and the woman's depressive mood). There was so much tension and internal pressure that she felt the client should take care of the concrete professional conflicts first, that she should continue and finish the

coaching and financial supervision and only after that start with her individual therapy. After this suggestion she described the client as persisting in her wish to start individual therapy now. Again, Eileen made her point concerning too many helpers at once but let go of her concerns the more Connie insisted on beginning very soon. They agreed to start in two weeks, and as they were about to part, the client said, 'Maybe your suggestion makes sense, and I will call you when the two other processes are finished.' Eileen agreed and Connie left. This ending was very confusing to Eileen and she asked how this dynamic was to be understood.

- *Free association:* The group started a discussion about the 'rights and wrongs' of Eileen's putting off beginning therapy versus her giving in to start soon. To me it felt like a repetition of the struggle in the therapy situation. When I analysed our discussion in terms of the therapeutic interaction we realised that a 'mirror phenomenon' regarding the therapy situation had taken place. I decided to open up this phase of association on the movement level. Two group members repeated Connie's horizontal movements and started to lower the tension and decrease the tempo. While closing their eyes the movements became more indulgent, with deceleration, indirect and light efforts.

  They described a deep need for support and much sadness when they intensified the passive weight at the end of the sequence. By going back and forth between more and less bound flow, they explored how the bound flow helped to ward off the inner needs and how it helped to stay in control.

- *Questions and clarifications:* This short movement sequence made it possible to get in touch with the client's resistance, sensing the warding off of neediness and depression. In our discussion the other witnesses and I had sensed an oral neediness for being seen, held and contained. At this point Eileen realised that she hadn't mirrored this sequence during the session at all. She was rationalising and occupied with trying to 'understand' the movement instead of empathising as she usually does.

  The ending was looked on as an important victory for Connie, having convinced the therapist (mother) of her despair and neediness, but finally giving in to be the 'good client' following the therapist's advice.

- *Countertransference analysis:* Eileen's response seemed to be a countertransference reaction. The group had done very intense work in identifying with the client to understand her repressed needs more fully. I myself started internally to explore the intellectual focus and the lack of emotional empathy of Eileen's role. I had an image of a strict mother giving 'good' advice. One interpretation that came to my mind was that Eileen's intellectual attitude could represent a complementary countertransference reaction. In our hypothesis we assumed that the client may have experienced an emotionally unreliable mother who preferred to give advice instead of emotional support.

- *Suggestions and conclusions:* At the end of the meeting, instead of making suggestions, I invited Eileen herself to explore in movement how to find her inner attitude for a possible therapy start with Connie. She sat down on the floor, closed her eyes and began to focus on her breathing. Then she started to shape her body in a spreading and enclosing way on the horizontal plane. She was calm and very centred. She said, 'If I'm just here, sensing and listening with my body, things get clear.'

Case example 2

Kathryn, an MD and dance/movement therapist, was working with a 28-year-old woman diagnosed with multiple personality disorder.

- *Verbal case presentation:* Kathryn had been meeting with her client for eight weeks and made her introductory comment by saying, 'I feel like I'm fishing in the mud'. She described the client as a high-functioning attorney, with a long history of individual therapy. Mary, the client, mentioned relationship problems regarding closeness and distancing, distrust and power struggles with her female friend. Kathryn had started with various interventions on body awareness, grounding, weight sensing, and the subject of individual space. Most of her presentation concerned her interventions and her insecurity about where the therapeutic process should focus. She pointed out that she did not want to dwell on psychodynamic issues of the multiple personality disorder with the client but first and foremost to stabilise her and to keep the movement process clearly in the 'here and now'.
- *Embodiment:* When I invited Kathryn to give us a movement impression of Mary, she got up and presented her client's body standing very upright, with neutral flow. She presented the client as being quite active, capable of using movement explorations and simple improvisations. I observed an upper and lower body split and locked knees at various moments. Movements with closed eyes were too frightening, as were interactive interventions, which seemed to feel uncomfortable. Still, I noticed that I was left blank after her showing (even now it is difficult to give precise movement descriptions).
- *Free association:* During the phase of association the group members were quite active as well. They gave feedback to Kathryn on how appropriate her interventions seemed, that her decision to focus on stability and the 'here and now' seemed completely right. It became a sequence of confirmation for Kathryn's way of working. I realised that so far I had not get any idea about the client, no image or association regarding Mary, except that I also felt I was 'fishing in the mud'. More and more I had the feeling that there was no internal space for the group to associate on our feelings.

- *Questions and clarifications:* I mentioned this, and that so far I did not get a feeling for the client. I asked if there might be anything left out at the case presentation. Kathryn was astonished, then stunned, and after a long pause she told us about the client's early childhood trauma of ongoing sexual abuse in the most cruel and brutal ways we had ever heard, namely sexual abuse by the father and two brothers, with objects and even animals involved. It was very difficult for Kathryn to find words to describe these horror scenes and for us to let in all this information.
- *Free association:* After a moment of resonating the group started to associate on the word 'mud': muddy, dirty, filthy, dull. The atmosphere became much more emotional; despair, anger and rage were freed up and Kathryn relaxed more and more. She didn't need to contain all that 'mud' herself any more. It also became much easier to look at the multiple personality disorder as a defence against the early trauma.
- *Countertransference analysis:* Kathryn and the group had been stuck in the concordant countertransference reaction, identifying with the client's resistance. In analysing this countertransference reaction it became obvious that the client had to repress the traumatic experience and she needed Kathryn at her side. Kathryn had lent herself to contain the trauma in the unconscious, unable to process and to fully understand this dynamic.
- *Suggestions and conclusions:* At the end we reassured Kathryn that it made so much sense to focus on strengthening and stabilising. In addition, I underlined the importance of keeping the information about the trauma conscious and present during the session without any need to act upon it.

I closed the session with a movement sequence for Kathryn and the other group members to imagine and create a vessel or container in movement for this material, where it is safely enclosed but still accessible (an image I was introduced to by Lewis Bernstein).

Both case examples show how the important transitions and changes took place after inserting a movement sequence. It seems to provide a much easier access to the somatic unconscious for dance/movement therapists than the purely verbal approach could. In particular, the final movement sequence gives the supervisees the possibility of processing the countertransference reactions on a bodily level, to let go of the confusion and turmoil and to centre themselves.

A concept of supervision for dance/movement therapy

The author's concept of supervision for dance/movement therapists will look at the setting of group supervision with a focus on case work (as shown above) by making use of the Balint group approach. The author favours this concept as a method for case work due to its client-centred approach and its focus on the client–therapist relationship.

Michael Balint[3] was interested in establishing a holistic approach within psychosomatic medicine. Thus, he wanted to train general physicians (GPs) by increasing their understanding of the 'doctor–patient elationship' and deepening their understanding of psychotherapy in general. The development of his 'training-come-research groups' was published in 1957 in his famous book, *The Doctor, his Patient and the Illness*. It was the first book on patient-centred medicine. The GPs were invited to present 'difficult cases' and, in discussions with group members, to gain a deeper understanding of their doctor–patient relationship. Later, these case discussion groups were used for social workers, teachers and other health professionals.

Here, the concept of supervision focuses on the improvement of the professional competence of the dance/movement therapist, based on Balint's ideas. This approach asks for openness to self-experiential processing of the professional role and action, as well as for a reflective attitude regarding one's own therapeutic identity. The attitude during the discussion should be non-judgemental, and constructive for the members. The group should have a supportive function for each member, it should be a safe container for professional growth, and should provide a creative pool of resources.

The concept of supervision in dance/movement therapy will now be outlined in seven stages which are:

1   Case proposals
2   Verbal case presentation
3   Embodiment
4   Free association
5   Questions and clarifications
6   Countertransference analysis
7   Suggestions and conclusions.

1 Case proposals

Before the actual case work starts members of the group propose cases, and the group discusses and decides which case to work on. During this phase many group dynamic aspects begin to come into play. Sometimes nobody has a case to present (there might be resistance in the group to show oneself and one's own way of working – expressing a lack of trust in the group).

Sometimes two or more members want to present and get into a kind of rivalry (expressing assertion or competition in the group). The dynamic of the decision-making process relates on the one hand to the situation of the group process and to the phase where each member is at present (as outlined later). On the other hand it may already relate to the case that will be presented afterwards. It may be looked at as a preconscious enactment of dynamics that will be revealed later in the case.

2 Verbal case presentation

The presenter is invited to talk about her/his questions or problems regarding the client–therapist relationship without any notes or session records. Notes usually already include a secondary processing and reflection of the therapy situation; it may be looked at as an intellectual preparation of the case presentation which diminishes the freedom for spontaneous verbal expression and thus keeps effective reactions under control (Balint, 1966, p. 19). Her/his own feelings and emotional reactions towards the client are of primary interest. The other group members are invited to follow the presentation with a free flow of attention. It is crucial not to take anything specific into focus, but to wander with the words as they unfold, to allow images and kinaesthetic responses to arise. The presenter may address a specific question or focus in the beginning.

At this point it is not important that the case information is complete. Much more important is how the supervisee presents the case (e.g. a depressed client may be presented hesitantly, with a passive voice and less tension flow). The omissions and incomplete parts are valuable, as the gaps and empty spaces during the case presentation give information about the psychodynamics involved.

3 Embodiment

After the verbal presentation the presenter is invited to embody the client for a brief moment. This is not role playing or physically pretending to be the client. Rather, it is a process of expressing how the dance/movement therapist has internalised the client. She/he will give movement examples, body postures or movement reactions from the client to create a physical presence of that person in the supervision context. Thus, she/he will give additional clues about resistance, transference and countertransference issues to the group. For example, Connie's horizontal sideways and across movements or Eileen's upper and lower body split.

Kinaesthetic awareness provides an additional sense of perception for group members. During the session, kinaesthetic empathy incorporates aspects of bodily felt sensing and physical attunement. This process gives access to more preconscious expression of enactive, primary processing, and to a receptive reverberation of felt meaning (Fiedler, 1988, p. 30). Here, the presenter re-enacts aspects of her client–therapist relationship and gives group members visual and sensing material for the process of association. As witnesses they are invited to allow the kinaesthetic material to resonate in their bodies.

4 Free association

Now, the presenter can lean back and follow the group discussion, their reactions and ideas. During the actual process of supervision, phases 4, 5 and 6 (free association, questions and countertransference analysis) mingle and intertwine constantly. However, for the purpose of conceptual clarity these will be outlined separately.

The ability to free associate is of great importance. At this point it is not intended for anyone in the group to fully understand the case but to add their own reactions. Freud once said that free association includes a completely different attitude towards attention than thinking does, since free association excludes thinking (Freud, 1922, p. 109). The members are invited to allow and express all kinds of subjective reactions: funny, critical, disgusted, bored, confused or silly. Many times the reactions that feel like complete nonsense are very valuable. They are regarded as unconscious representations or symbolic expressions of the case, of the client–therapist relationship and partly of the client's pathologic object relations. Here we use verbal, imaginable and kinaesthetic modalities as resources for association.

Within this supervision process the group members have an ongoing experience, of sustaining moments of transference and countertransference, sensing the quality of this dynamic, listening internally, and not trying to understand it too soon. Members name their reactions and specify their sensation on the basis of the presented material. At this point the group members are also invited to pick up movements and to use abbreviated moments of authentic movement themselves (in Eileen's case the exploration of the horizontal arm movements). Movers as well as the witnesses give their feedback to the presenter.

5 Questions and clarifications

Sometimes there is a tendency to first ask questions after the presentation. The author thinks of this as: (1) a defence against emotional reactions that might come up, or (2) as a possible re-enactment of split-off emotions in the case. If various group members start the case discussion by questioning the presenter, they parallel or mirror the psychodynamics of the client (in a concordant countertranference). Thus, the group has a way to understand the resistance and the transference of the client (as shown in Kathryn's case). In addition, the omissions point to blind spots of the supervisee. We ask, 'What hasn't been presented?' Questions like 'What about the father?' or 'What about her relationships and sexual life?' arise and make obvious which internal representations are being repressed and are still unconscious (as shown in Kathryn's case regarding the childhood trauma).

6 Countertransference analysis

The analysis of countertransference will be looked at on the basis of steps and levels conceptualised by Oberhoff (2000, p. 92). An in-depth discussion about the value of the analysis of countertransference reactions will follow later in this chapter.

Oberhoff suggests encountering the emotional reaction of countertransference in three steps. Each step or 'area' of understanding may be worked through on three different levels (Figure 9.1). Empathic understanding refers to the emotions involved. It relates to Stern's (1985) 'affect attunement' when group members and the supervisor allow the presented material to resonate. They then oscillate between a brief moment of identification and a cognitive naming of what has been sensed (such as experiencing a need to be held and contained and giving this feedback to the presenter). While associating, images of being held may emerge, for example, a concrete wish for more closeness between client and supervisee. The subsequent analysis may reveal oral neediness and/or regression on the part of the client and a necessity for providing a nurturing therapeutic relation.

Scenic understanding asks for the aspect of the client's re-enactment of early conflicts or traumata towards the therapist. It questions which internalised objects are being transferred (such as a strict mother or an emotionally absent father). It asks what kind of atmosphere is present in this scene. Here, the process of association creates images of social roles or fairy-tale figures (e.g. the witch, the bad stepmother, the good fairy and so on). Analysis will reveal clarification of the internalised early object relations of the client.

Biographic understanding looks at the personal material of the supervisee relating to, and perhaps conflicting with, the countertransferential reaction revealed. In a supervision group this should remain at the level of noticing and naming, except in groups with long familiarity and deep trust. The

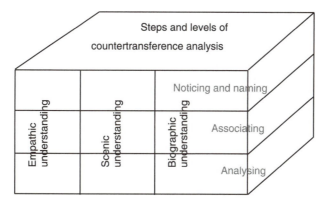

Figure 9.1 Steps and levels of countertransference analysis.[4]

supervisor should protect the supervisee and refer any further analysis to individual supervision or personal therapy. During this phase of exploring countertransference issues the supervisor suggests interpretations linking the mirroring process in the group with the dynamics of the client–therapist interaction.

7 Suggestions and conclusions

Finally, the group creates ideas and suggestions for the therapy process and offers further interventions. Again, at times this process happens in move-ment, as the body is their source of information and movement is their instrument for interventions. The author, as supervisor, looks at the moving body as the catalyst for changes in the supervisee's professional self. The supervisor has to ascertain whether the suggestions feel appropriate to the supervisee. The presenter summarises her/his insights and checks whether the question from the beginning has been answered.

The value of transference and countertransference analysis in the supervision process

> You can go on analysing forever and get nowhere. It is the personal relation that is therapeutic.
>
> (Fairbairn, in Guntrip, 1975, p. 145)

This quotation expresses the fundamental change in the understanding of the role of the analyst and psychotherapist away from the image of a neutral, passive, non-participant mirror and towards an active participant in an evolving process (Bernstein and Singer, 1982, p. 3).

Balint himself was a proponent of object relations theory with his approach of a client-centred medicine. Kohut (1977), Guntrip (1975) and Kernberg (1975) focused on the early stages of object relations with signifi-cant others on the basis of the developmental model by Mahler *et al.* (1975). Primarily, the individual is determined by its early experiences in relation to others. The theory looks at the development of individual needs and their satisfaction or frustration in outer reality.

Today, Stern's (1985) concept of the interpersonal world of the infant pro-vides a profound developmental model. Particularly for dance/movement therapists his ideas incorporate the early physical and sensory experiences as well as rhythmic attunement with significant others. Object relations theory and its application in dance/movement therapy will not be reviewed any fur-ther here, since it is beyond the scope of this chapter.[5] The focus of this chapter will now be on the changing concepts of transference and counter-transference to illustrate the 'mirror phenomenon' as a core concept of analytic supervision.

The term 'countertransference' was first defined by Freud (1910) as reciprocal feelings towards the transference of the patient. He implied that these reactions stem from unresolved conflicts of neurotic origin in the analyst, which needed to be eliminated and overcome. Later, Heimann (1950) and Racker (1968) underlined the therapeutic value of countertransference reactions.[6] Racker's (1968, p. 91) distinction between neurotic, concordant and complementary countertransference seems to provide clarity regarding the emotional reactions of the therapist. Taking each in turn:

- *Neurotic countertransference* is where the analyst identifies with his own infantile and child feelings in relation to the client. This needs to be worked through in one's own analysis.
- *Concordant countertransference* is where the analyst identifies with the client's ego; the reactions arise from the process of empathy and mostly have a steady and quiet quality.
- *Complementary countertransference* is where the analyst identifies with the internal objects of the client, stemming from the interactive relation and its projective and introjective dynamics. The analyst is being treated by the client as one of his internal objects; the quality is more disturbing, dramatic, and of an uncomfortable mode (Fiedler, 1988, p. 43).

For the supervision process the author stresses an understanding of the concordant and complementary countertransference reactions as essential to analyse the client–therapist relationship. Bernstein (1984, p. 321) added the bodily and movement dimension to this concept for dance/movement therapy when she coined the term 'somatic countertransference' regarding the bodily felt and kinaesthetic sensations of a therapeutic setting.

> The countertransference can be concordant, i.e. the therapist shares the unspeakable bodily felt experience with the individual; or it can be of a complementary quality in which the therapist experiences the polarized aspect of the complex; for example, if the patient is feeling victimized the therapist might have somatic imaginings of feeling like a rapist.
>
> (Bernstein, 1984, p. 328)

This addresses a whole new dimension to the inner experience of the therapist.[7] Kinaesthetic awareness makes it possible for the dance/movement therapist to receive and metabolise split-off parts of the client, projections and transference reactions in her own body.

During the supervision process in Balint groups and in psychoanalytically oriented supervision for dance/movement therapists, it is exactly this psychodynamic of the client–therapist relationship regarding transference and countertransference issues that is analysed. In supervision, counter-transference reactions happen within three forms of relationship (Balint, 1966, p. 410) which the supervisor needs to keep in mind in order to stay focused on the case:

1   the client–therapist relationship (regarding the case);
2   the supervisee–supervisor relationship (regarding the supervisee);
3   the supervisee–the rest of the group relationship (regarding the supervision group).

1 The client–therapist relationship

The concept of case work supervision for dance/movement therapists will look particularly at the case level. The group members try to be aware of the feelings aroused in them while the case is presented. Balint realised that the reactions of the group members and the process in the group are related to the emotional aspects and the psychodynamics of the case.

> There is a tendency, in the group, for the presenting doctor to behave like the patient and for the group to behave like the doctor. The situation in the consulting room is thus dramatically reproduced in the group.
>
> (Balint, 1966, p. 401)

This was called 'the parallel process'. Searles (1962) called it 'reflection' in the supervision session. In Germany, Argelander (1973) and Loch (1989) prefer the term 'Spiegelungsphänomen' (mirror phenomenon) (Figure 9.2), expressing that the client–therapist relationship, the primary conflicts of the client, resistance and/or unconscious transference issues are re-enacted and thus mirrored by the group members and the group situation at large. To distinguish between the original setting (in the therapy session) and the mirroring setting (in the supervision group), Dantlgraber (1977) suggests looking at them as transference–countertransference dynamics on the first and second ordering.

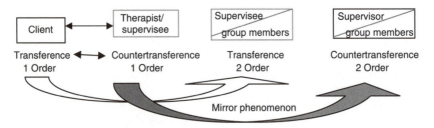

Figure 9.2 The concept of the mirror phenomenon.

2 The supervisee–supervisor relationship

The transference and countertransference issues between supervisee and supervisor are mainly concerned with parental and authority issues. Different phases of idealisation, compliance, rebellion, assimilation and self-assertion unfold. The needs of being seen and supported, of permission for separation and being different, and desires of creating one's own style are being expressed.[8] These issues need to be analysed especially in individual supervision with interns during their control analysis.[9] Within a supervision group, the author rarely analyses the supervisee's transference issues at this level. If the origin is of a neurotic nature the supervisee is given support to work this through in individual supervision or therapy.

In most cases the supervisor is also a representation of an authority conflict within the case. This needs to be clarified and made conscious for the purpose of understanding the role and the transference of the parental figure in the client–therapist relationship. If it is not understood and analysed properly by the supervisor, the supervisee may re-enact her/his unresolved issues with the client as shown in the 'reciprocal mirror phenomenon' (Figure 9.3). For example, an uncritical idealisation towards the supervisor may bring the supervisee/therapist into the position of expecting idealisation from her/his client as well.

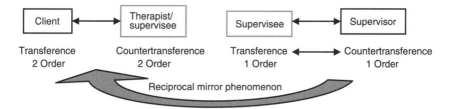

Figure 9.3 The concept of the reciprocal mirror phenomenon.

3 The supervisee–rest of group relationship

The third level, that of the countertransference reactions between the supervisee/presenter and the group, has been looked at in relation to the presented case. Sometimes the group reacts hesitantly, bored or overly critical towards the presenter. It is the supervisor's function to name this dynamic, and instead of changing the intention towards self-experiential group processing, to stay focused on the case and to make use of these emotional reactions for the analysis of the dynamics of the presented case.

The developmental process of supervision groups and their members

In the beginning of a new supervision group, a general ambivalence is apparent. Members are motivated by a wish for change and, in addition, they sense a fear of change. An old German saying expresses this ambivalence: 'Wash me but don't get me wet.' Supervision brings awareness of limits in one's own professional identity and may create changes and growth of the therapeutic self. For some members it is a risk to explore their limits in the beginning, and they may feel embarrassed or ashamed by not knowing better. The supervisor has to create an atmosphere where it is possible to learn by mistakes. Balint (1966, p. 407) calls it 'The courage of facing one's own stupidity'.

The supervisor has to watch the tempo and the developmental dynamics of the group process. Schutz (1958, p. 58) developed a concept of group dynamic processes in four phases. Briefly, his concept gives some general ideas about related emotional themes for individuals in groups:[10]

1   *Inclusion*: ambivalance, curiosity, openness, insecurity, wanting to trust, passivity, adjustment (throughout the first meetings of a new supervision group).
2   *Control*: power struggles, aggression, individuation, separation, activity, withdrawal, self-assertion (apparent during the following meetings of a settled group).
3   *Affection*: responsibility, safety, productivity, support (throughout the continuous process).
4   *Separation*: grief, anger, avoiding sorrow, feedback, concluding, letting go (while ending a process of group supervision).

The author has observed that groups of dance/movement therapists progress through these phases during their supervision process. In addition, each member deals with internal issues of her/his professional competence, by idealisation, rebellion, withdrawal and self-assertion towards the supervisor and the other group members. During the meetings it is helpful to keep these group aspects in mind, as they may overlap and interfere with the actual case work. They need to be named and interpreted in favour of the case discussion, not regarding self-experiential processes.

The role of the group leader

Balint was convinced that one of the most important aspects within the technique of Balint groups is the attitude of the leader of these groups (Balint, 1966, p. 409). She/he is not supposed to understand herself/himself as 'an all-knowing specialist' who can solve the presented problems. The role of the 'group leader' is characterised by a friendly attitude and by curiosity for the professional work of the members. The way of listening with a free flow of attention is of great importance to the atmosphere in the group (Balint, 1966, p. 403). She/he needs to bring lots of patience and restraint for the group process to unfold. She/he gathers the various ideas and gives suggestions for interpretations. On the other hand, she/he should understand herself/himself as an equal member of the group, willing to learn from the members of the group. She/he herself/himself must also be able to make mistakes, not to be perfect, and allow (perhaps even invite) criticism and contradiction. Thus, she/he can become a role model for the group members by not being embarrassed or ashamed when criticised. Beucke-Galm (2001, p. 23) lists the following abilities needed by a supervisor for a supportive dialogue: 'suspending' (to keep thoughts and assessments under suspense); 'listening' (to maintain a non-prejudiced, internally empty and open manner); 'voicing' (to express internal sensations, images and kinaesthetic responses); and 'respecting' (to acknowledge others the way they are).

Moving beyond the Balint group method

The major criticism of the Balint group approach is related to the lack of a reflection of the institutional setting. The reasons for this are related to the fact that the GPs Balint had worked with did not work in larger organisations. They worked in their private practices and did not need to consider any outer dysfunctional circumstances. When the therapeutic setting is within a larger organisation (such as a clinic, rehabilitation centre or psychiatric ward) various circumstances of the setting need to be reflected in addition to the client–therapist relationship in order to understand the dynamics totally. The Balint group approach would only look at the individual's capacity to process these dysfunctional structures of the setting, it would not analyse the setting itself.

Here, Rappe-Giesecke's (2003) integrative approach brings about more perspectives for the setting. The role identity of the dance/movement therapist and the expectations of the team need to be analysed as well as the hierarchical structure of the setting. Mostly, clients are referred to the dance/movement therapist by the responsible MD; at times therapy goals are defined by the individual psychotherapist, and the dance/movement therapist feels helpless and without power. Frustration or omnipotence (a defence against helplessness) come into play and interfere with the client–therapist relationship. The supervision of these conflicts needs to be understood before case work can continue. Usually, they are hidden within the case presentation and remain unconscious unless the supervisor brings them to the surface. Issues of projection and transference in teams, the team structure, as well as the structure of the institution, have to be incorporated by the supervisor. Thus she/he has to move beyond the pure Balint group method to support the dance/movement therapists more fully within their settings.

Conclusion

This chapter discussed the advantage of the Balint group method for dance/movement therapists and expressed its limitations as well. If supervision incorporates the vital kinaesthetic methods of movement representations in the body, of authentic movement and witnessing as well as of the concept of somatic countertransference, it provides an important link between a purely verbal and a movement approach. Thus, the dance/movement therapist experiences the reflection of her professional self on a more satisfying level of whole object relation as it is intended in her therapeutic effort as well. Here, supervision creates more internal freedom, specifically the freedom of having choices in relation to the client.

In addition, it was outlined that the more the supervisor takes dysfunctional circumstances of the setting into consideration, the more the process of supervision is supportive. Even though there is no direct intention for self-experiential experiences in supervision, a process of growth and professional autonomy takes place through the reflection of professional behaviour.

Notes

1 Available at www.btd-tanztherapie.de.
2 The author has been leading individual and group supervision with beginning and experienced dance/movement therapists for more than ten years. She was trained at the University of California, Los Angeles, by Dosamantes-Beaudry (Freudian psychoanalyst) and Wyman (Jungian analyst). After her training she was part of Balint groups for over five years in Hamburg, Germany.
3 Michael Balint was born 1896 in Budapest, where he studied medicine. In 1920 he came to Berlin for his psychoanalytic training with H. Sachs. He returned to Budapest in 1924 to finish his training with S. Ferenczi. In 1939 he emigrated to Britain and began to work at the Tavistock Clinic. He became a pioneer in psychosomatic medicine with various publications on psychoanalysis and medicine. In 1968 he became President of the British Psychoanalytic Society. Michael Balint died in London in 1970.
4 Figure 9.1 is developed by the author, and drawn from concepts by Oberhoff (2000, p. 92).
5 For a review of the literature see Bernstein and Singer, 1982; Bernstein, 1984; Dosamantes-Alperson, 1984.
6 For a further review of literature see Kernberg, 1975; Searles, 1979; Jacoby, 1984; Samuels, 1985.
7 Various authors have given extended examples of somatic countertransference from their practice: Bernstein, 1984; Siegel, 1984; Chodorow, 1986; Dosamantes-Alperson, 1987.
8 Examples of individual supervision in dance/movement therapy may be found in Siegel (1982).
9 The author finds it extremely helpful that dance/movement therapy students in Germany are obligated to fulfil 100 hours of individual psychotherapy during their training. Here, the onset is made of reflecting and analysing their individual transference issues.

10 In Germany, Bender (1990) has linked this concept with the group process in dance/movement therapy.

References

Argelander, H. (1973) Balint-Gruppenarbeit mit Seelsorgern. *Psyche*, 27, pp. 129–139.

Balint, M. (1957) *The Doctor, his Patient and the Illness*. London: Pitman Medical.

—— (1966) *Der Arzt, sein Patient und die Krankheit*. Stuttgart: Klett-Cotta.

Bender, S. (1990) *Ein gruppentherapeutischer Ansatz in der Tanztherapie*. Jahrbuch Tanzforschung Bd. 1, Wilhelshaven: Florian Noetzel Verlag, pp. 59–81.

Bernstein, P.L. (ed.) (1984) *Theoretical Approaches in Dance-movement Therapy*, Vol. II. Dubuque, IA: Kendall/Hunt.

Bernstein, P.L. and Singer, D.L. (eds) (1982) *The Choreography of Object Relations*. Antioch/New England: Graduate School, Keene, NH.

Beucke-Galm, M. (2001) Dialog in der lernenden Organisation. *Zeitschrift fuer Organisations-entwicklung*, 1, pp. 20–31.

Brandau, H. (ed.) (1991) *Supervision aus systemischer Sicht*. Salzburg: Otto Mueller.

Chodorow, J. (1986) The body as a symbol: dance movement in analysis. In N. Schwartz-Salant and M. Stein (eds) *The Body in Analysis*. Wilmette, IL: Chiron, pp. 87–108.

Dantlgraber, J. (1977) Ueber einen Ansatz zur Untersuchung von 'Balint-Gruppen'. *Psychosomatic Medizin*, 7, pp. 255–276.

Dosamantes-Alperson, E. (1984) Experiential movement psychotherapy. In P.L. Bernstein (ed.) *Theoretical Approaches in Dance-movement Therapy*, Vol. II. Dubuque, IA: Kendall/Hunt, pp. 257–291.

—— (1987) Transference and countertransference issues in movement psychotherapy. *The Arts in Psychotherapy*, 14, pp. 209–214.

Fatzer, G. and Eck, C.D. (eds) (1990) *Supervision und Beratung. Ein Handbuch*. Cologne: Agentur Himmels.

Fiedler, I. (1988) *The Interdependence of Kinesthetic Empathy and Somatic Counter-transference in Dance/Movement Therapy*. MA thesis, University of California, Los Angeles.

Foulkes, S.H. (1974) *Gruppenanalytische Psychotherapie*. Muenchen: Kindler.

Freud, S. (1910) *The Future Prospects of Psychoanalytic Therapy*. Standard Edition, Vol. 11, pp. 139–152.

—— (1922) *Vorlesungen zur Einfuehrung in die Psychoanalyse*. Vienna: Internationaler Psychoanalytischer Verlag.

Guntrip, H. (1975) My experience of analysis with Fairbairn and Winnicott. *International Review of Psychoanalysis*, 2, pp. 145–156.

Heimann, P. (1950) On countertransference. *International Journal of Psychoanalysis*, 31, pp. 81–84.

Jacoby, M. (1984) *The Analytic Encounter. Transference and Human Relationship*. Toronto: Inner City Books.

Kernberg, O. (1975) *Borderline Conditions and Pathological Narcissism*. New York: Jacob Aronson.

Kohut, H. (1977) *The Restoration of the Self*. New York: International Universities Press.

Lippenmeier, N. (1984) *Beitraege zur Supervision*. Kassel: Publik des Fachbereich 04 Gesamthochschule Kassel.

Loch, W. (1989) Balint Seminare: Zweck, Methode Zielsetzung und Auswirkungen auf die Praxis. In C. Nedelmann and H. Ferstl (eds) *Die Methode der Balint-Gruppe*. Stuttgart: Klett-Cotta, pp. 217–236.

Mahler, M., Pine, F. and Bergmann, A. (1975) *The Psychological Birth of the Human Infant*. New York: Basic Books.

Oberhoff, B. (2000) *Uebertragung und Gegenuebertragung in der Supervision*. Munster: Daedalus.

—— and Beumer, U. (eds) (2001) *Theorie und Praxis psychoanalytischer Supervision*. Munster: Votum.

Pallasch, W. *et al.* (eds) (1992) *Beratung, Training, Supervision*. Weinheim/Munich: Juventa.

Pühl, H. (ed.) (1990) *Handbuch der Supervision – Beratung und Reflexion in Ausbildung, Beruf und Organisation*. Berlin: Edition Marhold.

Racker, H. (1968) *Transference and Countertransference*. New York: International Universities Press.

Rappe-Giesecke, K. (2003) *Supervision für Gruppen und Teams*. Berlin: Springer.

Samuels, S. (1985) Countertransference, the 'Mundus Imaginalis' and a research project. *Journal of Analytic Psychology*, 30, pp. 47–71.

Schreyögg, A. (1991) *Supervision – ein integratives Modell*. Paderborn: Jungfermann.

Schutz, W. (1958) *A Three-dimensional Theory of Interpersonal Behavior*. New York: Rinehart.

Searles, H.F. (1962) Problems of supervision. *Science and Psychoanalysis*, 5, pp. 197–215.

—— (1979) *Countertransference and Related Subjects*. New York: International Universities Press.

Siegel, E. (1982) Object relations and the psychoanalytic supervision of dance-movement therapists. In P.L. Bernstein and D.L. Singer (eds) *The Choreography of Object Relations*. Antioch/New England: Graduate School, Keene, NH, pp. 167–193.

—— (1984) *Dance–movement Therapy: Mirror of Ourselves*. New York: Human Science Press.

Stern, D.N. (1985) *The Interpersonal World of the Infant*. New York: Basic Books.

Chapter 10

Interactive reflections

Moving between modes of expression as a model for supervision

Penelope A. Best

The art of supervision requires us to refresh our own souls or spirits, whatever we wish to call this part of ourselves, in music, art, laughter, nature, meditation and joy. As supervisors this helps us refresh our vision, our hearing, our wonder and awe at the miraculous qualities our patients, clients and supervisees present.

(Hewson, 2001, p. 73)

Introduction

Within this chapter I introduce a group model of supervision known as Relational Creative Processes Model (RCPM). While the concepts and many of the practices have been adapted also for individual supervision, this chapter will focus upon the group dimension. RCPM has been developed with experienced dance movement therapy practitioners as co-participants within ongoing practice-based research projects (Shrivener and Chapman, 2004).

As the supervisor within RCPM, I encourage active use of multiple perspectives and modes of expression which are supported by inter-creative reflections and shared verbal and non-verbal conversations. Supervisees are given opportunities to connect bodily with differing theoretical discourses. As psychodynamic ideas have become a dominant narrative within arts therapies literature, this chapter focuses upon constructionist and systemic discourses as additional lenses which might open alternative ways for arts therapists to observe and reflect upon their work.

I have chosen to locate the model's principles and practices within an overarching frame of reflexive inquiry (RI) as offered by systemic therapist Oliver (2004). Oliver posits five principles of RI; however, I have added a sixth principle to be more coherent with arts therapies practice. I also identify six separate practice foci, relate them to literature and illustrate practice examples. I differentiate the 'why', the 'what' and the 'how' of the model and highlight key elements within systemic, constructionist and artistic approaches as consistent with the Relational Creative Processes Model of supervision being presented.

Visions of supervision

The focus within supervision might vary (e.g. the client, the therapist, the supervisor, the mirroring processes within the supervisory relationship, or the demands of the institution) (Tselikas-Portmann, 1999). A major influential factor upon the style and focus chosen within supervision could be the developmental stage of the supervisee. A trainee might require more emphasis upon skills acquisition, case management and goal setting, whereas an experienced practitioner might want a more open, explorative environment. Balancing a questioning attitude alongside confidence building can prove difficult (Hewson, 2001). Cultivating curiosity means that supervisees may come up against their own biases and strongly held values particularly, around initiating and building relationships.

The issue of relatedness is central for psychotherapists and supervisors. Gilbert and Evans (2000, p. 9) advocate a 'meta-perspective' as a crucial stance in which the supervisor is also viewed as part of the relational meaning making. Within both therapy and supervision there is a tension between being aware of oneself and of others moment to moment. Gilbert and Evans suggest that maintenance of these polarities can only be held for short periods of time due to the tension involved. In this chapter I suggest that the use of multiple representations of experience used within RCPM may facilitate an increase in critical reflections due to an increase in the time supervisees can maintain a view of polarities (see Figure 10.1).

Supportive background research

Phase 1 of the research involved a pilot project with ten practising dance therapists (male and female) in a monthly supervision group and was aimed at characterising the RCPM supervision within a qualitative methodological frame. The first dataset included pre- and post-session questionnaires, supervisor contemporaneous fieldnotes, and a semi-structured group post-project interview. Interpretive analysis of the data was informed by illuminative evaluation and artistic inquiry methods (Meekums and Payne, 1993; Wadsworth Hervey, 2002) in which the focus shifted as information emerged through interpretation of the data.

Phase 2 of the research methods focused upon the perspective of the supervisees as active co-researchers. The data were collected over a year from another similarly mixed supervision group of qualified dance movement therapists. The second dataset included post-session questionnaires identifying significant learning moments and metaphoric images, personal learning diaries, inter-creative peer conversations, supervisor vocalisations during improvisations, episodic movement videos, and an interim group summary. Illustrative examples from the research data are included within this chapter.

The why – bodies of knowledge

Personal epistemology

The RCPM model emerged from both my tacit and explicit knowledge gained from within personal and professional experiences. My initial research question about whether, and to what effect, my own creative landscapes affected those of supervisees arose directly from my clinical practice. Within my practice in adult psychiatry I had noticed mutual influences between myself and clients, which could not be explained completely by psychodynamic ideas of transferential phenomena (Best, 2000).

Espoused theories

> When we practice reflexivity we become *responsible* and *accountable* for our choices, our actions, and our contributions to a relational system.
>
> (Oliver, 2004, p. 127)

For the purposes of this chapter I am defining and separating principles and practices in relation to RCPM. I locate the principles within an overarching model of reflexive inquiry (RI) used within business management by systemic therapist Oliver (2004). I have added a sixth principle (i.e. creativity) to the five principles of RI he posits (i.e. systemic, constructionist, critical, appreciative and complexity). The espoused theories behind the listed six principles have been informed by creative conversations with my colleague, Gabrielle Parker, as we searched within a DMT training context for ways to embody contemporary social creation discourses (Parker and Best, 2005). The practices listed are techniques and foci which emerged from my RCPM research.

Principles

1   *Systemic*: There are patterns within all communications and no one sits completely outside these patterns. Hence, if you are observing a system, you influence it, and this includes supervisors (Gilbert and Evans, 2000). Each system creates its own implicit and explicit rules and expectations. Each person interacts in a larger system and brings to each new encounter personal and social prejudices, values, personal metaphoric landscapes and storied feelings.

Reflections upon mutual influence can be incorporated into dance movement therapy through the concept of interactional shaping (IS). IS widens the traditional narrative of transference found within psychodynamic literature to incorporate the multiple moment-to-moment of conversational dances (Best, 2003). The concept of interactional shaping is a foundational element within RCPM practice.

2   *Constructionist*: There are multiple realities within any communication and meanings are socially created through both verbal and non-verbal languages and behaviours. Knowledge of the social world may be less stable than expected (Schnitmann and Schnitmann, 1998).

A supervisor may act differently, believing there are multiple realities in which language (verbal and non-verbal) has the power to both form and inform experience. This could open up possibilities of multiple, divergent interpretations and hypotheses as long as each person also takes responsibility for the co-creation and appreciate that sensory information may be coloured by prejudices.

3   *Critical*: Critical analysis requires the ability to shift one's position in such a way that one can see how one is being pressured, pushed, shaped by either dominant discourses, or particular contexts or roles. A critical stance may also reveal issues of power and difference. This principle contains three levels of order or critique. Within the first-order critique we are not yet able to see ourselves as an active part of the system we are complaining about, and therefore we tend to locate the explanation for a problem outside ourselves somewhere in the system. Within the second order we are aware of the system around us and that we may be caught in a pattern of behaviour. In the third order we are able to both notice the system and our place within it and consider how we might be influencing it ourselves.

In a supervision context it is important to help supervisees to move from first-order towards third-order critique. In RCPM supervision I suggest participants start by locating themselves in their bodies, then in relation to the spatial environment, then their aesthetic representations, clinical material, and finally overlapping systems of influence.

4   *Appreciative*: Oliver's (2004) view of appreciative inquiry differs slightly from approaches within other business consultancy literature in which a blanket appreciation of everyone's voice may in practice actually diminish the voices of those feeling oppressed or oppositional who now simply become one of many voices, as if all are equal (Quinn, 2004). From an arts therapies perspective we might be involved directly, or indirectly, with the creative dialogues and arts processes of clients or supervisees through offering texts, tasks, sounds, props, colours. How might these inadvertently silence certain voices? I question how we can appreciate all the clients' creative 'voices', whether oppositional or different from our expectations.

Another aspect of this principle which also runs across the critical, systemic and constructionist principles is that of positioning. The concept of positioning refers not only to perceptual positions (first, second, third or helicopter position) holding a meta-view (Gilbert and Evans, 2000, p. 9) but also to positions of role, stories lived and stories told. People are literally 'positioned' by their life narratives (Speedy, 2001, p. 34), as well as their actual physical and spatial positioning (Moore and Yamamoto, 1988). In dance movement therapy there is a particularly fascinating dilemma within supervision, when the therapist uses his/her own body (first) to embody something of the client (second) while peers (third) and the supervisors (helicopter) act as observers. Positional perspectives are useful for supervisory and therapeutic practice and are overtly highlighted within RCPM practice.

5   *Complexity*: Within the complexity of experience polarisations emerge as one way to reflect nature's fluid ebb and flow and to manage confusing systems which appear to have no order. If combined with critical reflexivity and appreciative inquiry the use of polarities may be viewed from a 'both/and' perspective instead of an ordered 'either/or' perspective. In RCPM supervision movement between polarities, and also modalities, keeps alive the complexity of both human experience and expression.

6   *Creativity*: The arts therapies locate themselves reasonably comfortably within a world of ambiguity, chaos, multiplicity, plasticity, fluidity, metaphor and 'non-logic processes' (Lahad, 2000; Jones, 2005). The slippery nature of experience is valued and utilised. The unconscious, non-verbal inner world of symbols which leak into the conscious, more concrete world may be held and understood when mediated by arts processes supported within a therapeutic relationship (Schaverien, 2003).

Creativity is not the purview of the arts therapies, as verbal therapy also plays with imagination, metaphor and imagistic language (Jung, 1961; Winnicott, 1971). However, the creative non-verbal metaphor may serve as a holding mechanism in itself without verbalisation i.e. movement metaphor (Payne, 1992; Ellis, 2001; Meekums, 2002). Metaphors can serve as useful tools for regulating safe distance from emotional material. Aesthetic distance (Jennings, 1992) is a crucial part of arts therapies practice which facilitates 'artistic knowing and creative experimentation' (McNiff, 1998, p. 13). Within RCPM metaphoric material is explored both verbally and non-verbally through multiple representation; symbols are viewed as 'raw knowledge' (Lett, 1995).

The what – body of practice

Within this section I shift from situating 'the why' of the model (the principles) towards describing 'the what' (the outline) of the model. I offer first an illustration (Figure 10.1) showing the communicative and interpretive flow between client, therapist and supervisor. Second, I offer a content outline of an RCPM supervision session as a context for the later sections which unpack 'the how' (the practice foci) of the model.

Figure 10.1 suggests how meanings might be inter-created within arts therapies from both verbal and non-verbal interactions and symbolic representations. Symbolic representations are created in relationship to either the

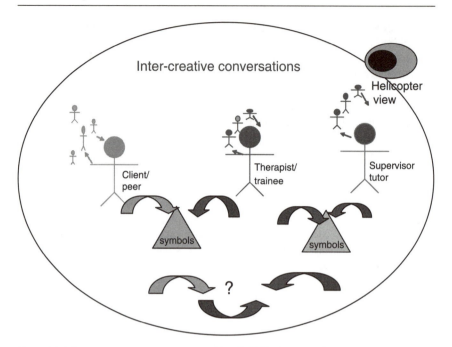

Figure 10.1 Inter-creative conversations within RCPM supervision.

Source: adapted from Gilbert and Evans' (2000, p. 11) meta-perspective model.

therapist's or the supervisor's presence (though perhaps not *with* the therapist or supervisor), and may include these individuals' own representations or responses, or not. My curiosity, demonstrated by the question mark at the bottom of Figure 10.1, refers to the possible blending and influencing of these differing representations of relationship. What kinds of mutual influences take place in the liminal, aesthetic experiences as well as the concretised and verbalised ones? As Mason (2002, p. 55) reminds us, 'we are not constructing reality but what our relationship is with reality'. Figure 10.1 illustrates how complex our relationship with reality might be and that there is always somewhere, another more distant point of view (e.g. the eye) which can see what we cannot see about ourselves in the wider system.

Sessions – the skeletal structure

The RCPM research group supervision sessions ran for two hours with ten DMT practitioners. The model has also been used effectively with counsellors, psychotherapists, art therapists and educational researchers. To ensure group consistency participants commit to once-a-month attendance. Individual trajectories are nurtured within a collective setting. Participants start with their own bodies, senses, feelings, images and creations in the 'here and now'.

There is a shared assumption that the personal and professional domains overlap. Client cases are not presented separately each month; however, case material emerges within the creative processes of the session. Often practitioners will say they have not 'brought anything consciously' to the sessions, and yet are 'surprised' and 'amazed' at what they are carrying in their bodies.

We often start with a brief verbal check-in. I listen carefully for indicative words, themes and descriptive phrases, and observe body postures, gestures and tensions which inform my verbal input and movement improvisations later. I am very aware of my own breathing and the shapes created by the body of the group as they enter and settle. These are techniques similar to those used by DMT within their clinical work. Within RCPM supervision I position myself as facilitator and guide initially, the mindful eye managing time and energy boundaries. It is my responsibility to maintain a sense of fluid containment sensitive to individuals' explorations.

I lead an improvisation, or a sensing task, as a way into bodily material, supporting the existing movement and focusing upon possibilities of more movement emerging. Initially I rely upon bodily rhythms already present and only add accompaniment later as either a frame, or a support, or even a provocation. While I enter without plans, a theme develops from the observed movement or the check-in. As different kinds of arts materials are on offer, we may move and then draw, talk in small groups, select photographs from a collection of images, make paper sculptures, finger paint, write a poem, or engage with props or sounds. These different modes of expression may be used once, or iteratively; they may become platforms from which the next exploration will take place. Hence these expressions, embodiments or representations may in themselves become impressions. Critically reflexive and inter-creative conversations help clarify relationships between emerging material and clinical practice. Sometimes connections are quite specific and immediate while at other times they are more general. We shift between embodiment and representation repeatedly, finishing often with a body sculpture, short dance phrase or verbal synopsis.

The how – fleshing out the structure with practice techniques

Within this section I present six core foci or practice techniques which have been illuminated through my practice-based research. Here I am separating out these aspects; however, in sessions they overlap and spiral around each other. The six techniques are: somatic engagement, transitional awareness, positional shifting, reflective conversations, improvisational play, and iterative choices. I acknowledge that as the supervisor I play a central and influential role, and therefore carefully apply, and model, the six principles listed above.

Somatic engagement

> Flitting in and out of consciousness, movement thinking, can be said to result in both body knowledge and body prejudice.
>
> (Moore and Yamamoto, 1988, p. 94)

By somatic engagement I am referring to physical, kinetic involvement in movement which is interconnected with psychological and emotional experience (Payne, 1992). Somatic engagement is a core feature within all dance movement therapy practice, yet it is not always present in DMT supervision processes. Within RCPM supervision somatic engagement is central; it the basis of the reflective and learning experiences. Supervisees engage through movement with drawings, written words, fabric sculptures, images on post-cards and photographs, yet the body is our reference point, our locus of self and group research. We go back to it throughout the session to check in with our bodily knowledge, trusting 'the wisdom of the cells' (Steckler, 2006, p. 31).

In RCPM I borrow from authentic movement practices in listening to the voices of the body, staying in touch with the deep sensory level of experience (Pallaro, 1999). We may differ from authentic movement practice in the ways in which we interpret or talk about sensations, images and voices as we are searching for overlaps between the somatic experience of the client and ourselves. One supervisee spoke about the 'essential nature of moving to understand the way a client is, to just be with this without talking about it'. This bodily knowing was what this supervisee took back into his or her practice rather than a theoretical interpretation.

I choose the term 'somatic engagement' rather than 'embodiment' within this section, though I use the term 'embody' often within supervision. I felt the need to differentiate the psychophysical and kinetic nature of movement engagement from other ways in which embodiment may now be used as if it is a form of substantiation (i.e. 'embodied theories') (Spinelli and Marshall, 2001). While there is increased appreciation that the body of the psychotherapist is participating and involved alongside that of the client (Shaw, 2004) within DMT the body of the therapist is centrally exploring 'embodied phenomena' including relational somatic transference (Payne, 2006, p. 1). RCPM practices offer exploration of intersubjective phenomenal material.

Transitional awareness

> 'In this context we keep shifting between the personal and the professional, as in a cycle, not linear. We think about transitions, what's between that space. Supervision bridges that space.'
>
> (RCPM participant)

Attention to transitions runs throughout RCPM practice techniques. Transitions are investigated by sensing a moment of change or observing the effect of difference in an interaction. Systemic therapists focus upon what amount of difference a therapist might bring into a therapeutic encounter which could initiate, rather than thwart, change (Andersen, 1995). Such input can be a subtle task relying upon body awareness. Within dancer practitioner Halprin's 'Psychokinetic Imagery Model' the individual notes minute sensory details when shifting between body, emotion and imagination (Halprin, 2003, p. 131). Body movement gives information to the participant observer about two main aspects of experience: how it is to be in oneself (i.e. movement quality) and how one relates to the world (i.e. shaping of movement) (Loman and Foley, 1996). Within movement observation theory, difference is what stands out; it is the 'variation, not maintenance, of kinetic quality that we perceive as a dynamic' (Moore and Yamamoto, 1988, p. 198).

In RCPM we pay attention to transitions in which the supervisee shifts in and out of embodying clients' movement. I ask participants to focus on the level of difference within a transition which might highlight important physical and emotional issues. Before they shift completely away from this exploration, I ask them to pause and be mindful of what has to change, what enables them to return to 'themselves'. It is within this in-between, transition space that the supervisees gain information about what their bodies hold somatically about their clients' experiences of being in the world.

Positional shifting

'I treat these sessions as space to shake the institution out of me [laughter], to drain the institution out, so I can be receptive to new movements, new people, new feelings, new ideas.'

(RCPM participant)

Shifting positions is another pivotal focus within RCPM and as a practice it is enacted in a number of ways (i.e. shifts between perceptual perspectives, role positions, theoretical approaches, modalities and media), as well as the implicit shifts held in all physical transitions indicated above.

Supervisees actively adopt different perceptual perspectives either by taking on the more distant role of a reflecting team as in systemic family therapy (Andersen, 1995) or through shifting perceptual positions (O'Connor and Seymour, 1994). When taking on a client's movement, supervisees sense and feel 'as if' the client in that moment. However, they are within their own bodies, hence in first person, and also taking on an empathic second person perceptual stance at the same time. This is a different mechanism than used by art therapists who might bring in a client's painting, gaining some distance from it, and thereby positioning themselves either in second (empathic) or third (observer) person. It is because of the cross-over and blending of body boundaries within DMT that I feel it is incredibly important within supervision to offer somatic exploration. The use of conscious positional shifting is an alternative and additional way of addressing unconscious material referred to as the 'somatic unconscious' within DMT literature (Lewis, 1984, p. 181). To shift between theoretical positions and to be mindful of how each theory shapes one's understanding and behaviour is another type of positional shifting used within RCPM sessions.

Acknowledgement of the different power held implicitly within differing roles is also addressed. If one constructs a story about clients, institutions or staff which labels the players as 'them' and 'us', this could limit room for creative manoeuvre. Role and perceptual positions can hold moral and ethical dimensions; for example, what rights and responsibilities do we have or are we given in different positions?

Reflective conversations

> '[Supervision] sessions enable me to be with the question, to be with the dance the question brings up.'
>
> (RCPM supervisee)

Critical questioning (i.e. questions stimulated by appreciative curiosity and reflexivity) can facilitate new perspectives. Questioning can take place in relation to others, in relation to one's own thoughts, as 'inner and outer dialogues' (Schnitmann and Schnitmann, 1998, p. 143) and in relation to one's expressive products (e.g. drawings, poems and dances).

Within RCPM supervision all of the above conversations take place. There is extensive opportunity for supervisees to generate 'inner dialogues' about their movement. There is also encouragement to articulate unfolding thoughts, thereby creating and performing narratives. Developing active listening techniques helps supervisees listen without interpreting, asking hypothetical questions to deepen or widen each other's experience.

In the extracts below three supervisees, who had not moved as a trio before, transferred their shared movement experience to drawing in silence upon one piece of paper. Subsequently they had an inter-creative conversation, during which the drawing became viewed as an incomplete map in which 'uncharted territory' could be an exciting journey: 'If we knew actually everything on that map we wouldn't be here, that would be kind of sad, we would have stopped learning, exploring.'

They go on to talk about a possible 'island' in the drawing and a 'porpoise', and the story grows between them with different images emerging. They wonder 'where these stories come from'. They play with the idea of whether it is a map or 'an outline' or 'a boundary' or about 'delineation'. From this specificity they move towards more general themes, tracking their individual and interactive processes:

'how much permission do I have to be close to you or look at your picture while you're drawing or how much permission do I have to be close to you in movement? And then how much permission do I give myself, to give so much or not?'

The exploration shifts to appreciation of respect, constraint and permission about using humour in relation to each others' words:

A: Pisces? as in fish?
B: Yeah.
C: Were you writing it backwards?
A: At first I thought you had written dices [laughter].
C: Ahhh, take a roll and find out where to go! Game board [laughter].
A: Is that 'little shift'?
C: I thought that said 'little stuff' [big laughter].
B: Point is, it's possible to have the both 'dices, Pisces, little stuff, little shit, little ship'.

As they play respectfully with each others' ideas, the reflective conversation moves on to include ideas about clients who developmentally might find relating to more than one person very difficult. As one says,

'There's more room for misinterpretation when you have people trying to relate to each other, as they'll each have a story about it. [What does it take] to have that multi-focus?'

Another one then notices:

'I was visually going quite autistic because I was looking at people's feet. It was pretty basic. It's a pretty straightforward way of relating to more than one person, or to new people. It was really curious how I went into that state.'

This supervisee works extensively with clients within the autistic spectrum and went on to unpack individual preferences which might connect with clinical work, saying:

'It seems to me that I rely much more on the visual when I'm in a different, or unusual situation, a new situation; I don't rely on the other senses nearly as much.'

Within these inter-creative conversations these supervisees connect personal and professional material, critically reflecting upon the ways these intermingle. They use their personal, creative playfulness while being very present with their here-and-now shared experience to generate understanding about clients. They note how they gain insight about their clients' experiences of being in relationship through embodying their clients' strategies for engagement.

Improvisational play

> Imagination is the meeting ground where old and new come together – what was, what is and what could be.
>
> (Halprin, 2003, p. 87)

For me, play is the essence of change, the essence of possibility; without playing one cannot imagine the possibility of something different, of change (Jones, 2005). In RCPM we play physically as well as cognitively. We use play and improvisation as a form of 'free association', similar to that used within art therapy, providing space for self-reflection, or 'reverie' (Edwards, 1993, p. 219). From a psychodynamic perspective imagination requires a capacity to trust, and holds within it the potentiality and 'existence of multidimensional and interconnected worlds' (Gordon, 1985, p. 13). Social creationist perspectives also view interconnectivity and multiplicity as core features of play and creative conversations.

The use of artefacts creates an in-between place in which the images are not actually the client nor the clinical issue, yet may be used by the client or supervisee to change an internal reality (Lahad, 2000). A core element of moving between mediums of expression (and impression) is the opening up of different perspectives, providing different levels of distance from the material, which in turn facilitates different possibilities for engagement (Jones, 2005).

Within RCPM we might use photographs as either a stimulus for exploration around a clinical theme or as means of describing specific emotional content. I might introduce finger paints which can stimulate movement during expression and simultaneously act as an impression upon the painter. In one session I observed two supervisees who were co-workers, each of whom had spoken separately during the check-in about difficulties within a specific DMT group that week with distressed young adults.

Following the improvisation task, supervisees transferred something of the movement experience individually on to paper with finger paints. I observed one of the co-workers pushing the paint with great intensity across the page, getting faster and faster, eventually ripping and throwing the paper in pieces around the room. The other supervisee placed her hands gently in the middle of her paper, smoothing and easing the paint outwards repeatedly in an even rhythm. Neither was consciously aware of the other during this process.

Afterwards they spoke about how differently they had experienced the paint. The supervisory story they created which helped them return to their shared clinical work the following week was that they had each absorbed different roles, feelings and responsibilities from the young adult clients. One felt like raging against boundaries chaotically, relishing the dirtying and invading of surrounding space. The other was in touch with a sense of calm and containment which could be achieved through repetition and central clarity. While this material might be interpreted differently from different theoretical approaches, what helped these two co-workers most was the deep physicality of their individual movement and painting explorations, followed by inter-creative critical reflections where each was able to really hear the experience of the other in the here-and-now. From this they felt able to imagine re-entering the clinical space which before had felt quite challenging to them as individuals and particularly as co-workers. They felt reconnected with their physical creative selves.

Iterative choices

> 'There's a difference between theory and doing. All theory stops at some point. It has to transmorph itself into action. I want to work on action.'
>
> (RCPM supervisee)

Aspects of supervision may be viewed as creative problem-solving (CPS) because therapists present with seemingly unsolvable scenarios in search of creative solutions. Within business contexts CPS might seek solutions, while supervision might seek helpful questions; however, certain precepts of CPS support RCPM practice (e.g. iteration, speed, and use of convergent and divergent thinking). Within supervision sessions we might repeatedly approach a drawing, a prop, an idea from different spatial directions (e.g. backwards, sideways, upside-down) with different energy or pace (e.g. creeping up, running at, jumping over) to see what emerges from bodily responses before cognitive analysis.

Speed is used in CPS to bypass personal judgement or criticism. Swiftly gathering together and respectfully accepting all ideas offered provides an enormous range of material which can then be scrutinised (i.e. 'cycle often, close late') (Martin, 2001, p. 108). The fast pacing may connect with the neurological basis for internal image-creating processes (Zabriskie, 2006). Within the supervision sessions I sometimes suggest quick shifts between drawing, writing and moving. In these sudden shifts I am aiming for supervisees to catch themselves off guard, because human experience is not compartmentalised, even though the way we choose to talk about it might be (Soth, 2006).

Techniques within RCPM supervision mirror those within CPS of combining divergent and convergent thinking. Sometimes after a long movement experiential, followed by drawing and writing, I will ask supervisees to circle three words, suspending judgement about why. Once done, I suggest they embody and sculpt these words, linking them, thereby focusing, narrowing and containing what can sometimes feel to be overwhelming personal and professional material. Supervision needs a creative balance between containment and exploration.

Summary and conclusion

Within this chapter I presented one model of group supervision, RCPM, which focuses upon relationships made evident through multiple creative processes. The chapter differentiated the 'why', the 'what' and the 'how' of the model and separated out its principles and practices. I located RCPM within an overarching frame of reflective inquiry (RI) and added a sixth principle, that of creativity, to the five offered by systemic therapist Oliver (2004). The full principle set then became: systemic, constructionist, appreciative, critical, complexity and creativity. I also identified six separate practice foci which arose from my research into the model in action, i.e. somatic engagement, transitional awareness, positional shifting, reflective conversations, improvisational play and iterative choices. RCPM as presented is a group model for practising therapists in which reflexive inter-creative conversations are central. This interaction, or relational aspect, refers not only to conversations between supervisees but also to those inner conversations which supervisees may have with themselves when relating to products of their expression.

RCPM makes use of embodiment and varied arts representations to assist clinicians' personal and professional reflections. Embodiment within dance movement therapy work relies upon somatic engagement. This involves also finding ways in which metaphors, whether movement, verbal, visual, can be re-enacted, re-embodied, re-presented while maintaining contact with essential bodily knowledge. The phenomenal body is the central reference point acting as a somatic knowledge bank. RCPM supervision focuses upon shifts and transitions noticing differences between experiences and representation of experiences. Supervisees are encouraged to move between, play with and be curious about the effect of different theoretical, perspectival and physical positions, as well as representational modes and creative processes. These shifts aim to open up supervisees' curiosity and ways of both looking at and engaging with clinical material; they are asked to consider possible relationships between their personal and professional conscious and unconscious metaphoric landscapes. Most importantly supervisees are asked to consider the effects of adopting one particular way of viewing and reflecting, and are encouraged to play with possibilities.

RCPM is informed by a range of theoretical positions, each one offering different perspectives upon clinical material. The emphasis within this chapter has been upon constructionist and systemic discourses, rather than psychodynamic, of which much has been written already within general arts therapies literature and about which I have written extensively elsewhere (Best, 2000, 2003, 2005). My rationale for introducing these discourses to arts therapies work was to offer alternative ways of thinking about the movements between the unconscious and conscious dimensions of experience and of representations of these shifts. Constructionist and systemic discourses focus upon both local and wider ecologies as well as on issues of difference and power.

The concept of interactional shaping (IS) was introduced which refers to both the psychosocial and physical phenomena between people within interactive conversations. Reflective practices within RCPM supervision are assisted by offering multiple perspectives upon the potential mutuality within liminal, creative processes, supported by varied opportunities for representation of embodied, relational experiences. Shifting positions both verbally and non-verbally can introduce levels of aesthetic distance and re-engagement with clinical material which assists therapists to become more 'interactionally self-knowing' (Lett, 1995, p. 335). In turn, articulating this knowing helps clinicians maintain safe, respectful and playful curiosity within an overall frame of reflective inquiry.

> The arts, as modes of knowing, are conceived of as vehicles for carrying meaning in supervision, as in therapy.
>
> (Lett, 1993, p. 371)

Acknowledgements

I wish to acknowledge the role Gabrielle Parker played in co-developing training concepts. I wish to thank all my supervisee co-researchers, Jonas Torrance for gallantly reviewing the chapter, and Dr R. Bolle for reading it through psychodynamic eyes.

References

Andersen, T. (1995) Reflecting processes; acts of informing and forming: you can borrow my eyes, but you must not take them away from me! In S. Friedman (ed.) *The Reflecting Team in Action: Collaborative Practice in Family Therapy*. New York: Guilford Press.

Best, P. (2000) Theoretical diversity and clinical collaboration: a dance therapist's reflections. *The Arts in Psychotherapy*, 27 (3), pp. 197–212.

—— (2003) Interactional shaping within therapeutic encounters: Three dimensional dialogues. *The USA Body Psychotherapy Journal*, 2 (1), pp. 26–44.

Edwards, D. (1993) Learning about feelings: the role of supervision in art therapy training. *The Arts in Psychotherapy*, 20, pp. 213–222.

Ellis, R. (2001) Movement metaphor as mediator: a model for the dance/movement therapy process. *The Arts in Psychotherapy*, 28 (3), pp. 181–190.

Gilbert, M. and Evans, K. (2000) *Psychotherapy Supervision: An Integrative Relational Approach to Psychotherapy Supervision*. Buckingham: Open University Press.

Gordon, R. (1985) Imagination as mediator between inner and outer reality. *The Arts in Psychotherapy*, 12, pp. 11–15.

Halprin, D. (2003) *The Expressive Body in Life, Art and Therapy*. London: Jessica Kingsley.

Hewson, J. (2001) Integrative supervision: art and science. In M. Carroll and M. Tholstrup (eds) *Integrative Approaches to Supervision*. London: Jessica Kingsley.

Jennings, S. (1992) *Dramatherapy with Families, Groups and Individuals: Waiting in the Wings*. London: Jessica Kingsley.

Jones, P. (2005) *The Arts Therapies: A Revolution in Healthcare*. Hove: Brunner-Routledge.

Jung, C. (1961) *Memories, Dreams, Reflections*. Glasgow: Collins and Routledge & Kegan Paul.

Lahad, M. (2000) *Creative Supervision: The Use of Expressive Arts Methods in Supervision and Self-supervision*. London: Jessica Kingsley.

Lett, W. (1993) Therapist creativity: the arts of supervision. *The Arts in Psychotherapy*, 20, pp. 371–386.

—— (1995) Researching experiential self-knowing. *The Arts in Psychotherapy*, 25 (5), pp. 331–342.

Lewis, P. (1984) *Theoretical Approaches in Dance-movement Therapy*, Vol. II. Dubuque, IA: Kendall/Hunt.

Loman, S. and Foley, L. (1996) Models for understanding the nonverbal process in relationships. *The Arts in Psychotherapy*, 23 (4), pp. 341–350.

Martin, J. (2001) *Managing Problems Creatively: Creativity, Innovation and Change*. Milton Keynes: Open University Press.

Mason, B. (2002) A reflective recording format for supervisors and trainees. In D. Campbell and B. Mason (eds) *Perspectives on Supervision*. London: Karnac.

McNiff, S. (1998) *Art-based Research*. London: Jessica Kingsley.

Meekums, B. (2002) *Dance Movement Therapy*. London: Sage.

Meekums, B. and Payne, H. (1993) Emerging methodology in dance movement therapy research: a way forward. In H. Payne (ed.) *Handbook of Inquiry in the Arts Therapies: One River, Many Currents*. London: Jessica Kingsley.

Moore, C-L. and Yamamoto, K. (1988) *Beyond Words. Movement Observation and Analysis*. Philadelphia: Gordon & Breach. Originally published 1988.

O'Connor, J. and Seymour, J. (1994) *Training with NLP: Skills for Trainers, Managers and Communicators*. London: Thorsons.

Oliver, C. (2004) Reflexive inquiry and the strange loop tool. *Human Systems: The Journal of Systemic Consultation and Management*, 15 (1–3), pp. 127–140.

Pallaro, P. (ed.) (1999) *Authentic Movement: A Collection of Essays by Mary Starks Whitehouse, Janet Adler and Joan Chodorow*. London: Jessica Kingsley.

Parker, G. and Best, P. (2005) Moving reflections: the social construction of identity. In L. Kossolapow, S. Scoble and D. Waller (eds) *Arts – Therapies – Communication: On the Way to a Communicative European Arts Therapy*, Vol. I. New Brunswick: Transaction Publishers.

Payne, H. (1992) Shut in, shut out: dance movement therapy with children and adolescents. In H. Payne (ed.) *Dance Movement Therapy: Theory and Practice*. London: Tavistock/Routledge.

—— (2006) Tracking the web of interconnectivity. *Body, Movement and Dance in Psychotherapy*, 1 (1), pp. 7–15.

Quinn, R. (2004) *Building the Bridge as you Walk on It: A Guide to Leading Change*. Berkeley, CA: Jossey-Bass.

Schavarien, J. (2003) The embodiment of desire: art, gender, and analysis. In T. Adams and A. Duncan (eds) *The Feminine Case: Jung, Aesthetics and Creative Process*. London: Karnac.

Schnitmann, D.F. and Schnitmann, J. (1998) Reflexive models and dialogic learning. *Human Systems: The Journal of Systemic Consultation and Management*, 9 (2), pp. 139–154.

Shaw, R. (2003) *The Embodied Psychotherapist: The Therapist's Body Story*. Hove: Brunner-Routledge.

Shrivener, P. and Chapman, P. (2004) The practical implications of applying a theory of practice based research: a case study. *Working Papers in Art and Design*, 3. Available online at <http://www.herts.ac.uk/articles1/research/papers/wpades/vol3/ssabs.html (accessed 17 July 2006).

Soth, M. (2006) What therapeutic hope for a subjective mind in an objectified body? *Body, Movement and Dance in Psychotherapy*, 1 (1), pp. 43–56.

Speedy, J. (2001) Narrative approaches to supervision. In M. Carroll and M. Tholstrup (eds) *Integrative Approaches to Supervision*. London: Jessica Kingsley.

Spinelli, E. and Marshall, S. (eds) (2001) *Embodied Theories*. London: Continuum.

Steckler, L.H. (2006) Somatic soulmates. *Body, Movement and Dance in Psychotherapy*, 1 (1), pp. 29–42.

Tselikas-Portmann, E. (ed.) (1999) *Supervision and Dramatherapy*. London: Jessica Kingsley.

Wadsworth Hervey, L.W. (2002) *Artistic Inquiry in Dance/Movement Therapy: Creative Alternatives for Research*. Chicago, IL: Charles C. Thomas.

Winnicott, D.W. (1971) *Playing and Reality*. London: Tavistock Books.

Zabriskie, B. (2006) When psyche meets soma: The question of incarnation. *Body, Movement and Dance in Psychotherapy*, 1 (1), pp. 67–77.

Chapter 11

Three makes one

A journey of growth through supervision

Kedzie Penfield

Introduction

The story of any individual supervision involves three people: the supervisor, the supervisee and the patient. These three roles interact with and affect each other within the unfolding drama of a therapy, in this case a dance movement therapy, supervision. Here I wish to look at some aspects of the dynamic relationships between these roles and how their stories are expressed, informed by and understood through movement in the context of individual, post-qualifying supervision.

Many practitioners in the arts therapies and in the analytic field have written about the dynamics within a supervision process. In applying some of this thinking to clinical incidents from my experience as a supervisor, I am interested in Searles' (1955) and Mattinson's (1975) ideas about the reflective process, in Tom Ogden's (2005a) differentiation between *holding* and *containing* in trying to understand the complexity of interactive stories in one supervision process, and the 'third perspective' (Cavell, 1998) or dialogue that takes place outside the direct therapist–patient dyad in individual therapy work.

As both supervisor and supervisee may call themselves 'therapists' and both the patient and the supervisee may call themselves 'clients', I have chosen to call the three roles to be explored 'patient', 'supervisee' and 'supervisor' to avoid confusion. Those who choose to attend supervision in my private practice work in a variety of settings including private practice, NHS and community mental health. In the form of supervision I am investigating here, the supervisee is a qualified professional and is clinically responsible for what happens.[1] I have also chosen to use the female 'her' when referring to an individual with the exception of one example about a man. Although based on incidents from my practice, the stories presented are fictitious in order to protect those involved.[2] It is helpful if one is familiar with structures such as authentic movement, improvisation and role play when reading this chapter.

The model

I use a psychodynamic model that comes from individual patient therapist work and has been applied to supervision. There are many concepts that may be used to consider processes in both therapy and supervision with this model: developmental growth, transference, countertransference and identification to name but a few. It would therefore be useful to start with what an arts therapy process is. David Johnson (1998, p. 89) has facilitated my thinking about this when he writes:

> The environment that is re-created in the creative arts therapy session; that is an aesthetic, imaginal, metaphoric space between therapist and patient in which inside and outside, self and other, are mixed.

And:

> The therapeutic relationship between the therapist and patient, combined with the arts therapy medium, offers a process through 'which suffering can be transformed into resilience.'
>
> (Johnson, 1998, p. 97)

In supervision we are adding a third person to the therapeutic dyad. In training this is essential: the supervisor embodies the 'objective' or 'intersubjective' view (Cavell, 1998, p. 451) which the supervisee/therapist is trying to develop in order to do the work. Developmentally one could talk about the second parent; the father or second carer who is present when the mother or primary carer is still the main focus of the infant. Marcia Cavell puts this in terms of a mind learning that there is a third position, separate from that of the mother–child pair:

> the child needs not just one but two other persons ... the child must move from interacting with this mother to grasping the idea that both his perspective on the world and hers are perspectives; that there is a possible third point of view, more inclusive than theirs, from which both his mother's and his own can be seen and from which the interaction between them can be understood.
>
> (Cavell, 1998, pp. 459–460)

Hester Solomon (1997) writes, the 'two stage, dyad-to-triad process' (pp. 298–299) is paralleled by supervision work; thus the intensive dyadic work would have a counterbalancing relationship created by the triangular space of supervision. Learning and growth occur as we witness our own or someone else's work whether we are in the role of supervisor, supervisee or patient. In dance movement therapy supervision, part of this takes place through the consideration of 'two kinds of articulation, that of the body in movement and that of the mind in thought' (Bloom, 2006, p. 4). The former is addressed through using movement whenever it seems appropriate to do so in the supervision session. The latter process is addressed through the relationship of the individuals involved for which the psychodynamic model is helpful.

Putting these relationships into diagrammatic form, we get the picture shown in Figure 11.1. The double-headed arrows indicate relationship: there is a direct, physical relationship between the supervisor and supervisee and the supervisee and patient but there is no physical interaction between the supervisor and the patient. They never meet, but the supervisor will know a lot about the patient and have thoughts and feelings about her. The patient will feel the effect of the supervisor's thinking although she will usually be unaware of it. Sometimes this effect will be consciously felt, however: for example, I have heard of instances where the patient has remarked on a change in the style of therapist which, she suspects, could have come from that therapist's supervisor.[3]

Because of the overlapping nature of the three roles in a supervision process, it is useful to look at their roles separately in order to understand how they integrate into one story. The supervisor, as indicated above, may be seen as a kind of parental figure who provides a third perspective.[4] In authentic movement terms, she is a 'witness [who] may be similar to the benign "observing other" of the individuated internalized supervisor' (Payne, 2001, p. 6). When I am in the role of supervisor, my focus and 'embodied attentiveness' (Bloom, 2006, p. 65) is similar to that of my focus as a therapist. However the context, the *container* (see below) of the role is different so I will adopt more of a teaching practice, give different, if any, verbal interpretations and share more of my own opinions and experiences than I would as a therapist. The role of supervisee is that of a student who is learning technical and personal skills. She brings her thoughts, stories and own history to discussion and movement with the supervisor so that 'the experiencing self [which] is the

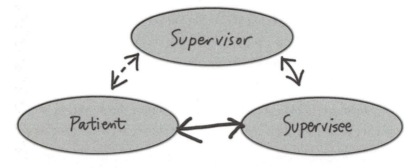

Figure 11.1 The configuration 'created by the triangular space of supervision'.

Source: Solomon, 1997, p. 299.

experiential container of awareness . . . can be refocused into fuller awareness' (Lett, 1993, p. 371).

There is a developmental process for all three individuals. They are all attempting to understand each other and themselves through a dialogue: the patient with the supervisee who, in turn, is learning through her conversations and movement work with the supervisor to have a constant 'dialogue between the external supervisor and the internal supervisor' (Casement, 1985, p. 32). The supervisor will also be continuing these conversations. Tom Ogden (2005b) describes a supervision session he attended when, as an experienced professional, he had a consultation with an admired colleague whom he considered senior to himself (where he refers to analytic work I would refer to arts therapies work):

> It did not seem to matter whether it was his or my own conscious; preconscious and unconscious responsiveness that took the lead at any given moment, as we talked about our analytic work and what was happening between us. Claims of 'ownership' or credit due for originality or insightfulness held no purchase. All that seemed to matter was making a human connection and gaining a sense of what was true to the present moment, both of the analytic work and the supervisory work.
>
> (Ogden, 2005b, p. 1275)

Figure 11.2 shows the overlap between the roles including the relationship arrows (their length is of no significance) from Figure 11.1. The area of overlap in the centre between the three individuals is where conscious, unconscious and artistic processes serve as the arena for learning and growth in the supervision process. The circle surrounding the three roles indicates the external world which includes the physical and situational structures influencing the work. The arrows coming in from the containing circle indicate these influences (see Anne's story below).

The other essential element that is not specifically shown in these diagrams is dance movement. Lett (1993) states that 'The arts, as modes of knowing, are conceived of as vehicles for carrying meaning in supervision, as in therapy' (p. 371). Both the arts therapy and verbalisation provide the language of mental and psychological work that takes place between and because of these three people. The art form will be part of the process of 'developing skills and knowledge, learning and greater awareness leading to greater choices of how to work with the client' (Clark, 2001, p. 3). Thus movement work will usually be part of a dance movement therapy supervision session whether that is in service of the supervisee on a personal level (see examples below) or more directly in service of the patient.

Two concepts that contribute to my way of conducting supervision are *holding* and *containing*. Tom Ogden (2005a) sees Winnicott's holding 'as an ontological concept that is primarily concerned with being and its relationship

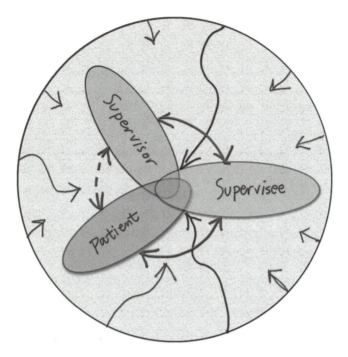

Figure 11.2 The outcome of the supervisor–supervisee–patient triadic relationship sur-
rounded by the outside world.

to time' (p. 93). *Holding* takes place in time and changes over time. One holds
a baby's body completely in its first months of life, then as time goes on and
the baby grows, one holds less and less until, one hopes, the baby can walk by
herself and is able to choose when and how she will be held. This process
continues through life whether one is a parent, teacher, therapist or supervisor
and one is doing the holding or being held.

A *container*, on the other hand, does not change over time of its own
accord.[5] I am aligning it with the external world: literally the container of the
work that does not change, although it does have a dynamic form. It is
concerned with the procedures and place that surround the work such as
money, space, contract, session time and the arts therapy being used. For
example, if the physical space is not safe, private, warm, and does not have an
appropriate temperature, ventilation and furniture it will have an impact on
the supervision process. I remember being supervised by someone in a rented
room that resembled a warehouse of cast-off furniture waiting to be taken to
a dump. The physical container of our meetings was not in tune with the
tenor of getting a clearer view of my work.

When agreed aspects of the contract such as time, money, responsibilities
and procedures are changed without thought it can be unhelpful to the work.

Changes are provocative, so if these are not attended to, information about the nature of the therapeutic contact is lost. If, for instance, I find myself running over time so that the session will be longer than agreed, I may be acting out a concern for the supervisee that needs to be discussed rather than put into the action of running over time. If a fee has not been paid it may 'reflect' (Searles, 1955, p. 137) a process going on between the patient and supervisee. These agreed arrangements are *containers*, and when they are changed without thought it can be informative to consider why the *container* is not holding.

There are times when one is *holding* the supervisee through one's presence and experience. There are other times when one has to *contain* the experience of the supervisee by addressing what she (the supervisor) sees as unconscious action in hopes that the supervisee will internalise this *containing* for herself. This may include exploring actions of the supervisee that feel uncomfortable for both supervisor and supervisee.

One example where I did not confront the supervisee's behaviour, although I did hold to the containing role of supervisor, concerned the literal 'container' of clothing. A young dance movement therapist I will call Adam (although most arts therapists are women I occasionally have male supervisees) came for supervision quite early on in my own supervision practice. He was a good-looking, talented man both in the field of performance, where he co-led a small performing group, and in the field of therapy, where he worked in various social work and statutory settings with disadvantaged adults who were often single women. This particular day he arrived dressed in jogging trousers and a strap tank top, although he usually wore a shirt or a polo top. I was struck by his attractive, athletic body and realised that, if I were twenty years younger, I would have felt pulled by a personal and sexual agenda rather than a professional one; a clear moment of countertransference. He seemed totally unaware of his physical appearance and I asked him if he thought about what he wore when leading sessions. He looked puzzled and said no, he simply wore clothing appropriate to movement. We then went on to discuss his work in which it was clear that he had no inkling of the impact his physical appearance might have on his patients. Interestingly, he had described feeling uncomfortable with the sensuous movements of one patient in previous supervision sessions. I hinted at awareness of his looks in the context of his work with young women but he did not pick up on my points and instead we worked technically on the questions he had about the work he was doing.

In his movement work he seemed empathic, a good observer and not given to 'performing' when he was in the role of a movement leader. Technically he was well able to pick up movement from others, thoughtfully engage with them through their movement vocabulary without imposing his own preferences and draw out clear verbal insights and questions when appropriate. I realised that the whole theme of what he wore, which I took to be an unconscious act, was an important indication of what might be going on in his work with these women. In one way it was an aggressive act: he was flaunting his physical sexuality to a group of people to whom he was unavailable just as he was unavailable to me. His actions could have indicated his need to control the situation through a narcissistic use of his body that I picked up through my feeling of being attracted to him. He turned a blind eye to his own choice of dress and I – although aware of some dynamic story behind this choice – turned a similar blind eye to addressing this in our supervision session. I *held* the *container* of ethical behaviour by not taking my physical reaction to Adam into action outside my mind. However, the work as it unfolded did not lead to further understanding at that time: he was unable to 'watch himself' (Casement, 1985, p. 32) as a young man working with a group of single women. I can only hope that, because I held (consciously realised) the thought in my mind that his clothing indicated an unconscious attitude that could dynamically inform his work, he might think about this issue himself in the future. If he did and it came into our sessions, my *holding* could change over time in order to consider this issue with him.

Figure 11.2 shows the overlap area where the unconscious and conscious processes of the supervisor, supervisee and patient roles operate. If there is some leakage in my *containing* presence in terms of *holding* contractual issues, projections, misuse of physical work, then the chances are that there will be a similar leakage in the work of the supervisee with his patients. There are many possibilities of overlapping stories with attendant levels of dynamics playing themselves out through the thinking and moving 'arts/play-space' (Johnson, 1998) between supervisor, supervisee and patient.

Anne

Anne worked with long-term patients in an NHS hospital. Although she had regular verbal supervision from the psychiatric consultant who was very supportive of her dance movement therapy work, Anne felt she wanted additional private supervision that would focus on movement as an essential and informative part of the working process. She came once a week and brought whatever aspect of her case load felt most pressing or interesting to her; individual, group or staff issues.

At this particular session she arrived and sat down heavily. She was quite still; very different from the usual bouncy quality that served her well, I imagined, in getting people into movement in the hospital. She said she wanted to talk about one particular patient: a slow-moving, middle-aged woman who had started attending individual DMT sessions for an initial six-week period to see if she would benefit from them.

Anne described the session (fifth in her series of six) very quietly. The patient had arrived twenty minutes late for her forty-minute session which had surprised Anne, as the patient was usually on time and seemed to enjoy the sessions. This time she sat stolidly in her chair and said little, answering Anne's questions with a yes or no and, in Anne's perception, refusing to engage with the work. At the end of the session the patient had started moving her hands to some waltz music but the session time had ended before the movement could develop. Anne was left with a sense that nothing had happened; she had failed to get anything moving or understood for her patient and there was an atmosphere of 'block, stop and doom' as she put it. She felt she had 'failed' because the patient did not move and 'no work was done'.

We noticed the 'mirroring' (Cavell, 1998, p. 461) of this patient's actions in our session: unusually, Anne did not want to move but sat, telling me about the session with none of her usual physical demonstration or dynamism. She mentioned how she felt that the nurses had indirectly negated her work by suggesting that activity trips organised by the occupational therapy department were more appropriate and beneficial to the patients, including this one, in the summer. She also felt that the nurses saw her as an 'airy-fairy' teacher who entertained patients through her dancing. This was her patient's penultimate session before deciding whether or not individual DMT sessions would continue for her. As the consultant was on holiday for a week other hospital supports for the dance movement therapy work were absent.

I began to feel outrage on Anne's behalf but when I put this into words she said she did understand the staff's view and wondered if she should cancel her groups for the summer months. I was curious about my outrage and wondered privately if my emotion was an 'emotional experience [which had] informational value' (Searles, 1955, p. 137). Perhaps the patient was expressing outrage through her passivity in the session which was echoed in Anne's unusually low energy in our session. I also wondered if Anne's wish to cancel her sessions could be an angry reaction to her perception that the staff did not consider her work important: a statement saying 'you don't want my work so I'll make sure you don't have it!' The passivity expressed by both Anne and her patient might have been a cover to deny the outrage we each felt in different ways.

I saw this as Anne not holding the *container* of time for her patient's sessions and as a potentially informative event to understanding what was going on. The external world was intruding in a way that we needed to understand: one of the arrows from the circle (Figure 11.2) was twisting its way into the centre of the work and affecting Anne's ability to *hold* the 'arts/play-space' (Johnson, 1998) for her patient.

I suggested that Anne sit in a chair as her patient had done and move her hands to some waltz music I would put on. She agreed but asked for another kind of music – perhaps something more abstract and abrasive. I chose some Steve Reich music and began to witness her moving. She waved her hands in a graceful figure 8 as she had indicated her patient did. Almost immediately her hands flattened and pushed into the space with the sharp accents of the music. These staccato, flat-handed pushes began to accelerate. The shape of her hands then changed to pointing with her forefingers; this soon changed to two fingers as if she had a pistol in each hand. Her torso narrowed and leaned forward as she seemed to focus more carefully and 'shoot' something straight ahead of her. Then she closed her eyes, brought her fingers to her mouth as if silencing speech and pushed herself into the back of the chair. She sat very still in that position for a few moments before finishing the improvisation.

She spoke about the intensity of the 'shooting and silencing' part of her sequence. Images of how a silencer works on a gun and the anger expressed by shooting led us to think about the patient's possible anger at the potential loss of her sessions. It also confirmed Anne's part in the dynamic of the story: she did feel angry that her work was being diminished in importance. As a result she considered standing aside and being replaced by a ward trip in order to avoid 'a confrontation with ward staff' as she put it. Perhaps this paralleled her patient feeling replaced in some way we did not know about. I also wondered if Anne had an unconscious fear that she was only offering an 'airy-fairy' activity rather than a serious therapeutic process so that the aggression expressed in her movement was a defensive way of coping with some lack of confidence.

As our session finished Anne realised that she needed to spend more time simply being on the ward so that she was not seen as an 'airy-fairy' entertainer who could come and go as she pleased. Her relationship to the staff would be different if they interacted with her in various ways over time. She suddenly saw the ward and the staff on it as another important element (or 'person') with whom she needed to relate in order to do the best work possible for her patient. She also realised that she needed to fight for these important sessions that were beneficial for her patients.

Wendy

Wendy had qualified as a dance movement therapist five years before she came to me for supervision. She had worked in the field continuously both in the public and private sectors and now wished to build up her private practice. She had a passionate need to move; she had been a professional dancer and teacher before realising that she 'preferred to encourage others to move over performing for them herself'. She worked with individuals and groups in a variety of ways including authentic movement, had been in her own therapy for some years and seemed competent in most aspects of her work that tended to be with depressed women.

She had been working for a year with a woman who was married to a businessman and came into therapy to understand why she felt so unhappy in the relationship. She had been to several counsellors and was 'tired of words'; she found the authentic movement form of great help and satisfaction to her.

My supervisee liked her but always felt pulled down and depressed after their sessions. We discussed the possibility that she (my supervisee) in some way identified with the patient and allowed her to 'unload and leave' her bad feelings with the supervisee.

About a year into their work together my supervisee came to supervision with a dream which she recalled to me as follows:

> I'm walking down the street with my patient who is on a shopping spree. I'm helping her choose different things to buy and I feel envious because she has the money to buy things I can't. She is suddenly unable to walk normally as she is moving in slow motion – almost as if she is struggling against a strong wind. I seem to be drifting backwards away from the scene. She fades and I wake up.

Wendy explored the manifest content of the dream and wondered if she did feel envious of her patient's rich husband despite the difficulties she was having in her marriage. Everything we talked about seemed rather too simple and literal in its interpretation so I suggested she try to move some part of it. She chose to take the slow-motion movement at the end of the dream.

She began a slow-motion walking movement with her eyes closed. Her arms began to spread wide over her head as she moved contra-laterally with arms and legs in the same rhythm. Gradually this changed to standing with feet apart and her arms moving alternately forward and back over her head. This movement became smaller until only her hands were moving from her wrists and her face looked very sad to me. She maintained a simple 'X' shape in the vertical plane, each hand and foot in a different corner, in stillness except for her hands moving slowly from her wrists as if trying to twist out of something. After about a minute of this she stopped and opened her eyes.

It took a few moments before she spoke – it seemed as if an important event had occurred. She spoke of being tied by her wrists to her bedstead when she was very young: she had begun to sleep-walk when she was three and her carer had tied her to the bed in order to keep her safe from accidents while sleep-walking. She remembered she did not fight but whimpered to herself. The vertical position with her arms outstretched and her hands moving from her wrists was a replica of her horizontal shape lying on a bed. She wondered if her use of movement to heal as a dance movement therapist was a direct result of this experience in which the ability to move was the only thing that made the situation bearable.

I did not know much of her personal story and wondered if it felt safer for her to touch this material in supervision rather than in her own therapy. I suggested she had made an important discovery both personally and professionally, if indeed her choice of movement therapy came from this early experience, and that we consider how this might have something to do with the patient. Given her experience and the knowledge she already had about herself, including this experience of being tied to a bed, my guess was that the patient had evoked something in Wendy that touched both their stories.

I suggested she move again this time as if she were her patient but to add the idea of being 'tied up' and see what happened. She took a moment in the space to centre herself, then stood with her eyes closed and her arms wrapped around her, swaying slightly. Rather than evolving a story through movement from memories in her inner world, she appeared to be in a moving state of thought. She continued this physical ruminating, so to speak, for a couple of minutes, then sat down to put her reflections into words.

She realised she had identified with her patient in the dream. The patient felt 'tied' to her husband through financial need which had little basis in reality, as she would have been perfectly able to get work but thought she preferred a life of shopping and social events. We managed to untangle some of the story of how Wendy and her patient both had resentments around money – particularly money controlled or given by men. They both had more choices than they were exercising: the one to earn her own money if she so wished, the other to understand how her adult choices were influenced by her early experience. It is interesting to think about how I might have explored these matters in supervision; however, my judgement was that this was better placed in her therapy. The latter piece of work was not in the remit, or container, of our supervision and I assume she took it back to her own therapy just as I considered my relationship to money in my self-analysis after the session.

The theme of money was 'reflected' (Mattinson, 1975, p. 13) throughout these interweaving stories. Wendy had 'forgotten' to pay me that month. When we discussed it she 'admitted' to feeling envious of me and my work: she wanted to be in my position of receiving payment rather than in her position of giving it. Interestingly her patient, who was paying a reduced fee, often lost the cheque she was supposed to give Wendy on a monthly basis. We considered the implications of withholding money from someone to whom one owes something, to whom one may feel beholden. She realised that she needed to consider her relationship to paying me in order to open up the possibility for her patient to think about her paying practices. Wendy mused about her word 'admitting' and concluded that she felt uncomfortable about the possible hostility behind this withholding or, to put it in its aggressive form, stealing. She played with the slow motion walking again, exploring what she found to be a character of 'politely floating over' uncomfortable movements of tension and contortion. This brought her to a deeper consideration of the parallels between the stories of her patient and herself.

Thinking about her use of the word 'admitting' gave us a process of understanding that her withholding payment to me echoed her patient's withholding money from her. Later I realised that my own story around the theme of withholding had been deepened through this event in my supervision work. The reasons for this withholding were different for each of us but the emotional dynamic of expressed hostility was similar. Our mental and physical thinking began a process of understanding and change in her ability to *hold* the agreed boundaries of the contract with her patient. My understanding of her, my and the patient's relationship to the external reality of money deepened.

Lett (1993) notes that 'To exclude the natural progression into self-exploration would be to prevent understandings of fundamental importance to the therapist' (p. 374). This 'importance' may be personal and professional, informing the supervisee about herself as well as her patient, as in Wendy's story above. The *container* of being a supervision process rather than a personal therapy process can keep the appropriate focus and integrity of the work between the supervisor and the supervisee. Thus any material brought into the supervision session may be used to understand what might be going on between the patient and the supervisee or the supervisor and the supervisee, sometimes with echoes in the supervisor's journey as well.

Conclusion

There are many rooms in the house of one supervision story. The house would have a kind of Hogwarts' character with 'doors that weren't really doors at all, but solid walls just pretending' (Rowling, 1997, p. 98). Similarly, the supervision process adapts to the dynamic relationships between the three growing inhabitants. In wandering through each other's rooms, cohabiting in some, visiting in others and learning how to accompany and be accompanied down dangerous corridors, these three learn to understand more of their lives' events and develop a 'resilience' (Johnson, 1998) to the impact of those events. Each individual learns from the experience of her own history and that of the other two. Each pair within the triangle touches and is touched by the presence of the third person in the triangle: the patient–supervisee pair are witnessed by the supervisor, the supervisee–supervisor's work has a direct effect on the environment in which the patient moves and thinks, the patient–supervisor pair learn and affect each other indirectly through the supervisee.

Movement is a form of thinking and creative expression that informs and forms the process between these three people. The 'arts/play-space' (Johnson, 1998) of dance movement lies alongside the conscious and unconscious processes at the overlapping centre between patient, supervisor and supervisee. The commitment and effort of the three individuals engaging in one process of supervision enables each one to become more properly who she is; learning from and contributing to the growth of the other two.

Notes

1 I have also worked as a supervisor for training programmes in dance movement and drama therapy where I am clinically responsible and an assessor for the work of the supervisee. This results in a different basis for the relationship between supervisor and supervisee; one where the latter is more safe but sometimes more anxious than the qualified professional who continues with supervision.
2 Where facts make it impossible to keep the individual anonymous the person whose story is told has seen this writing and agreed to its being published.
3 I have known quite punitive and controlling supervision situations which were not helpful to either supervisee or patient. The former became so fearful of doing anything incorrect that the therapy almost stood still. We can only speculate about the experience of the patient but, in one case I know of, the patient broke off the therapy, saying she felt it was unsafe to continue.
4 Therapy can take place without supervision just as a child can grow up without two parents. However, this is often very difficult for those involved.
5 Tom Ogden goes on to discuss *containing/container* as a kind of thinking process (Bion, 1983) but I will take a far more concrete and literal use of this word.

Acknowledgements

Thanks to Rob Hain for the two diagrams (Figures 11.1 and 11.2), and to Jane Puddy for her unflinching support and thought in reading and commenting on this chapter.

References

Bion, W. (1983) *Experiences in Groups*. London: Tavistock Press.
Bloom, K. (2006) *The Embodied Self: Movement and Psychoanalysis*. London: Karnac.
Casement, P. (1985) *On Learning from the Patient*. London: Routledge.
Cavell, M. (1998) 'Triangulation, one's own mind and objectivity', *International Journal of Psycho-analysis*, 79(3), pp. 449–467.
Clarke, I. (2001) 'Supervision in dance/movement therapy', *E-Motion*, 13(3), pp. 3–5.
Johnson, D.R. (1998) 'On the therapeutic action of the creative arts therapies: the psychodynamic model', *The Arts in Psychotherapy*, 25(2), pp. 85–99.
Lett, W. (1993) 'Therapist creativity: the arts of supervision', *The Arts in Psychotherapy*, 20, pp. 371–386.
Mattinson, J. (1975) *The Reflection Process in Casework Supervision*. London: Institute of Marital Studies Tavistock.
Ogden, T. (2005a) 'On holding and containing, being and dreaming'. In: D. Birksted-Breen (ed.) *This Art of Psychoanalysis*. London: New Library of Psychoanalysis.
—— (2005b) 'On psychoanalytic supervision', *International Journal of Psycho-analysis*, 86(5), pp. 1265–1280.
Payne, H. (2001) 'Authentic movement and supervision', *E-Motion*, 13(4), pp. 4–7.
Rowling, J.K. (1997) *Harry Potter and the Philosopher's Stone*. London: Bloomsbury Publishing.

Searles, H. (1955) 'Informational value of the supervisor's emotional experiences', *Psychiatry*, 18, pp. 135–146.

Solomon, H.M. (1997) 'The ethics of supervision: developmental and archetypal perspectives'. In: E. Christopher and H. Solomon (eds) *Contemporary Jungian Clinical Practice*. London: Karnac.

Appendix

International professional associations

Art Therapy Italiana
Via Barberia 13
40123 Bologna
Italy
Email: associazione@arttherapyit.org
www.arttherapy.it

Austrian Association for Dance Therapy (Oesterreichischer Berufsverband
fuer Tanztherapie)
Dr Ursula Lischke
Alser Strasse 28
1090 Wien
Austria
Tel: 0043 7612 88672

American Dance Therapy Association (ADTA)
ADTA National Office
Suite 230
2000 Century Plaza
Columbia
ML 21044
USA
Tel: 410 997 4040
Fax: 410 997 4048
www.adta.org

Association for Dance Movement Therapy in the United Kingdom
(ADMT.UK)
The Administrator
ADMT.UK

32 Meadfoot Lane
Torquay
Devon TQ1 2BW
UK
Email: queries@admt.org.uk
www.admt.org.uk

Dance Therapy Association of Australia (DTAA)
PO Box 641
Carlton South
VIC 3053
Australia
Tel: 0419 531 218
Fax: (613) 9598 0636
Email: data@alphalink.com.au

Dance Therapy Association of Finland
Suomen Tanssiterapiayh distys ry
PL 1366
FIN-00101 Helsinki
Finland
www.tanssiterapia.net

International Dance Therapy Institute of Australia (IDTIA)
PO Box 274
Elsternwick
Melbourne
VIC 3185
Australia
Tel: (613) 9578 7109
Email: mbraban@bigpond.com

IDTIA studio
Danceworks Studio
29 Macquarie Street
Prahan
VIC 3181
Australia
Tel: (613) 9578 7109
Email: mbraban@bigpond.com

Japanese Dance Therapy Association (JDTA)
Tokyo Welfare Special School
2-7-20 Seisinchou Edogawaku

Tokyo 134-0087
Japan
Tel and fax: 81 3 5605 8283

Dance movement therapy professional training programmes (UK)

Goldsmiths College
University of London
New Cross
London SE14 6NW
Tel: 020 7919 7171
www.goldsmiths.ac.uk

Roehampton University
Erasmus House
Roehampton Lane
London SW15 5PU
Tel: 020 8392 3000
www.roehampton.ac.uk

University of Derby
Mickleover
Derby
DE3 5GX
UK
Tel: 01332 514323
www.derby.ac.uk

International professional training programmes

Austria

InTAT – Institut fuer Tanz- und Ausdruckstherapie
Dr Elisabeth Gruenberger
Kaiserstrasse 6/2 37
1070 Wien
Austria
Tel: 0043(0) 676 31 22 515

China

Dr Tony Yu Zhou

China Europe Dance Therapy Program (CEDT)
Inspirees International
China
Email: info@inspirees.com
www.dancetherapy.ch

Germany

Deutsche Gesellschaft fuer Tanztherapie
Koenigsberger Strasse 60
50259 Pulheim
Renate Gronemeyer
Tel: 02234 83008
Email: dgt.office@t-online.de
www.dgt-tanztherapie.de

Frankfurter Institut fuer Tanztherapie F.I.T.T. e.V.
Sybille Scharf-Widder
Schneckenhofstrasse 20H2
60596 Frankfurt/Main
Tel: 069 616058
Email: info@tanztherapie-fitt.de
www.tanztherapiefitt.de

Langen Institut
Fachschule fuer Dance Alive und Tanz- und Ausdruckstherapie
c/o Praeha Bildungszentrum
Rathausstrasse 20–22
50169 Kerpen (Horrem)
Tel: 02273 93250
Email: info@langen-institut.de
www.langen-institut.de

pantarhei-institut
Irmgard Halstrup
Anke Teigeler
Hauptstrasse 29
37083 Goettingen
Tel: 0551 7908920
Email: info@pantarhei-institut.de
www.pantarhei-institut.de

Tanztherapie Zentrum Berlin
Am Tempelhofer Berg 7d
10965 Berlin
Germany
Email: Imke.Fiedler@t-online.de
www.tanztherapie-zentrum-berlin.de

Zentrum fuer Tanz und Therapie
S. Bender
Geyerspergerstrasse 25
80689 Muenchen
Tel: 089 54662431
Fax: 089 54662432
Email: info@tanztherapie-zentrum.de
www.tanztherapie-zentrum.de

Italy

Dr Rosa Marie Govoni
Art Therapy Italiana
Via Barberia 13
40123 Bologna
Italy
Email: r.m.govoni@freesurf.ch; rosamariagovoni@tiscalinet.it

Netherlands

Codarts University of Professional Arts Education
Annalies Schrijnen-van Gastel
Postgraduate Programme in Dance Therapy
Kruisplein 26
3012 CC Rotterdam
The Netherlands
Email: codarts@codarts.nl

Hogeschool voor Muziek en Dans
Kruisplein 26
3012 CC Rotterdam
The Netherlands
www.hmd.nl

Poland

Poland Instytut DMT
Polski Instytut Psychoterapii Tancem I Ruchem
Ul. Batorego 37/167
02 -591 Warszawa
Poland
www.instytutdmt.pl

Portugal

University of Lisbon
Isabel Figueira
Portugal
Email: isabelfigueira@hotmail.com; dance_therapy_portugal@hotmail.com

Slovenia

University of Ljubljana
Dr Breda Kroflic
Associate Professor Convenor of Postgraduate Arts Therapies Education
Faculty of Education
Kardeljeva pl. 16
Si- 1000 Ljubljana
Slovenia
Email: breda.kroflic@guest.arness.si

Spain

Autonomous University of Barcelona
Heidrun Panhofer
C/d'en Grassot 26, 3, 1
08025 Barcelona
Spain
Email: info@en-e-mocion.com

Switzerland

Institut fuer Bewegungsanalyse
Cary Rick
5728 Gontenschwil
Tel: 0041(0) 61 8430508
www.bewegungsanalyse.net

Sweden

University College of Dance
Prof. Erna Gronlund
Sweden
Email: erna.gronlund@telia.com; erna.caresia.gronlund@danshogskolan.se

USA

Antioch University New England
40 Avon Street
Keene
NH 03431-3552
USA
Tel: 1 800 553 8920

Columbia College Chicago
Susan Imus
600 South Michigan Avenue
Chicago, IL 60605
USA
Tel: 1 312 344 7697
Email: pholmquist@columbia.edu

Drexel University
Hahnemann Center City Campus
1505 Race Street Ms 501
Philadelphia, PA 19102
USA
Tel: 1 215 762 6921
Email: theuges@drexel.edu

Laban Institute for Movement Studies (LIMS)
520 Eighth Avenue
Room 304
New York, NY 10018
USA
Tel: 1 212 643 8888
Email: info@limsonline.org

Lesley University
29 Everett Street
Cambridge

Massachusetts 02138
USA
Tel: 1 617 868 9600
Email: info@lesley.edu

Moving the Self Psychotherapy Center
3010 Mitchellville Road
Suite 104
Bowie
MD 20716
USA
Tel: 1 (301) 390 2742
Email: badreezyuh@verizon.net

Naropa University
Boulder, Colorado
USA
Tel: 1 303 546 3500
Email: webreg@naropa.edu

Pratt Institute
200 Willoughby Avenue
Brooklyn
New York 11205
USA
Tel: 1 718 636 3669
Fax: 1 718 636 3670

Professional journals and newsletters

American Journal of Dance Therapy
Suite 230
2000 Century Plaza
Columbia
ML 21044
USA
www.springerlink.com/link

German Journal for Dance Therapy
Forum Tanztherapie
DGT
Koenigsberger Strasse 60
50259 Pulheim
Germany

Tel: 02234 83008
www.dgt-tanztherapie.de

International Journal of Body, Movement and Dance in Psychotherapy
University of Hertfordshire
Meridian House
32 The Common
Hatfield
Herts AL10 0NZ
UK
Tel: 01707 285861
Email: BMDP@herts.ac.uk
www.tandf.co.uk/journals/titles/17432979.asp

The Arts in Psychotherapy
Customer Service Department
6277 Sea Harbor Drive
Orlando
FL 32887-4800
USA
Tel: 407 345 4020
Fax: 407 363 1354
Email: usjcs@elsevier.com
www.elsevier.com/locate/artpsycho

Author Index

Adler, J. xi, 29, 30, 34, 35, 39, 40, 44, 47, 52, 58, 59, 60, 91, 101, 111, 112, 116, 153
Alexandris, A. 30
Allstetter, N.S. 59
Alvarez, A. 44
American Psychoanalytic Association 46, 74
Aposhyan, S. 44
Argelander, H. 135
Arlow, J.A. 74
Aron, L. 101
Atkinson, P. 74

Bakthine, M. 88
Balint, M. 14, 118, 119, 121, 123, 125, 127, 128, 133, 134, 135, 136
Bartenieff, I. 44
Beard, C. 30
Bender, S. 135
Bernard, J. 58
Bernstein 34, 45, 53, 59, 123, 128, 129, 134, 135, 136
Bernstein, P.L. 45, 59, 135
Berrol, C. 45
Best, P. 59, 60, 151, 153
Beucke-Galm, M. 135
Beumer, U.
Bick, E. 45, 101
Binder, J.L. 59
Bion, W. 45, 101, 166
Bloom, K. 166
Bollas, C. 45, 101
Bolognini, S. 45
Bonovitz, C. 45
Bovensiepen, G. 101
Bram, A.D. 45
Brandau, H. 135

Brems, C. 116
Buber, M. 30
Bush De Ahumada, L. 47

Caldwell, C. 45
Carroll, M. 15, 116
Casement, P. 15, 30, 166
Cecchin, G. 59
Chaiklin, S. 59
Chodorow, J. 45, 59, 101, 116, 135
Clarke, I. 15, 166
Coffey, A. 74
Condon, W.S. 30
Connella, J.A. 45
Cooper, M. 23, 28, 30
Corradi, M. 101
Cox, M. 30
Creative Problem Solving (CPS) 149

Dantlgraber, J. 135
Dattilio, F. 116
Daveson, B. 74
Davis, M. 74
De la Noe, Q. 88
Deikman, A.J. 45
Dithrich, C.W. 74
Doehrman, M.J. 74
Dosamantes, I. 45, 74
Dosamantes-Alperson, E. 30, 135
Driver, C. 45
Durkin, J. 117

Eck, C.D. 135
Edward, J. 74
Edwards, D. 16, 152
Elizur, J. 116
Ellis, M.V. 59
Ellis, R. 152

Erikson, E. 45
Evans, K. 152

Fairbairn, W.R. 59
Fatzer, G. 135
Federman, D.J. x, 13, 49, 50, 52, 54, 56, 58, 60
Feldman, B. 101
Ferro, A. 45
Ferstl, H. 136
Fiedler, I. 135, 172
Figueira, I. x, 13, 76, 78, 80, 82, 84, 86, 88, 173
Fogassi, L. 31
Fonagy, P. 35, 45, 89, 92, 101
Foulkes, S.H. 135
Foulks, E.F. 35, 45
Freud, A. 45
Freud, S. 75, 135
Frick, W. 116
Friedlander, M.L. 59
Friedman, S. 151
Fulkerson, Mary 25, 29, 30

Gaber, L.B. 13
Gaddini, R. 45
Gallese, V. 31
Gendlin, E. 24, 28, 30, 39, 45
Gergely, G. 45
Giannoni, M. 92, 101
Giesecke, M. 119
Godbout, C. 36, 45
Goldberg, C. 63, 75
Goodyear, R. 50, 58
Grater, H.A. 50, 59
Gray, L.A. 59
Grunebaum, H. 69, 75
Guntrip, H. 128, 136

Halprin, D. 145, 148, 152
Hantoot, M.S. 67, 75
Hartley, L. 65, 75
Haugh, S. 30, 31
Hawkins, P. 6, 15, 30, 38, 46, 72, 75
Heidegger, M. 70, 75
Heimann, P. 34, 46, 129, 136
Herman, J. 30
Hersen, M. 30
Hess, A.K. 50, 59
Hewson, J. 137, 138, 152
Holmes, J. 89, 101

Hosseini, K. 30
Hutto, B. 69, 75

Itzhaky, H. 67, 75

Jacobs, M. 16, 31
Jacobs, T.J. 46
Jasper, M. 75
Jennings, S. 152
Johnson, D.R. 166
Johnson, M. 30
Jones, P. 152
Jumaa, M. 75
Jung, C. 152
Jurist, E. 45

Kadushin, A. 59
Kernberg, O. 136
Kestenberg Amighi, J. 46
Kestenberg, J.S. 46
Kestenberg, Kestenberg Movement Profile (KMP) 46
Klein, M. 46
Knill, P. 116
Knox, J. 101
Kohut, H. 136

La Barre, F. 46
Laban (Laban Movement Analysis, LMA) 34, 136
Laban, R. 46
Ladany, N. 17
Lakoff, G. 30
Lane, G. 59
Lett, W. 16, 116, 152, 166
Leventhal, M. 116
Levine, S. 110, 114, 115, 116
Lewis, D. 44
Lewis, P. 30, 46, 59, 152
Lippenmeier, N. 136
Loman, S. 46, 152
Lucchi, B. 101

Mahler, M. 128, 136
Marshall, S. 153
Martin, E. 46
Martin, J. 152
Mason, B. 152
Mattinson, J. 20, 30, 164, 166
McCall, D. 40, 46
McDougall, J. 89, 99, 102
McNiff, S. 141, 152

Meekums, B. 30, 75, 152
Meltzer, D. 46
Merry, T. 30, 31
Milner, M. 34, 46
Mitchell, P. 116
Mitrani, J. 89, 102
Mollen, P. 116
Mollon, P. 62, 63, 75
Momigliano, N.L. 34, 46
Moore, C-L. 141, 144, 145, 153
Moro, M.R. 80, 81, 83, 88
Mouchenick, Y. 88
Musicant, S. 40, 46

Nadeau, L. 88
National Health Service (NHS) 9
Nelson, M.L. 59
Nikolitsa, A. 40, 46

O'Connor, J. 145
Oberhoff, B. 119, 127, 134, 136
Ogden, T.H. 21, 22, 31, 36, 46, 54, 59,
    60, 157, 166
Oliver, C. 137, 139, 150, 153

Pallaro, P. 7, 12, 31, 48, 51, 52, 53, 54, 56,
    57, 58, 59, 60, 62, 64, 65, 76, 77, 89,
    101, 102, 144, 153
Pallasch, W. 119, 136
Panhofer, H. xii, 13, 61, 62, 64, 66, 68,
    70, 72, 74, 173
Parker, G. 54, 60, 139, 151, 153
Payne, H. xii, xiii, xiv, xvii, 1, 2, 3, 4, 6, 8,
    10, 12, 14, 16, 28, 30, 31, 52, 60, 138,
    141, 144, 152, 153, 156, 171
Pearmain, R. 23, 24, 31
Perach, D. 117
Pine, F. 136
Polanyi, M. 31
Psychokinetic Imagery Model (PIM) 145

Racker, H. 34, 47, 129, 136
Ramseyer, F. 23, 31
Rappe-Giesecke, K. 119, 133, 135, 136
Reason, P. 72, 75
Reber, A. 116
Reber, E. 116
Reichelt, S. 60
Relational Creative Processes Model
    (RCPM) x, 137–42, 146–51
Resnik, S. 36, 47
Ribner, D. 75

Rizzolatti, G. 24, 31
Robert, B. 59
Robin, P. 45
Robutti, A. 34, 46
Rogers, C. 25, 107, 116
Ross, M. 31
Rousseau, C. 84, 88
Rowan, J. 18, 25, 26, 27, 31
Rowling, J.K. 165, 166
Rubinstein, G. 51, 60
Rycroft, C. 63, 64, 65, 75
Ryle, A. 31

Samuels, A. 21, 31, 102
Samuels, S. 136
Sander, W.L. 24, 30
Sarnat, J.E. 36, 47
Scharff, D.E. 34, 47
Scharff, J.S. 47
Schavarien, J. 153
Scheflen, A. 31
Schilder, P.F. 47
Schmais, C. 59
Schmid, P. 25, 31
Schoop, T. 65, 75, 111, 113, 116
Schore, A. 35, 47, 89, 102
Schott-Billmann, F. 108, 116
Schutz, W. 136
Schwartz, F. 45
Schwartz-Salant, N. 135
Searles, H.F. 70, 75, 130, 136, 154, 159,
    161, 167
Segal, H. 21, 31, 34, 47, 92, 102
Seibel, J. 34, 36, 38, 39, 44
Seymour, J. 153
Shaw, R. 28, 31, 144, 153
Shipton, G. 116
Shlien, J. 22, 23, 25, 31
Shohet, R. 6, 15, 30, 38, 46
Shorr, J.E. 45
Silvano, E. 59
Singer, D.L. 128, 134, 135, 136
Skjerva, J. 50, 60
Sobel, G.E. 45
Solomon, H.M. 156, 167
Sossin, M. K. 34, 46
Soth, M. 149, 153
Sowa, A. 34, 47
Speedy, J. 140, 153
Spiegel, D. 69, 75
Spinelli, E. 112, 116, 144, 153
Stanton-Jones, K. 65, 75

Stein, M. 135
Stern, D.N. 34, 35, 47, 136
Stewart, J. 36, 47
Strupp, H.H. 50, 59
Sturm, G. 86, 87, 88
Sullivan, B. 116
Sullivan, H.S. 60
Sumerel, M. 70, 75
Symmington, J. & N. 102

Target, M. 45
Theilgaard, A. 22, 24, 30
Thomas, M. 47
Tselikas-Portmann, E. 59, 138, 153

Ungar, V.R. 37, 47

Van der Kolk, B. 31
Vaslamatzis, G. 21, 22, 30, 31

Wadeson, H. 114, 117
Wadsworth Hervey, L.W. 138, 153

Walker, J.A. 5, 17
Wallerstein, R.S. 51, 60
Watkins, C.E. 50, 59, 60
Whitehouse-Stark, M. 30, 34, 44, 47, 52, 58, 59, 60, 101, 153
Wilkinson, M. 60, 89, 102
Wilson, J.P. 22, 30
Winnicott, D.W. 31, 47, 60, 102, 153
Wolman, W. 112, 117
Wrye, H.K. 102
Wyman-McGinty, W. xiii, 3, 14, 29, 32, 34, 35, 39, 47, 89, 90, 92, 94, 95, 96, 97, 98, 100, 102

Yamamoto, K. 141, 144, 145, 153
Yerushalmi, H. 37, 48, 49, 60
Yorke, V. 40, 48
Young, M. xii, xiii, 14, 57, 61, 64, 65, 69, 83, 103, 104, 106, 108, 110, 112, 114, 116, 148, 149, 159, 160, 163

Zohar, D. 26, 27, 32

Subject index

accent 77, 78
active imagination 52, 97, 101
active listening 146
active 31, 40, 51, 52–4, 72, 95, 97, 98, 101, 122, 128, 137, 138, 140, 146
adaptive 67
adolescent 62, 64
affect attunement 127
affect regulation 45, 47, 89, 102
affective 14, 19, 23, 24, 28, 35, 53, 66, 89, 91, 92, 94, 96, 100, 125
aims 2, 11, 56, 106, 111
alliance 2, 3, 5, 6, 7, 15, 16, 35, 37, 38
alone 24, 25, 31, 49, 60, 71, 85
ambivalence 132
analyst 5, 21, 30, 49, 74, 128, 129, 134
analytical third 54
anger 41, 67, 80, 99, 100, 123, 132, 162
anxiety 7, 21, 51, 65, 68, 77, 96, 99, 103
anxious 72, 103, 111, 166
appreciative inquiry 140, 141
art form 115, 157
art therapy 33, 44, 114, 148, 152, 168, 172
artistic 137, 138, 141, 153, 157
arts therapy xiv, 116, 117, 153, 155, 157, 158
assess 4, 7, 50, 78, 96, 97
assessment 7, 14, 50, 62, 67
assimilation 131
associating 127
attachment 89, 92, 101
attentiveness 156
attunement 14, 23, 27, 89, 91, 92, 96, 107, 125, 127, 128
authentic 3, 14, 16, 28–32, 34, 39, 40, 42, 44, 46, 47, 52, 53, 56–60, 90, 91, 93, 95, 97, 99–102, 116, 118, 126, 134, 144, 153, 156, 162, 166
authenticity 67, 112, 111

authoritarian 103
authority 49, 103, 112, 131
awareness 4, 5, 14, 24, 28, 33–5, 38, 39, 42, 44, 51, 52, 61, 63–5, 67, 70, 85, 86, 89–93, 95–100, 103–6, 108, 111, 122, 125, 129, 132, 143–5, 150, 157, 159

becoming 3, 15, 25, 39, 44, 60, 81, 86, 91, 94, 100, 116, 152
behaviour 31, 41, 50, 58, 67, 68, 106, 112, 134, 146, 154, 160
being with 53
bodily felt experience 41, 90, 129
body image 39, 93, 96
body shape 76, 105, 109, 111
borderline 41, 44, 94, 95, 136
boundaries 9, 25, 26, 36, 90, 95, 96, 143, 146, 149, 165
breath 41, 53, 64, 93

catalyst 12, 128
childhood 45, 103, 114, 123, 126
choice 61, 66, 80, 85, 86, 112, 160, 163
choreography 40, 135, 136
client-therapist relationship 13, 14, 118, 124, 125, 126, 129, 130, 131, 133
clinical practice xvii, 2, 4, 8, 10, 12, 13, 28, 34, 47, 58, 61, 65, 68, 73, 78, 87, 102, 139, 167
cognitive 20, 31, 51, 79, 101, 127, 149
collaborative 10, 151
compassion 91, 92
competence 8, 10, 16, 66, 119, 124, 132
complexes 90
complexity 4, 27, 35, 67, 73, 139, 141, 150, 154
compliance 131
complementary 19, 74, 120, 121, 129

concordant 29, 120, 123, 126, 129
confidence 10, 16, 103, 112, 113, 114, 138, 162
conflict 6, 68, 72, 78, 112, 120, 131
congruent 57, 97
consciousness 26, 27, 29, 39, 42, 61, 62, 65, 144
containing 14, 21, 22, 30, 62, 63, 77, 89, 90, 113, 150, 155, 157, 159, 160, 166
conversation 5, 146, 147, 166
co-researchers 138, 151
counselling xiv, xvii, 2, 5, 6, 9, 10, 14, 15, 16, 17, 23, 28, 29, 31, 60, 89, 116
course 6, 13, 14, 31, 34, 37, 39, 49, 61, 68, 69, 70, 77, 78, 84, 90, 103–7, 109, 114, 115
creative xiv, xvii, 1, 11, 16, 17, 26, 28, 30, 31, 33, 34, ,35, 37, 38, 40, 43, 44, 45, 52, 54, 55, 58–78, 80, 83, 104, 110, 124, 137, 138–43, 146, 148–53, 155, 165, 166
creatively 33, 152
critical reflections 38, 149
cube 39
culture 5, 35, 45, 47, 48, 102
cultural 4, 12, 45, 64, 65, 69, 78, 79, 86, 87

debriefing 104, 106, 112–14
defence 63, 92, 94, 123, 126, 141
definitions 2, 3, 13, 21, 22, 119
dependency 91, 96
depressed 94, 97, 125, 162, 163
depression 16, 94, 120, 121
desire 25, 36, 40, 84, 85, 86, 94, 96, 98, 100, 102, 153
development 3–6, 9–12, 17, 27, 28, 31, 34, 35, 36, 39, 45–7, 49, 50, 52, 54, 58, 60, 80, 81, 89, 92, 96, 102, 115, 116, 124, 128
developmental 5, 34, 37, 39, 46, 95, 128, 132, 138, 155, 157, 167,
dialectical 49, 54
dialogical communication 76
dialogue 28, 31, 46, 51, 53, 54, 60, 65, 76, 77, 87, 97, 133, 154, 157
diary 73
didactic 2, 51
dissociated 4, 35
drama xiv, xvi, 59, 103, 111, 113, 115, 154, 166

dramatic 83, 114, 129
drawing 12, 70, 114, 115, 146, 147, 149
dream 65, 97, 99, 102, 152, 163, 164
dyad 37, 41, 42, 92, 94, 102, 111, 114, 154

edge 9, 43, 95
educational 7, 51, 85, 119, 142
effort 23, 39, 69, 77, 105, 106, 115, 134, 165
ego 49, 94, 96, 102, 129
embodiment 13, 23, 31, 102, 120, 122, 124, 125, 143, 144, 150, 153
embodied self xvi, 2, 10, 166
    mind xvi, 30, 60
    knowing 18
    also see self
emotional 6, 7, 20, 21, 24, 35, 36, 38–40, 47, 51, 52, 53, 60, 63, 64, 66, 69–71, 79, 81, 82, 91–3, 96, 102, 121, 123, 125, 126–7, 129–32, 141, 144, 145, 148, 161, 165, 167
empathy 4, 14, 18, 21, 22–6, 29, 30, 31, 35, 45, 52, 53, 57, 89–92, 96, 97, 107, 118, 121, 125, 129, 135
enactment 81, 114, 125, 126, 127
energy 19, 93, 107, 112, 143, 149, 161
    energetic 53
engagement 8, 37, 39, 143, 144, 148, 150, 151
epistemology 139
ethics 167
ethnic 35
expression 8, 21, 8, 14, 25, 33, 34, 39, 42, 52–4, 60, 70, 90, 92, 97, 104, 108, 110, 116, 125, 137, 139, 141, 143, 145, 147–51, 153
expressive 11, 28, 50, 59, 70, 100, 110, 114, 116, 146, 152
eye contact 61, 66, 104, 108

fantasy 57, 97
father 65, 74, 85, 123, 126, 127, 155
fatigue 120
fear 6, 8, 21, 41, 42, 66, 67, 71, 83, 91, 95, 98, 99, 103, 111, 113, 132, 162
feedback 5, 7, 67, 73, 104, 118, 122, 126, 127, 132
feeling 6, 14, 19, 22, 23, 25, 26, 39, 41, 43, 49, 51, 52, 63, 69, 70, 73, 79, 86, 89–91, 94, 96–100, 109, 110, 122, 123, 129, 140, 159, 160, 162, 164

flow 22, 25, 28, 39, 41, 105, 106, 108, 109, 111, 120, 121, 122, 125, 133, 141
forgotten 13, 61–5, 67, 69–71, 73, 75, 82, 112, 164
frozen 57, 79, 83, 85, 99
fundamentals 34, 39, 58

genuine 111
gesture 23, 33, 38, 44, 79, 164
goal 9, 66, 115, 138
grounding 19, 122
group dynamics 62, 107, 109
group models 13
groups, Balint 118, 129, 132, 134

healing 33, 36, 39, 40, 101, 107, 108, 115, 116
health professionals 119, 124
helplessness 62, 63, 67, 69, 91, 133
here and now 122, 142, 148, 149
holding 4, 22, 24, 28, 36, 41, 64, 81, 82, 93, 111, 140, 141, 154, 157, 161, 166
humanistic 6, 26, 60, 106, 116
humanity 96, 111

idealization 131, 132
identity 49, 50, 64, 67, 69, 77, 85, 87, 124, 132, 133, 156
identity, cultural 74
image 39, 40, 42, 43, 47, 68, 85, 92, 93, 94, 96, 108, 121, 111, 114, 122, 123, 128, 149
   also see body image
imagination 4, 33, 35, 44, 45, 52, 55, 58, 59, 89, 92, 97
improvisation 18, 62, 66, 143, 148, 154, 162
improvise 66, 110
impulse 25, 43
individual supervision xvii, 8, 9, 13, 69, 70, 74, 113, 115, 119, 128, 131, 134, 137, 154
individuation 132
infant 21–3, 32, 45, 47, 91, 92, 96, 128, 136, 155
in-session supervision 3, 10, 13, 103–5, 107, 109, 111, 113, 114, 115, 117
insight 5, 6, 13, 14, 15, 19, 22, 40, 51, 54, 58, 63, 64, 70, 73, 106, 148
institution 36–8, 43, 68, 103, 113, 133, 138, 145
institutional 10, 14, 86, 118, 133

integration 8, 12, 29, 33, 65–7, 78, 80, 85, 95, 100, 113
integrative xiv, 6, 12, 119, 133, 152, 153
intellectually 80, 103, 104, 115
interactive 62, 122, 129, 137, 146, 151, 154
inter-creative 137, 138, 142, 146, 147, 149, 150
interfere 36, 78, 84, 132, 133
internal reality 148
internalised 28
interpretation 14, 25, 27, 31, 36, 45, 46, 91, 121, 138, 144, 163
interpretive analysis 138
inter-relational 54
intersubjective 45, 54, 58, 62, 74, 89, 144, 155
intersubjectivity 28, 54
interview 65, 112, 116, 138
intra-psychic 95, 97, 98, 100
intuition 21, 22, 31, 115
iterative 143, 144, 150

kinaesthetic empathy 4, 14, 24, 35, 89, 91, 118, 125
kinetic 144, 145
knowledge 4, 10, 12, 21, 23, 35, 37, 42, 44, 51, 67, 69, 103, 114, 139, 140, 141, 144, 150, 157, 163

leader 42, 93, 106, 132, 159
learning experience 36, 55
left brain 18, 19, 66
linguistic 19, 66
linking 18, 25–9, 33, 93, 128, 150
logic 13, 29, 141
longing 36, 94, 100
lying 63, 67, 75, 163

mastery 46, 50
meaning 22, 23, 33, 35, 37, 46, 52, 61, 62, 68, 74, 75, 83, 93, 95, 97, 107, 112, 125, 138, 151, 157
memories 56, 152, 164
mentally ill 94
meta view 140
meta-perspective 138, 142
mirroring 3, 11, 23, 92, 96, 97, 98, 104, 108, 109, 128, 131, 138, 161
modelling 55
mother 21, 41, 49, 81, 82, 85, 91, 92, 94, 96, 102, 121, 127, 155

movement patterns 36, 74
mover 42, 52, 90–4, 111, 112, 114
music xiv, xvi, 54, 56, 72, 74, 82, 97, 104, 137, 161, 162
mutism 79
mutual 28, 51, 53, 114, 139, 142

narcissism 136
   narcissistic 67, 94, 160
narrative 11, 46, 51, 54, 62, 72, 137, 139, 153
neurological 4, 35, 149
neurophysiologic 24, 45
neurotic 90, 129, 131
non-judgmental 106
non-logic 141
non-verbal 11, 21, 22, 31, 35, 37, 38, 55, 56, 58, 65, 92, 137, 140, 141
not- knowing 25, 28, 29, 40, 69
noticing 104, 127, 150
novice xviii, 3, 11, 103

object relations 33, 47, 101, 126–8, 135, 136
object relations theory 33, 128
observation 4, 34, 36, 39, 45, 47, 65, 77, 78, 84, 103, 108, 145, 153
observer 7, 54, 55, 145, 159
omnipotence 133
ontological 157
opposite 73
opposites 70, 72, 73, 86
oral 121, 127

parallel process 3, 5, 7, 9, 16, 22, 54, 70, 75, 130
parent 23, 32, 155, 158
   parental 22, 57, 131, 156
participant observer 7, 55, 145
pattern 24, 39, 46, 97, 107, 108, 140
peer 8, 9, 14, 62, 63, 65, 67, 86, 138
perfect 77, 100, 111, 112, 133
performing 24, 144, 159, 162
personal development 6, 36
personal therapy 3, 9, 16, 17, 36, 37, 128, 165
personality 47, 52, 59, 103, 104, 113, 122, 123
perspective 2, 8, 10, 13, 14, 18, 19, 23, 24, 62, 87, 93, 95, 112, 118, 138, 140, 141, 142, 148, 154–6
physical contact 58

physically disabled 115
placement 3, 10, 51, 64, 65, 66, 68, 69, 73, 75, 76, 104, 112, 113
play 6, 9, 16, 19, 26, 34, 37, 38, 40, 41, 43, 65, 72, 81, 83, 85, 108, 110, 124, 133, 143, 146–8, 150, 154, 160, 161, 165
poem 70, 143, 146
   poetry 75
polarity 71
positioning 140, 141, 145
   positions 14, 40, 54, 65, 72, 76, 140, 145, 146, 150, 151
posture 23, 31, 35, 41, 105
potential space 4, 33, 35, 45, 74
power 1, 8, 29, 30, 49, 53, 54, 62, 67, 69, 74, 106, 107, 108, 111, 115, 122, 132, 133, 140, 146, 151
pre-conscious 64
pre-verbal 3, 22, 35, 65
primitive 22, 90, 91, 96, 102, 108, 116
private practice 1, 11, 13, 14, 90, 98, 99, 101, 120, 154, 162
problem 37, 40, 50, 79, 80, 84, 85, 101, 106, 120, 122, 125, 132, 136, 152
process centred 51
processes
   primary 38
   secondary 64
professional development 3, 10, 11, 12, 115, 116
programme centred 51
projection 21, 63, 92, 97, 133
projective identification 16, 21, 22, 31, 41, 46, 92, 95, 97, 99
proprioceptive 35
psychiatry 88
psychic skin 89
psychoanalysis 15, 16, 45, 46, 47, 51, 58, 74, 75, 89, 101, 118, 134, 136, 166
psychoanalytic 6, 14, 44–9, 54, 58, 60, 63, 74, 118, 134–6, 166
psychodrama 6, 62, 63, 64
psychodynamic 2, 3, 6, 7, 11, 21, 23, 26, 31, 33, 43, 51, 59, 62, 94, 122, 129, 137, 139, 148, 150, 151, 155, 156, 166
psychological xiv, xvii, 4, 10, 13, 16, 33, 35, 38, 39, 65, 79, 80, 92, 100, 136, 144, 157
psychology xiv, 9, 15, 16, 30, 32, 45, 47, 48, 54, 59, 60, 75, 89, 96, 101, 102, 116, 135, 136
psychosocial 151

psychotherapy 4, 6, 8–17, 23, 27, 29, 30, 31, 36, 38, 43–7, 49–69, 72, 59–61, 69, 74, 75, 89, 90, 93, 95, 106, 116, 117, 124, 134, 135, 151–3, 166, 175, 176
puberty 64
punishment 57

questionnaires 138

rage 41, 95, 99, 123
rapport 23, 31, 108, 114
rebellion 131, 132
recuperation 61
rediscovering 62, 73
re-enactment 81, 114, 126, 127
    re-enacting 53, 61, 81
reflection 11, 30, 33, 36, 44, 51, 52, 53, 56, 66, 67, 70, 76, 86, 91, 94, 98, 111, 114, 119, 125, 130, 133, 134, 148, 151, 166
reflective 8, 28, 45, 54, 92, 97, 99, 101, 104, 106, 124, 143, 144, 146, 147, 150, 151, 152, 154
reflexive 101, 137, 139, 143, 150, 152, 153
rejection 57, 98
relatedness 138
relaxation 104, 108
representation 63, 65, 69, 92, 98, 131, 141, 143, 150, 151
repression, repressed 4, 35, 64, 65, 121, 126
research 2, 4–6, 9, 11, 12, 14, 15–18, 24, 28, 30, 31, 44, 47, 40, 59, 74, 96, 102, 124, 135–9, 142–4, 150, 152, 153
resistance 62, 66–8, 70, 75, 85, 86, 121, 123–6, 130
reunion 96
rhythm 39, 56, 66, 105, 107, 108, 148, 163
rhythmic 27, 53, 108, 113
ritual 83, 105, 107, 108, 113
rivalry 67, 124
role, professional 14, 118, 124
role play 154

safe 2, 6, 8–10, 33, 35, 41, 43, 52, 74, 82, 84, 85, 86, 87, 102, 113, 135, 136, 169
safety 9, 16, 39, 43, 67, 91, 98, 132
school 6, 33, 46, 64, 78, 79, 80, 82, 84, 85, 86, 87, 102, 113, 135, 136, 169
secondary working through 56
secure 26, 35, 90, 96, 101
see, seeing, seen 2, 19, 41, 62, 94, 108
self – directed 42, 90, 93

self awareness 4, 5, 51, 67
    care 13, 29
    doubts 7, 9
    efficacy 4, 5
    supervision 3, 59, 152
sensation 21, 23, 38, 39, 41, 52, 53, 90, 93, 129, 133, 144
sensory 19, 20, 128, 140, 144, 145
sensory information 19, 140
separation 25, 26, 96, 131, 132
sexual 29, 30, 46, 64, 123, 126, 159
    abuse 29, 30, 123
    sexuality 19, 64, 160
shadow 4, 45, 77, 101
    movement 77
shame 100
shape 37, 39, 41, 76, 105, 109, 111, 115, 122, 162, 163
sharing 2, 22, 37, 56, 58, 114
skills
    communication 104, 108, 110
    motor 104, 106, 108, 109
    personal 104, 108, 110, 156
    social 104, 106, 108, 109
    supervisors' 39
    technical 78
soma 34, 153
somatic countertransference 4, 9, 14, 18, 60, 22, 27, 29, 30, 31, 38, 47, 89–92, 94, 99, 102, 118, 129, 134, 135
    intelligence 13, 18
space
    interpersonal 101
    safe 33, 43, 52, 92
    personal 77, 97
    potential 4, 33, 39, 45, 74.
    therapeutic 63, 76
spatial 27, 140, 141, 149
split 4, 22, 35, 40, 77, 81, 84, 122, 125, 126, 129
    splitting 63, 95, 97
spontaneous symbolism 13, 18, 19, 20, 22, 25, 26, 27, 29
stages 17, 34, 50, 59, 118, 124, 128
states of mind 3, 46, 89, 90, 91, 92, 95–8, 100
stillness 27, 30, 104, 108, 163
story 31, 53, 54, 72, 73, 79, 81, 107, 110, 146–8, 153, 154, 156, 157, 160, 162–6
stress 8, 83, 87, 98, 100, 118
student xvii, 13, 16, 36, 38, 40, 50, 60, 61, 63–70, 72–8, 84, 85, 103, 116, 156

subjective 54, 67–91, 92, 126, 153
subjectivity 23, 28
sublimation 92
supervisee xviii, 3, 4, 6–10, 13, 16, 18–20,
    22, 26, 28, 29, 36–42, 44, 50, 51, 52, 54,
    55–6, 64, 70, 74, 90, 91, 95, 97, 98, 114,
    116, 119, 125–8, 130, 131, 138, 144–9,
    151, 154, 160–3, 165, 166
supervisor xvii, 2, 3, 5, 6, 7, 8, 10, 13, 15,
    16, 20, 26–9, 33, 34, 36, 37–44, 49–52,
    54–7, 59, 61, 62, 67–70, 72–4, 76, 78,
    80, 82, 84, 87, 97, 104, 110, 112–15,
    110, 127, 128, 130–4, 136–8, 140–3,
    154–60, 165, 166
supervisory frame 35, 36
support xviii, 5, 7, 8, 12, 16, 41, 66,
    119–21, 131–3, 143, 145, 166
symbolic way of relating 91
symbol 19, 20, 34, 47, 53, 89, 94, 135
    symbolism 13, 18–23, 25–9, 31, 53,
    66
synergy 37
syntonic 21, 27
systemic 6, 137, 139, 140, 145, 150, 151,
    153

talk 31, 43, 71, 79, 98, 100, 125, 143, 144,
    146, 149, 155, 160
    -ing 61, 78, 106, 108, 144
teacher 72, 77–9, 81, 103, 111, 158, 161,
    162
techniques 3, 7, 15, 18, 23, 39, 44, 54, 62,
    65, 139, 143, 145, 146, 149
tension flow rhythm 39
text xvii, 12, 71, 72
therapeutic frame 18, 36
therapeutic relationship xiv, 2, 15, 16, 22,
    28, 35, 37, 38, 41, 53, 69, 70, 78, 87, 89,
    120, 141, 155, 161, 178, 106, 108, 144
third perspective 154, 156
tool 35, 66, 103, 114, 115, 118, 141
touch 42, 45, 58, 64, 65, 67, 70, 72, 77, 80,
    85, 91, 121, 144, 149, 163
trainee 1, 5, 6, 10, 14, 17, 28, 29, 45, 50,
    55, 61, 69, 103, 110, 138
training
    DMT xvi, 29, 37, 40, 42, 62, 73, 76,
    103, 139

groups 40, 42, 76, 77, 93
transcultural 13, 76, 77, 79, 81, 83–7
transference 20, 21, 22, 29, 30–4, 36, 38,
    39, 42, 45, 47, 94, 96, 98, 118, 125, 126,
    128–31, 133, 139, 144, 155
transitional 4, 34, 35, 56, 83, 92, 143, 144
    transitions 123, 144, 145, 160
trauma 30, 31, 84, 123, 126
triadic 2, 158
triangular space 155, 156
trust 28, 40, 53, 81, 91, 94, 97, 104, 108,
    115, 116, 124, 127, 132, 146
truth 26, 63, 70

unconditional 55
unconscious 3, 14, 18–21, 33, 36, 38, 39,
    40, 42, 46, 51, 52, 54, 63, 64, 65, 67, 70,
    75, 89, 90–3, 97, 111, 123, 126, 130, 133,
    141,
    146, 150, 151, 157, 159, 160, 162, 165
understand 10, 14, 20, 37, 38, 43, 55, 66,
    70, 77, 78, 79, 85, 91, 118, 121, 161,
    180,141, 126, 132, 133, 144, 154, 156,
    157, 164, 165
    -ing xv, 1, 2, 3, 6, 7, 9, 10, 12, 13, 14, 19,
    20, 23, 24, 25, 27, 29, 33–5, 37, 39,
    41, 45, 51, 52, 54, 55, 57, 58, 63, 71,
    73, 81, 89, 91, 92–7, 109, 115, 119,
    124, 127, 128, 129, 131, 146, 148,
    152, 160, 161, 164, 165

video 7
vital 9, 31, 35, 134
vocalization 91
vulnerable, vulnerability 80, 82, 87,
    98

warm-up 18, 28, 53, 56, 93, 104, 112
weight 105, 106, 111, 120, 121, 122
whole 26, 27, 51, 53, 57, 58, 67, 84, 96,
    110, 113, 129, 134, 159
    ,-ness 103, 113, 115
witness 13, 24, 27–30, 42, 44, 52, 58,
    90–4, 100, 101, 111, 112, 114, 116, 155,
    156, 161, 101, 102, 111, 134
    -ing 20, 29, 32, 42, 47, 91, 92
writing xiii, 23, 24, 44, 70, 72, 73, 101,
    111, 147, 149, 166